WITH NAVAL WINGS

TARANTO

The Duce has his fleet
In a quiet safe retreat,
And he sits behind his cannon
Where the mighty cruisers lie,
But he'll never wear another smile
Within a little while,
For we'll sink them in Taranto when the sun has left the sky.

Taranto, Taranto,
The modern Lepanto.
He'll fall before our eagles as the pagans fled the Cross.
When the battle bombs descend
He'll know the bitter end
Of those who threat our banners with destruction and with loss.

The eagles from their eyries
Will wheel in sudden flight,
And the devil brood of Italy will tremble at the sight
For with anger unabated
And hate as cold as steel
We'll crush the coward Fascist like a worm beneath the wheel.

Taranto, Taranto,
The modern Lepanto.
He'll fall before our eagles as the pagans fled the Cross
When the battle bombs descend
He'll know the bitter end
Of those who threat our banners with destruction and with loss.

Wilfred B. Currie
November 1940

WITH NAVAL WINGS

by
John Wellham

Lt. Cdr. J. W. G. Wellham DSC Royal Navy (ret'd)

*The Autobiography of
a Fleet Air Arm Pilot in World War II*

Foreword by
Rear Admiral I. D. G. Garnett
Flag Officer Naval Aviation

SPELLMOUNT
Staplehurst

Thanks are due to the artist of the
illustration on page 156 but whose
whereabouts could not be traced

Photographs: Crown copyright, Fleet Air Arm Museum

British Library Cataloguing in Publication Data:
A catalogue record for this book is available
from the British Library

ISBN 1-873376-33-2

First published in the UK in 1995 by
Spellmount Limited
The Old Rectory
Staplehurst
Kent TN12 0AZ

3 5 7 9 8 6 4 2

Typeset in 10/11pt Palatino by
SX Composing Ltd, Rayleigh, Essex
Printed in Great Britain by
T. J. Press (Padstow) Ltd, Padstow, Cornwall

Foreword

One of the many pleasures of my present appointment as Flag
Officer Naval Aviation is being asked to write forewords to new
books about the Fleet Air Arm. I am delighted and honoured to
provide one for John Wellham's book.

Without the men of John's generation, there might not have been a
requirement for a FONA. Naval aviation was born comparatively
painlessly into an Edwardian Royal Navy which slowly accepted that
aeroplanes and ships could co-exist to their mutual benefit. With the
RNAS's incorporation into the new Royal Air Force in 1918, the Royal
Navy's world lead in carrier development was lost between the wars,
and both the strategic awareness and tactical application of naval air
power were ill-founded by the beginning of World War 2.

The Fleet Air Arm's victory at Taranto in November 1940
emphasised once and for all the important place of naval air power in
sea-borne operations. The Japanese Navy was quick to realise that
their nation's Pacific ambitions must be based on the use of carriers,
and that the US Navy's carriers similarly presented the only means
of denial of those ambitions. The success of 21 Swordfish in crippling
the Italian Fleet in their own harbour of Taranto prompted the
Japanese to rework their plans for the attack on Pearl Harbor. John
Wellham piloted one of those Swordfish. Thus was the scene set for
the great conflicts between carrier forces later in the war.

John Wellham was in at the beginning of this epoch. All young
aviators have been told in their early training: 'There are old pilots,
and there are bold pilots, but there are no old bold pilots.'
Remarkably and fortunately he seems to have beaten the maxim. He
was in at the beginning, and his memoir reads like a history of FAA
operations of the Second War; Mediterranean, Western Desert,
Atlantic Convoys, Russian Convoys. He was still there at the end,
responsible for flying operations from an escort carrier in the East
Indies Fleet.

It would be an exaggeration to say that the 42 airmen who flew
into Taranto Harbour in November 1940 changed the face of naval

warfare overnight, but they certainly began the process which saw the aircraft carrier replace the battleship as the capital ship of the Fleet. I am pleased that one of those 42 has written it all down in a book of candour and humour, and made these crucial events available to a wider audience.

Rear Admiral I. D. G. Garnett
Flag Officer Naval Aviation

Preface

I consider that I was 'conned' into writing this book by Graham Mottram, Curator of the Fleet Air Arm Museum, as a result of my having dictated on to cassettes my memories of some of the operations in which I took part. My arm was twisted further by my son who seemed to feel that there should be some written answers to the question 'What did your Daddy do in the War?'

I had always felt that sufficient books had already been written about the subject but was assured that few writers had simply recorded their personal memories in their own words. This book, therefore, is just such a record. It is based on my own recollections, aided by my Flying Log Book and photographs taken at the time. Items such as dates and squadron numbers have been checked from official records but I have found that those frequently differ. I am grateful to the FAA Museum for their efforts to clarify many of the points of disagreement.

After these many years my memory may not be serving me as well as I would wish so I can only apologise for any errors and hope that readers will obtain some entertainment from the story.

Any criticisms or opinions of events and personalities are, of course, entirely my own.

John Wellham
Sunderland, 1994

Acknowledgements

My thanks are due to all those who have assisted me and, in particular, to:

The staff of the FAA Museum for their willing help in checking dates, squadron numbers, etc.

My wife for typing and correcting my spelling

My daughter for copying many photographs to the required size

My son for checking details and suggesting improvements, including the title

The Rev. Canon W. B. Currie (now deceased) for his previously unpublished poem 'Taranto'.

Simon J. Dawes for his assistance with the ramifications of the word processor

The numerous people who have given criticisms and advice, usually constructive.

Contents

To the aircrews and maintenance crews of
the Fleet Air Arm past, present and future

Chapter 1

In The Beginning

I strolled through the Fleet Air Arm Museum, pausing for a few minutes beside each of the aircraft that I had flown so often, to listen to the story it told me of what we had done together. They were all there: the Sea Gladiator, the Fulmar, the dreadful Skua, the Seafire, Albacore, Hellcat, Avenger and Firefly. They all had tales to tell.

The longest story came from my old friend the Fairey Swordfish. There she lay in a bed of sand to commemorate her exploits in the Western Desert. Beside her was printed a chapter telling of the day that 'Ollie', 'Cheese' and I had flown three of her sisters into Bomba Bay and managed to sink four ships with three torpedoes. Further along she was there again in a wonderfully realistic model of Taranto Harbour with the ships that were our targets, the AA fire and explosions. I looked down and remembered it well.

An extraordinary aircraft was the 'Stringbag'. She had started World War II as an obsolete bi-plane, and when the end came six years later she was still operational, festooned with radar aerials and rocket launchers. No one could build anything to replace her. She had destroyed a greater tonnage of enemy shipping than any other Allied aircraft. In the horror of North Russian convoys, when Neptune could churn the sea into an insane cacophony more vicious than the violence of the enemy, she had been instrumental in sinking sixteen U-Boats. She could be bent and battered but still take you home, as I knew to my advantage. She richly deserves her place in the Roll of Honour of Naval Aviation.

I moved on into the era of the jet. It seemed incredible to me that in but a few years aircraft could have advanced so far. In 1942 I had commanded a squadron equipped 60% with Swordfish with a top speed of some 100kts, but less than 10 years later my aircraft had an instrument showing my airspeed related to the speed of sound.

I ended these nostalgic hours sitting in the observation room to watch Harriers at play on the airfield and wondering what twists of fate could have caused me to spend most of my youth earning the memories that had returned during the last few hours.

It all started after World War I when I was born in the Western Isles of Scotland – to be precise the Isle of Bute. Although I did not appreciate it at the time, it was an idyllic place to spend one's childhood. The scenery was superb and had caused poets to wax eloquent and singers to burst into song. There were heather-covered hills and moors ideal for small boys to play Cowboys and Indians and other warlike games: there were secluded bays not yet found by the Glasgow trippers, where the relatively warm waters of the Gulf Stream lapped the sand: the water was apparently designed for messing about in boats.

Another advantage – or disadvantage, depending on one's point of view – was that I received a Scottish education. At that time it was one of the best in the world. The Scots had a thing about education: every labourer visualised his son taking a degree at Glasgow University. This might have been due to the fact that, after the Romans left Britain, most places south of the Border were rapidly reverting to the stone age whilst, in Scotland, they were building a university at St Andrews. I had to gain a certificate known as 'The Dreaded Highers' which was considerably more advanced than the English equivalent and was taken a year earlier. I labour this point because it affected my future career.

In moments between my struggles to obtain this epic qualification I did all the right things by getting into the school Rugby fifteen and the cricket eleven, and becoming rather a good swimmer. There was little excuse for not swimming well as we all spent a great part of every year on, in or under the water.

This abundant water, we regarded as a road. Excellent paddle steamers provided a frequent service which we used almost as a bus service to travel only a few miles. Ocean-going ships passed all day up and down the Firth of Clyde to and from Greenock and Glasgow, where they built the finest ships in the world such as *Queen Mary* and *Queen Elizabeth*.

At the age of fourteen I was faced with a vastly important decision. What career should I choose in order not to deny the world my obvious talents? There were two futures that I wanted. I fluctuated between them depending upon whether I was currently reading a novel about Biggles, in which case I must become a pilot in the Royal Air Force or one by Percy F. Westerman, when I had to become a Naval Officer.

I was fifteen when I was introduced to my first aeroplane. In those distant days people still looked up to the skies if they heard an aircraft passing over. Children did not take it for granted that, every year, their parents would take them, in a jet airliner, to some sub-tropical paradise. On our island was a place called Ettrick Bay, where there was a pavilion in which dances were held for the entertainment of summer visitors. A few hundred yards away was a relatively flat field in which a light aircraft gave flights of five, fifteen or thirty minutes depending on how much one was prepared to pay.

One evening I attended one of these dances with my current girl friend and won the spot prize, which was a fifteen-minute flight. Next day we presented ourselves to this flying machine, which was a Fox Moth: a small bi-plane where the pilot sat in an open cockpit behind the wings and two passengers sat in a glassed-in cabin in front. On this flight I was so impressed by the feeling of superiority from looking down on my fellow citizens that I was convinced flying was the only career for me. This lasted for three weeks until we had our annual visit from the Navy, showing the flag.

On this occasion it was HMS *Nelson* with a bunch of attendant destroyers and other vessels. She was 'Open to the Public' each afternoon, so I rushed on board. Consequently it became obvious to me that my only future could be as a Naval officer. I was back to square one.

This difficult situation continued until I had just achieved the age of seventeen, was in my last term at school and was attacking the 'Dreaded Highers'.

I had just survived this ordeal when I found, in the press, an advertisement inviting young men of not less than seventeen years, with healthy bodies and suitable educational qualifications, to apply for Short Service Commissions in the Royal Air Force. These lasted for only four years, so I felt that, at the end, if I did not like it, I would not be too old to do something else. I applied. Some time later I received an enormous package of application forms and other bumph. Having enjoyed the Scottish education, I was able to decipher the forms and complete them. I then rushed around finding the local people with the most clout to act as referees. Some weeks after returning these documents I received instructions to report for interview at the Air Ministry in London.

I arranged to travel from Glasgow by the grace of the London, Midland and Scottish Railway Company. In those days one travelled to London in a train called the Royal Scot which steamed non-stop to its destination, arriving at the exact minute scheduled. There was reasonable comfort, adequate restaurant facilities and a cinema showing short films to while away the time.

At the Air Ministry I found 25 other young men waiting for interview. A few were fellow Scotsmen, but most were from English public schools. One was from Eton but was not, apparently, of a sufficiently high standard, as he was rejected. One by one we were called into another room. As I suffered from a name beginning with

'W', I was last. The others all staggered out with the story that the Service officers were OK but that there was a professor from Oxford who gave a horrifying grilling on education.

Eventually it was my turn and I nervously entered the other room and was bidden to sit down opposite a table where were seated three senior RAF officers – an Air Commodore and two Group Captains – and a horribly intelligent-looking civilian. The officers were in uniform with pilots' Wings below which was a selection of coloured ribbon to indicate that they had done something useful in previous wars. They all spoke with plums in their mouths and wore moustaches of the Earl Haig type in recruiting posters. They were obviously 'Awfully Decent Chaps' but I couldn't help feeling they would have been more suitably dressed in hunting pink. They asked me: 'Was I aaawfly good at Rugga? Eh! What!' and 'Did I play a jolly straight bat at cricket? Eh! What!'

They appeared to have a very limited vocabulary, as after each of my replies they only said: 'Ah! Jolly good show. Eh! What!'

After some five minutes of this innocuous conversation, the Air Commodore turned to the intelligent-looking civilian and said: 'Ah! Professor Snooks, questions on education Eh! What! Jolly good show. Hrrmph.' The professor fixed me with a beady eye, looked down at what I assumed was my file, and said: 'Oh! Scottish education, no questions.' I sat with my mouth open looking even more moronic than usual until I was told to report to the Warrant Officer outside. There were only about ten of the originals there and the WO told us to go down to the canteen, have some lunch and return for a medical examination. I did not realize until later that this meant that those of us remaining had passed the interview, subject to the medical showing that we were likely to live for the next four years.

We all went downstairs, where we were served an indifferent lunch and were watched fixedly by some gentlemen who were, presumably, assessing our skill at balancing peas on our knives. After this we were sent to another department for an incredibly thorough medical examination. They were most particular to find out if we were suffering from venereal disease or had been engaging in any sports likely to give it to us.

The RAF had a fixation about VD. I later became convinced it was a much greater danger than killing oneself when flying.

When all this was over we were told to go home and that we would receive a letter in due course. Everything in the RAF happened 'in due course.'

After some three weeks, 'due course' was reached and a letter informed me of my commission in the Royal Air Force in the rank of

Acting Pilot Officer, with the appropriate pay and allowances, to take effect from the day on which I was appointed to an Ab Initio Flying Training School, which would happen in due course. I was told to ensure I could provide myself with dinner jacket, lounge suit, sports gear and felt hat – the last appeared to be vital. If I did not yet have a driving licence I was to arrange to obtain one. They also gave a list of books, largely mathematical, which I studied assiduously, only to find in later training that they were quite irrelevant.

In this case 'due course' was three months' time. I then received an envelope, heavily stamped 'On His Majesty's Service'. It was addressed to 'Acting Pilot Officer', which gave me a tremendous superiority complex and thrilled our local postman, who spread the news far and wide. It was some time before I found that an Acting Pilot Officer was the lowest form of aviation life.

The document instructed me to report to Blackburn Elementary Flying School at Brough, East Yorkshire, on 20th December 1936. Only some hung-over official behind a desk could have chosen to start a course four days before Christmas! Having collected all the specified equipment including, of course, the felt hat, I made my way to the village of Brough, on this occasion on the London and North Eastern Railway.

Chapter 2

They Taught Me To Fly

Brough was a large grass field. On one side were the lecture rooms, offices and suchlike of the Flying School; nearby was our living accommodation; on the opposite side were hangars and factory-like buildings where Blackburn Aircraft Ltd designed and built some of the worst aircraft to be inflicted on any flying service.

Living at Brough was reasonably comfortable, as we all had single rooms. There was a sitting room, bar and dining room and there were also squash and tennis courts. Our main complaint concerned the eating system, since the last meal of the day was at 5.00pm and consisted of 'high tea', apparently a Yorkshire habit. On most evenings, a bunch of healthy young men found themselves suffering from malnutrition and provided a roaring trade for the local fish and chip shop. We were all convinced that Blackburn had shares in this establishment and had arranged the meal times accordingly.

On the morning after arrival we assembled in the lecture room to be given the customary pep-talk, told about the routine and issued with flying gear, which consisted of a Sidcot suit, boots, gloves, helmet, goggles and a parachute. In the afternoon we were introduced to the aircraft and to our instructors. We were to be trained in the Blackburn B2.

This was a bi-plane not unlike a fat Tiger Moth, the reason for the extra girth being that pupil and instructor sat side by side as opposed to the usual tandem arrangement. The instructors were civilian officers in the RAF Reserve and used their Air Force ranks. I was inflicted upon Flying Officer Morris, who was quite a character and known as 'Cha Cha' because of his strange habit of adding 'Cha Cha Cha' to the end of any statement. If we made a mess of an exercise he would say 'Black show, Cha Cha Cha!' and, if we repeated this mess, he would say 'Doubly black show, Cha Cha Cha!'

The 'Ab Initio' flying course lasted a little over two months, during which we spent half of each day flying and the other half at lectures covering the Theory of Flight, Navigation, etc., and, of course, VD. We were somewhat alarmed to find we were only kept in the air by a 'Theory'. It was some time before the aircraft designers decided that they had got their arithmetic right and the title was changed to the 'Principles of Flight'.

I thoroughly enjoyed the first few hours flying. After five or six hours in the air some of the pupils who had arranged to have a few hours private flying instruction before joining the course were sent off on their first solo. I became very concerned and depressed, as I had been given about seven hours dual instruction and could see no hope of ever being allowed to fly alone. It seemed impossible to land without bouncing at least six times.

My next flight was another 30 minutes of 'circuits and bumps' which elicited numerous 'Doubly Black Shows'. We taxied in and Cha Cha told me to stay in the aircraft, climbed out and said 'Go and do one circuit and one landing and don't break the bloody thing, Cha Cha Cha', then turned and walked away. Overcome with emotion, I forgot to be frightened. I took off and made a very careful circuit, and the disadvantages of side-by-side seating in a training aircraft immediately became apparent: there was a horribly empty space where the instructor ought to have been! I made the best landing that I had achieved so far and when I taxied in I was met with 'Not too black a show', which was a high compliment.

It is amazing what improvement in morale and confidence a First Solo provides; the danger, in fact, is over-confidence. After an hour of flying solo I was authorised to go up to practise steep turns. I had once been shown how to make an aircraft spin and how to recover, so I amused myself by doing two or three spins. This had, quite definitely, not been authorised. I was given the mother and father of all 'blasts' involving even more Cha Cha's than usual, warned of the horrors of over-confidence and not obeying orders, and had the old adage thrown at me – 'it is better to be an old pilot than a bold pilot.'

By the end of the course I had achieved some 60 hours flying, more than half of it solo. We were given a test by the Chief Flying Instructor and an exam on the ground subjects. Those of us who passed were then presented with a Private Pilot's Licence, at that time called an 'A' Licence. Our log books, which had been impounded, were returned and I found on mine a large stamp in which had been written, under the heading of 'Ability as a Pilot', the words 'Above the Average'. Despite my confidence in my own brilliance I was surprised and could only assume that the average was very low.

Our next assignment was to RAF Uxbridge, a barracks with ghastly, dormitory-style accommodation. We spent some time being lectured about the RAF, Air Force Law and, of course, VD. We also did a great deal of 'square bashing' still dressed in civilian clothes and, naturally, our felt hats. This was most embarrassing and we felt complete idiots.

However, the reason for our being there was to be fitted with uniforms. Every day a body of smooth gentlemen arrived, wearing black jackets and striped trousers. They were from Messrs Gieves and Messrs Moss Bros, and they hung uniform around us, then rent it into shreds.

I have never understood why a tailor tears his work to pieces and sews it together again a number of times, before producing the final result. It must be a Trade Union rule.

In two weeks a complete set of uniform, immaculately fitting, was handed to each of us. As we had been joined by pupils from other Elementary Flying Schools, there must have been some 50 of us to be clothed so it was a remarkable tailoring achievement. I wonder why it takes so many weeks to build a single suit when I order one?

My course group was then sent to No. 5 Flying Training School, RAF Sealand, which was situated on the Wirral near Chester and commanded by Group Captain A.N. Gallehawk, whom we seldom saw.

I did not enjoy my time at Sealand. Although the flying was superb and I could not fault it, the atmosphere of the place was stiff and unnatural and, particularly in the junior term, we seemed to be treated like pupils at a prep. school. If this was typical of life in the Royal Air Force, I was appalled at the thought that I had tied myself to it for four years.

As at Brough, half of our time was spent flying and half on ground subjects. These latter included a new one, Armament, which covered stripping down and clearing stoppages in machine guns, the design and workings of various types of bombs, and shooting on the range with rifles and revolvers. Great fun, and I fully approved of the subject.

The facilities for sport were very good but we were forced to take up boxing, which I have always loathed. The idea of two people trying to thump each other strikes me as barbaric. I may be slightly biased, as I have a rooted objection to being hurt, so that, if anyone tries to attack me, I retaliate with low tricks learned during a short Commando course.

The aircraft we were to fly were the Hawker Hart Trainer and the Hawker Audax. Despite being bi-planes these were neat and compact machines which looked good, and an aircraft that looks well normally flies well. The Hart was dual controlled, with the instructor in the rear cockpit. The Audax, in which we did most of our solo flying, was very similar but fitted with a front gun and rudimentary gun sight; the rear cockpit had a Lewis gun and, in the floor, a bomb sight.

Most of us were sent solo after about one hour dual flying, after which we carried out much more advanced training than that at Brough. We climbed to 15,000 feet, made camera gun attacks, learned to fly in formation, were taught instrument flying in real clouds, flew at night and did numerous other exercises. There were frequent tests of our progress by the Flight Commanders.

This excellent course lasted for three months, at the end of which we were tested by the Chief Flying Instructor and sat an examination on the ground subjects. Our log books were impounded once again and, when mine was returned, I was not a little pleased to find it had again been stamped 'Above the Average'.

On 25th June came the great day. There was much parading and marching past, then we were each presented by the Group Captain with our coveted 'Wings'. This, of course, had to be celebrated with large quantities of liquid. We were in something of a daze next day when we went on a few weeks' leave, most of which I spent sailing on the Clyde with some old school friends.

Returning to Sealand, we had another three months in the Advanced Training Squadron. Most of the flying was done in the Audax but we also used Hawker Furies, which were delightful aircraft. They were single-seater fighters, faster than the Audax and fitted with two forward-firing guns. As we were now officially 'Qualified to wear the Flying Badge' we could carry crew or passengers and did many of our exercises with other pilots or photographers in the back, and occasionally members of our ground crews, to give them some experience of flying in the machines they worked on so competently.

The final month was spent at the Armament Training Camp at Penrhos in Wales, where we actually fired our guns in the air and dropped practice bombs on targets on the beach. This was, I think, thoroughly enjoyed by all.

The place was a hotbed of militant Welsh Nationalists led by the local Vicar and they often picketed the main gate, banging on it and demanding entry; on one occasion they attempted to poison our water supply. One evening we retaliated and nearly caused open warfare. At the end of a cinema show in those days, it was the practice to play the National Anthem; in Penrhos the locals rushed to the door during this ceremony so we arranged that some twenty of us would leave our seats before the end of the show and form a solid phalanx across the doors. This developed into a major punch-up and we received a group blast from the Station

Commander for inciting the natives, but we felt that he thoroughly approved.

When we returned to Sealand we found that we were considered sufficiently competent to be allowed loose, and received postings to squadrons. I was to join No.50 (Light Bomber) Squadron at Waddington in Lincolnshire.

Chapter 3

Front Line Squadron

Another pilot had also been posted to Waddington, so we set off by road, in convoy, which I was enabled to do by possession of my first motor car. This was a Wolseley Hornet Sports Saloon of which I was very proud. At that time inflation had not hit the world and, although the car was only three years old, it had cost me £32, which vast amount I had raised by giving a deposit of £5 and arranging to borrow the rest on hire purchase. For some reason I cannot recall, I christened my chariot 'Galloping Bedsprings'.

During the journey my great worry was that I would find the same 'prep school' atmosphere that I had disliked so much at Sealand. In fact, Waddington was totally different.

We arrived about tea-time and found our way to the Officers' Mess, where two pilots who happened to be in the hallway immediately introduced themselves and welcomed us. They found our rooms and a batman, took us to tea and told us about the station. Later, at dinner, we met our Squadron Commander and others.

We were treated as officers and pilots; we joined in the sports that interested us; there was a friendly rivalry between squadrons, in the air and on the ground. I decided I had made the right choice after all.

We were to fly Hawker Hinds, which were very similar to Harts but with much more equipment, such as radios and bomb racks for full-sized missiles. We flew them almost daily in war-like exercises and had an enjoyable time.

On December 14th two memorable events took place: I nearly terminated my career, and I became superstitious.

In the squadron we had one Hind that had been converted into a dual (almost) aircraft. The rear cockpit had been fitted with a pilot's seat, stick, rudder bar, throttle and air speed indicator, for the practice of instrument flying. The pilot blotted out his cockpit by pulling a canvas hood over, while another occupied the rear cockpit to keep a look-out for solid objects in the air or on the ground which would be invisible to the 'hooded' one and to keep track of where they were. On this particular day I was acting as safety pilot.

It was miserable weather with poor visibility and snow lying thick around: conditions not ideal for an instrument exercise. I suggested that the pilot come out from his hood and fly home. This was agreed and I showed him our exact position, over Cranwell College. I snuggled down to keep warm, leaving him to fly home, which only entailed following the main road. After about fifteen minutes my stomach complained that it needed lunch so I looked over the side to see if we were nearly home but could see nothing recognisable. I asked the pilot where we were only to find that he had no idea. After flying around for a few minutes in an unsuccessful attempt to find a familiar object, we decided to look for a suitable field and force-land before we hit something. A field was found and he started an approach. I remonstrated that it might be better to land into wind. He went round again at a height of some 500 feet then, without warning, suddenly turned the aircraft on to its back and pulled his stick right back. There was nothing I could do about it and we flew straight into the ground.

By great good fortune we passed through some trees and scrub and a very high hedge. It was found later that the air speed indicator had stuck at 180 mph, which is an excessive speed at which to hit any solid object.

I next remember the local 'Bobby' and some others trying to cut through my safety harness with penknives. This was quite impossible as it was made of hard canvas reinforced with wire, but they were making noble efforts in a position of some danger since the wreckage could have burst into flames at any time. I tried to indicate that it was only necessary to extract the securing pin with one finger but I was not very lucid, as my face was suffering from a severe blow and some teeth were scattered around. At this point the Fire Brigade arrived; they were more skilled, and removed us both from the wreckage and put us into an ambulance which by then had joined us. We were taken to the casualty ward of the mining hospital at Northallerton, where we found that my colleague, although extensively injured, was not suffering from anything fatal. I had broken my left leg, was bruised and scratched from head to foot and had two lovely black eyes.

The hospital was a dreadful place: Victorian, dark and depressing. The other beds in the ward were occupied by miners, many of them litte more than boys, who had suffered the most ghastly injuries. The nurses and staff, though, could not have been kinder. They covered me with bandages, set my leg and plastered it, and cleaned me up. It was at this point that I became superstitious.

The Doctor commented to me that I was very lucky in not having had any hard objects in my trousers pockets, which would probably have smashed my pelvis and crippled me for life. The night before this crash I had found in my desk a leather cigarette case; I usually carried a fairly large silver one but decided that the leather one would be more comfortable when flying. After the crash it was bent completely double! This suggested to me that I either had a guardian angel or, more likely, it was a case of the Devil looking after his own. I could not discard the feeling that I was not designed to be killed or badly injured in an aircraft. This feeling was confirmed on many future occasions during the War. Although I would have denied it utterly, I gradually adopted a particular routine, wearing articles that seemed to have been 'lucky' and avoiding anything 'unlucky' when about to do anything dangerous. Perhaps I was right, as I am still here!

The following morning I was visited by Squadron Leader Sutherland, my Squadron Commander, accompanied by our RAF Doctor from Waddington and a friend of mine. They were armed with vast quantities of grapes. I have never understood why grapes are given to people in hospital; they may not like grapes – fortunately I do – and they are awkward things to eat in bed, as it is difficult to spit out the pips.

I begged them, almost on bended knee but not quite as one was covered in plaster, to get me out of there with the utmost despatch and no regard to 'due course'. I am happy to say that this *cri de coeur* had the desired effect, as on the following day an RAF ambulance arrived to take me to the Officers' Hospital at Cranwell RAF College.

Before leaving I spoke to my companion in the escapade. I must admit my inclination was to cause him worse physical injury, but I behaved like an officer and a gentleman and did not even air my views on his ability as a pilot. He said that he couldn't remember what had happened, which may have been true. Later I found that, on leaving his FTS, his log book had been stamped 'Below the Average – must be watched'. Had anyone bothered to tell me that before our flight, I might have watched him more carefully.

It is amazing the difference that atmosphere can make to morale. On arrival at Cranwell, I was placed in a bright and well furnished room with bed-side table, radio and magazines; tea was served by a steward in a spotless white jacket bearing a tray holding a silver tea-pot and neatly cut fresh sandwiches. I immediately started to recover.

I was kept there for a few days while doctors did all the things that they do if one gets into their clutches, then told to go home.

I was unhappy at the thought of travelling all the way to Aberdeen, where my family had moved by then, with my plastered leg sticking out in front of me. I need not have worried, as I was

23

placed in a reserved first class compartment, and the guard must have been told the story or bribed as he kept bringing me cups of tea and arranged for a waiter to bring me lunch from the restaurant car. When, being a relatively honest citizen, I attempted to pay for the meal, I was told that it was 'With the compliments of the Railway Co.' The waiter would not even accept a tip!

Arriving in the Granite City I was met by my family who, of course, fussed about me generally, although I was shod with a metal stirrup on my plaster and supplied with a crutch. Provided everyone kept out of my way I could get around reasonably well. However, they got me into a taxi and home without causing me any more bodily harm.

After a rather immobile Christmas I returned to Cranwell where, in a short time, they sent me back to Waddington for 'Ground Duties'. A few weeks later, passed 'Fit for Full Flying Duties', I was back in the air.

I was relieved to find that our little frolic had not affected my liking for flying. By then I had been confirmed as a Pilot Officer, so had dropped the 'Acting' stigma from my rank.

At this time my CO had been promoted to Wing Commander and replaced by Squadron Leader Young, who had just spent some time with the Fleet Air Arm, which was, perhaps, an omen of things to come. I also learned at that time that my companion in the crash had been posted to Southern Arabia to the Armoured Car Unit which the RAF maintained in what was then called 'Trucial Arab Emirates'. This was similar to being exiled to Siberia from Tsarist Russia but I couldn't feel very sorry for him.

I enjoyed the next few months at Waddington, had some summer leave and was then sent on a navigation course. The RAF was keen on these courses but I could not see how it could be done in the small pilot's cockpit of a light bomber. The course was held at Air Service Training, a sort of Civilian Air University, at Hamble. It was interesting and well organised and Hamble was a pleasant place to be in summer. At the end we received a Civil Aircraft Navigator's Licence.

The students came from all over the world and I had my first experience of colour prejudice. Until that time I had had very little contact with black people, although an ebony coloured boy had been at school with me, who had been very popular and joined in all our activities. Naturally, he had been nicknamed 'Snowball'. At AST there was a student who was a prince from some African country and was, of course, very black. He was forbidden entry into most pubs, restaurants and hotels, often with rudeness and abuse, so seldom went out of the college. There was no Race Relations Act at that time. My group became friendly with a Burmese student called Jimmy Chang, because no one could pronounce his proper name, who possessed oriental features but was only light brown in colour. At no time did he experience any difficulty or embarrassment anywhere. I was unable to understand why one's acceptability should be based on the colour of one's skin.

On my return to Waddington an event occurred that changed the whole course of my life.

At the end of the first war the RNAS and the RFC had combined to make the RAF, the FAA simply becoming the poor relation.

In 1938 the Admiralty took control of the FAA and made it an integral part of the Royal Navy. We had heard about this but did not consider it of any importance as far as we were concerned, until an Air Ministry Order appeared stating that suitably experienced officer pilots of the RAF were invited to apply for commissions in the new Air Branch of the Royal Navy, and that those accepted would be given every opportunity to qualify for full 'Executive Status'. It did not require too much thought to see that this was a wonderful opportunity to solve my schoolboy problem and was the best of both worlds.

I applied immediately. Squadron Leader Young, with his experience of the FAA, thought I was completely mad and did his best to dissuade me. However, finding that I was adamant, he agreed to recommend me. Two others from the station also applied.

Chapter 4

The Best of Both Worlds?

I soon received a letter from the Admiralty, accompanied by a long list of uniforms and pages of rules and regulations about the Air Branch. The letter informed me that I had been granted a commission in the Royal Navy in the rank of Sub-Lieutenant with seniority of my present RAF rank. I had no objection to this, as a Sub-Lieut. was equivalent to a Flying Officer in the RAF and one rank higher than I held at the time.

I had joined the RAF straight from school at the minimum age of seventeen which gave me the necessary seniority to become a full Lieutenant in the Navy at the age of twenty; this was not usually attained until about twenty-three. A few years later even stranger things happened. When the war started and all the Services were obliged to expand very quickly, the RAF and the Army scattered 'Acting' ranks about like confetti. The Navy was never keen on this but saw that it was necessary, to give suitable clout when dealing with the other services.

Experienced lieutenants were appointed to command FAA squadrons, submarines and such like and I was given command of a squadron when I was only twenty-three, with the acting rank of Lieut-Commander, not usually achieved until about thirty years of age. This produced some very silly situations, not least because, from an early age, I had been equipped with blonde hair and a smooth, fair complexion. I must have looked like an overgrown schoolboy.

On one occasion, when I was wearing a naval raincoat, which has no badges of rank, it was pouring with rain and I was dashing towards the entrance gate of an air station. Just outside I passed an officer of the same rank who was one of those who had returned for the war, having been axed by Geddes in the early 1920s. He screamed after me 'Come here, young man; don't you usually salute senior officers?' I made some fatuous comment over my shoulder such as 'Yes, if they are senior enough' and ran towards the shelter of the guard-room, passing the sentry, who recognised me and presented arms, a courtesy not given to officers below the rank of Lieut-Commander. This made the irate gentleman even more purple. I had achieved the shelter of the guard room and was taking off my rain coat to shake it before he caught up with me. This gave him full view of two-and-a-half gold stripes and some pieces of coloured medal ribbon to which I had become entitled. He stood gaping like a cod-fish out of water.

He had the grace to apologise, and stood me drinks in the bar afterwards. He had mistaken me for one of the RNVR Midshipmen who were under training at that station.

To revert to the story: I threw myself on the mercy of Messrs Gieves once again. There were many more items of uniform needed than in the RAF, including a sword, which was a weapon not required by Short Service officers in the Air Force. We were allowed some four weeks to be fitted out. When our uniforms arrived we spent a deal of time standing in front of mirrors admiring ourselves. I was pleased with the effect, but we were all rather disgruntled by our pilot's 'Wings', which looked like a small, bedraggled sea-gull, worn above the 'executive curl' on our arms together with a little silver 'A' in a gold laurel wreath. Fortunately, this was soon changed to a gold embroidered 'A' inside the curl and a beautifully designed pair of golden wings above it.

We were appointed to the Torpedo Training Unit at Gosport, as the Navy had not had time to beg, borrow or steal any Air Stations from the RAF. Gosport was a station of very long standing and the accommodation was good.

We were to be introduced to the Navy, and taught naval flying systems and how to drop torpedoes. The instructors were FAA officers but still in the RAF.

Here I met the Swordfish, which was to be my airborne home for many hours and to carry me safely through much enemy aggro. We looked at it with awe and one wag asked 'Does it fly?' It was not a thing of beauty. No artist on sighting it would have dashed off to get his sketch pad. The Harts and Hinds had been solid, neat and purposeful but the Swordfish looked as though the various parts had been added as afterthoughts. The ailerons, elevators and rudder seemed remarkably big. The instructors told us that it had a very short take-off and landing run and could carry a crew of three and a 2,000lb bomb load. We took their word for it with some incredulity.

One aircraft had been fitted with dual controls and we were taken up for twenty minutes to get the feel of it and make a couple of landings, after which we were given one to familiarise ourselves with. I took mine up to a reasonable height and made it do every manoeuvre that I could think of other than pure aerobatics. It did everything absolutely according to the 'book of words'. I tried to stall it but it was very light with only a pilot and no load, and I had to stand it virtually on its tail.

Most aircraft when stalled will suddenly drop the nose, but mine simply subsided gently.. I tried again, this time applying full rudder with the stick right back, which should have made her fall straight into a spin; she only flopped into a sort of spiral and straightened out immediately I centralised the controls, without any recovery procedure. I felt that she had a distinct personality, and that she found the performance a bit of a bore.

When I returned to the airfield and landed, I found the others in my group had had similar experiences. We asked the instructors if the aircraft had any vices, but they could think of none. We thought 'Ah – the Pegasus engine! Was it reliable on long flights over the sea?' They looked at each other and shook their heads, then one said 'I remember in my last squadron that one did cut and had to ditch in the sea. She had run out of fuel, of course.'

I am sure that the 'Stringbag' must have been an accident on the drawing board as I cannot believe anyone could have designed an aircraft with no vices at all. In years to come I was to be profoundly grateful to this accident. The designer should have had a statue raised to him.

We were the first course from the new Air Branch and our teachers knew nothing about us nor our backgrounds in the RAF. They had therefore decided to give us the whole course, and started by taking us up as passengers in four Swordfish to show us how to fly in formation. We were then told to go and practise, with many warnings about being careful and not getting too close. As most of us had come from fighter and light bomber squadrons, we were in the habit of flying in very close formation and even doing aerobatics in that mode. We felt it was time to get things onto a proper footing, so arranged to meet out of sight of the airfield, where we tucked ourselves into a very tight 'box', then dived down to cross the field very low; the man in the box then slid neatly into echelon and we landed still in close formation. The instructors were duly chastened and decided that it would save a great deal of time if they had a conference with us and amended the programme accordingly.

We achieved a first class programme. The basic flying items were deleted and we started by practising very low flying over the sea, virtually skimming over the water, both alone and in formation. This required judgement and concentration and was very necessary, as our next exercise concerned torpedo attacks. This was much more difficult than any of us had expected. We had to dive from 7-8,000 feet, adjusting our position to allow for the avoiding action taken by the target, flatten out at about 50 feet, calculate the speed of the enemy and aim off to allow for it, then fly absolutely straight and level, before releasing the torpedo when we had estimated that we had reached the correct range. All this seemed to need much more time than was available and our first efforts were appalling.

In the early stages, our target was No Man's Fort, which was one of the Martello towers built in the sea off Portsmouth during the Napoleonic wars. We were fitted with camera guns to record our efforts. We then graduated to attacks on the light cruiser HMS *Dunedin*, which was even harder, as she steamed at about 20kts and took avoiding action.

Finally, we attacked her with dummy torpedoes. Their warheads had been replaced by flotation compartments so that they could be retrieved on the surface. Torpedoes are very expensive items.

Another frolic to which we were introduced was being catapulted into the air. This lengthy and complicated process involved the Swordfish being lifted by crane and lowered, with a great deal of shouting and pushing, on to a trolley which ran on rails along the top of a structure resembling the jib of a dockyard crane. This device was fitted on a turntable to allow it to be swung into wind. On the inboard end of the jib was a breech like that of a large gun, into which was inserted a sausage-shaped paper bag containing explosive, which we were told was used to fire the shell of a battleship's 15-inch gun. When the aircraft was adjusted on the trolley with its catapult points engaging in the hooks provided, the engine was started and the pilot ran it up to take-off revolutions and locked the throttle, laid his head against the head-rest, put his left hand on the stick and raised his right; when ready in all respects he dropped his hand, whereupon the cartridge was fired.

There was then a violent explosion and the trolley, complete with aircraft, was hurled along the rail until, on reaching the end, it stopped dead, leaving the Swordfish to shoot off into the air with the pilot shaking the stars out of his eyes and attempting to gain control.

We each made two of these launches without ill effects but could not see any particular use for the idea in aircraft carriers. It was, however, used to good effect in cruisers which embarked Sea Fox floatplanes or Walrus amphibians for reconnaissance. The days of hydraulic and, even later, steam catapults had not yet arrived.

Between flying sessions we arranged lectures from experienced naval officers and visited many of the RN establishments which lay thick on the ground in that area. We all spent a few days at sea in HMS *Dunedin*, which was excellent value as we learned about life and routine in ships. We also had a day in a submarine. I was apprehensive about this, since I suffer from claustrophobia.

However I was surprised to find when submerged that it seemed little different from being below decks in a ship.

We spent two packed months at Gosport, and began to feel more like naval officers.

We all received appointments to 822 Squadron, HMS *Courageous* and were very excited. At last, a real carrier! Unfortunately, it was not quite what we had expected, as the Squadron was disembarked in Scotland, at Donibristle on the north side of the Firth of Forth, while *Courageous* was anchored on the seaward side of the Forth Bridge.

We were required to do more torpedo attacks, camera gun attacks on each other and attacks with real ammunition on towed targets, as well as navigation exercises out to sea with experienced Observers. We discovered the accuracy with which we needed to steer compass courses if we were to fly for some hours over the sea and then find our ship, which had probably steamed some 60 miles whilst we had been away. We were most impressed by the standard of navigation shown by the Observers and the time and care which was spent on checking and adjusting compasses. It was all very different from the RAF, where most of the flying was done over the land, with roads, railway lines and towns usually in sight.

However, our main object was to learn to deck land. We had to spend many hours doing ADDLs (Aerodrome Dummy Deck Landings). Most of these we did at Turnhouse, an airfield near Edinburgh which was destined in the future to become Edinburgh Airport. It soon became clear that, to land on deck, we had to break nearly every rule we had ever learned about landing an aircraft. The system was to approach off a left-hand turn in a tail-down attitude, virtually 'hanging on the propeller'. On passing over the stern of the ship, the engine was cut and the aircraft flopped down on to the deck, where hopefully it would remain, after catching an arrestor wire.

On flights to and from Turnhouse we often passed over *Courageous* and were startled to realise that this floating postage stamp was all we would have as an airfield.

When we were reasonably competent at ADDLing, we embarked in the ship, being carried out to her from Rosyth in a steam drifter. During the next four days we were given useful knowledge of life in an aircraft carrier. We were surpised to meet a term of Air Branch midshipmen recruited direct from school, who were being trained in basic naval subjects. I doubt if any of us had appreciated that the Air Branch had already, in the few months since we had joined, become sufficiently organised to have had an entry of young officers. This was the first example I had met of the amazing ability of the Navy, once it had decided to do something, if only a children's party, to organise it at great speed and then run it efficiently.

· We were the first 'qualified' Air Branch officers that they had met so, every evening after dinner, a number of us were always invited to the Gunroom which, of course, resulted in a great deal of:

'There I was, at 20,000 feet, upside down in the middle of a cloud'. I don't think we encouraged them much to begin a flying career.

On the first morning at sea each of us was shown how to land on a deck by an instructor in a Tiger Moth. He circled the ship so that we could see what it looked like, then made a smooth and unexciting landing. We were then put into Swordfish and told to go and do it ourselves. Actually, if one strictly obeyed the ADDL's training, it did not seem to be all that difficult. In the four days allowed I made 30 deck landings without frightening anyone, including myself.

Having decided that we could be allowed loose in a carrier, they sent us ashore again, where we met another example of no one having decided what to do with us. While someone worked this out, we were sent to various second line units around the country. My fate was with No.750 (Observer Training) Squadron at the School of Naval Co-operation at Ford, in Sussex.

Ford was a pleasant place in May; it is on the edge of the Solent, with almost deserted sandy beaches within walking distance. The job of 750 Squadron was to fly around the Solent carrying observers under training. Already there were far more pilots than needed so we were not exactly overworked, and did a good deal of swimming.

The aircraft at Ford were Blackburn Sharks, which had just been leaving the drawing board at Brough when I was there over two years before. The machine had been relegated to second line duties as soon as it had come off the production line. Its only merits were that it looked neater than the Swordfish and had a glass canopy over the cockpits, which made it a little warmer in British weather.

Unable to find any useful job for me, they gave me a Shark to gain 'Experience on Type'. I spent five hours in the air, although less than half an hour would have been enough. At least I had some very good views of ocean liners in Southampton, battleships in Portsmouth and yachts racing at Cowes. They then made me fly around the country collecting Shark spare parts, of which a continuous supply appeared to be needed.

When I had been at Ford for three weeks, I was required to ferry two pilots to Abbotsinch, near Glasgow, to collect two more Sharks. After packing them into the rear cockpit and arranging to refuel at RAF Linton-on-Ouse, I took off. The weather was disgusting and my passengers, two RAF pilots, hoped that I would turn back. With my usual confidence in my own ability I told them not to worry. I resorted to navigation, and, at the due time, Linton-on-Ouse materialised out of the murk as I had hoped. The RAF were duly impressed by Naval navigation, just as I had intended. Having refuelled, we left in improving weather conditions and reached Abbotsinch. I had been warned about this airfield, as it was sited immediately beside another field called Renfrew and strict circuit rules were necessary, so that one had a right hand circuit and the other a left hand to avoid meeting each other head on.

I had hoped that some reason could be found for delaying the return flight by a day, so that I could sneak down the river Clyde to Bute to see my childhood haunts, but unfortunately the two Sharks for collection were fuelled and ready.

No fault could be found in mine either, so I had no excuse for delay. I climbed away with the others in formation on me, as they had both refused to lead having, apparently, more faith in Naval navigation than in their own. I was therefore obliged to repeat my Vasco da Gama effort and find RAF Church Fenton, where I had arranged to be refuelled. When we arrived I decided that I had flown quite long enough for one day and would get no bonus for going any further, so ordained that we would spend the night there. We left the following morning and reached Ford before lunch.

I walked to the officers' mess, which we were entitled to call the wardroom since the Navy had taken over. There I found, in my letter rack, a large OHMS envelope which I opened. To the alarm of all around, I let out a piercing scream and leapt into the air. In the envelope was a letter from their Lordships to inform me that I had been appointed to 824 Squadron, HMS *Eagle* which I knew to be in the China Fleet. This was a plum appointment. I was instructed to obtain tropical uniform and a passport, which I was to send to them for a Chinese Visa to be granted, and told that passage had been booked for me on the Blue Funnel liner SS *Antenor*, sailing from Liverpool in about three weeks' time.

I spent the next day getting myself organised. I sold Galloping Bedsprings to an RAF type and appealed to the more experienced RN officers for advice on tropical uniform. They told me that I need only, once again, submit myself to the tender mercies of Messrs Gieves.

I travelled up to London the following day and presented myself in Bond Street, where Gieves very calmly assured me that they had my measurements and that all would be ready in ten days. I asked their advice on civilian clothes for the Far East and they sold me some things that proved to be ideal with one exception: they insisted I would need a solar topee. I found later that they had not been worn by Europeans since the time of David Livingstone, but it turned out most useful for baling out sailing dinghies when racing.

I took a few days' embarkation leave at home where my family seemed convinced that going to China was equivalent to a voyage to Mars. I tried to convince them that a commission in a ship of the Royal Navy usually only lasted two years and that they would still be in the land of the living when I returned.

Returning to Ford, I received a large package from the Blue Funnel Line containing a pile of labels marked 'Wanted on Voyage', 'Not Wanted on Voyage' and numerous brochures and suchlike about the ship, assuring me that the Blue Funnel Line provided a higher standard of everything on a voyage to the Far East than could be found in any other steamship line. I was recommended to catch a train at a particular time on the day of sailing.

Arriving at Euston Station with a retinue of porters, I was surprised to find that the entire train had been reserved by the shipping line for *Antenor's* passengers. We travelled to Liverpool non-stop in comfort and continued along a line by the docks, stopping immediately alongside the ship. A regiment of white-coated stewards was waiting. They at once organised our luggage and, by some extraordinary system of telepathy, found the passengers who belonged to them and their 'Wanted on Voyage' boxes. Mine took me to my cabin, insisted on unpacking and stowing my gear, showed me a plan of the dining saloon and told me that I did not require to dress for dinner as we would be sailing during the evening.

In the dining saloon I found that, at my table, there were some Army and RAF Officers, and in two cases their wives. This table was presided over by the Chief Officer but he was not present on that occasion as he was busy getting his ship ready to leave port. The food was superb but the stewards were most apologetic about the small menu – only two pages – and assured us that everything would be better the following day.

After dinner and a quick look around the ship I found a vantage point on the boat deck to watch us getting under way. Two tugs came alongside and, with a total lack of fuss, we slid away from the dock-side and were soon steaming out to sea.

Next morning I went up to enjoy an enormous breakfast and was surpised at how few people were in the dining saloon. I had hardly noticed that the ship was moving about a bit, as I have the good fortune not to suffer from sea-sickness. When I went on deck I found that we were steaming into a heavy sea and waves were crashing on to the forecastle. It was very impressive and I watched it for some time with a few other hardy passengers. Some poor souls never left their cabins during the first few days and others were occasionally seen staggering along the upper deck displaying a greenish hue.

From the passenger list I had found that, apart from a few Service people and some Chinese, most of the passengers were civilians returning to the East after leave in Britain. One interesting name on the list was HH The Tunku Abdul Rahman. I found that 'Tunku' was the Malay word for 'Prince' and that he was a son of the Sultan of Kedah, one of the Malay States. He had been up at Oxford, where he had distinguished himself by becoming table tennis champion and very much undistinguished himself by marrying an English girl.

The sultan had taken a poor view of the Prince marrying a white commoner, and had banished him. By this time, however, he had relented and the Tunku was on his way home complete with wife. She was a very pleasant girl, but I did not envy her the welcome she could look forward to in Kedah. After they disembarked in Penang I heard nothing more until the early 1950s, when the politicians were engaged in tearing the British Empire to pieces and thereby causing civil wars and general mayhem in most of our previous possessions. When the war in Malaya ran out of steam a reasonably stable government was formed in the new country with Tunku as the first Prime Minister of Singapore. I believe he proved a very good one.

Some of the passengers seemed most odd because, when not eating, they spent all day and well into the night playing bridge in the saloon. As I seldom found a moment when there wasn't something new and interesting to see or do I decided that they must all be mentally stagnant. Various entertainments were laid on for us with deck games during the day and a swimming pool when the weather became warmer: I spent a lot of time in it. After dinner there were dances, housey-housey (bingo), 'horse racing' and even table tennis when the sea was calm enough.

One day the crew challenged us to cricket on the forecastle, with nets rigged round the ship's side. There was obviously some low cunning involved, as we were soundly beaten and it cost us a crate of beer. I kept very quiet to avoid anyone finding out that, when at school, I had played for Bute County; my side would probably have made me pay for all the beer.

After a few roughish days in the Bay of Biscay we passed through the Straits of Gibraltar with a fine view of the Rock. I was disappointed that we did not call there, as it had cropped up so often in books that I had read. Our first port of call was Marseilles, which I found rather a scruffy, uninteresting place, but we only stayed a few hours before leaving to pass through a sunny Mediterranean, past Sicily to Port Said.

This was my first introduction to the Near East, which I was to know so well in future days. Most of the inhabitants seemed to have given themselves unlikely Scottish names and have no other object in life than to 'con' passengers from visiting ships into buying things they did not want. On the trip through the canal I spent every possible minute on deck until we cleared into the Red Sea, where we had the bad luck to suffer a following wind. The heat was almot unbearable and, this being before the days of air-conditioning in ships, it was like living in a floating oven.

Fortunately, it was not long before we passed Aden, then through the Straits of Bab-El-Mandeb into the Indian Ocean and on to Colombo.

The first sight of this town was a huge neon sign towering into the air, bearing the words 'Ceylon for Good Tea'. Situated on a very fine harbour, it was a large and unusual mixture of buildings: very British Victorian structures and much older Portuguese ones, as well as smaller native shops and houses. I decided to test the arrangements that I had made with my bank in London; they had told me that I would find, in all major cities in the East, a branch of the Hong Kong and Shanghai Bank which was their oriental agent. Indeed they were right. I found a large and imposing building where they cashed my cheque without any difficulty. I had to keep strict control of myself to avoid spending a fortune in shops stocked with mouth-watering goods; in particular silver, ivory and emeralds which seemed ridiculously cheap. However, I had been warned by the 'old stagers' to wait until we reached Hong Kong where I would find that things were even cheaper.

Leaving Colombo we steamed across to Penang, one of the Straits Settlements which were ruled by the British. After a few hours we left for Singapore where we spent more than a day and I had the chance to tour the place, not appreciating that I would soon come to know it very well. This was a most impressive city with even more imposing Victorian buildings set around a magnificent harbour. The place was thriving and the number of white people everywhere surprised me. Most of the industry and business was handled by industrious Chinese, while the local Malays were a cheerful race who seemed satisfied to allow anyone else to do the work. The Police and the guards at every building were bearded and turbaned Sikhs.

The next part of the voyage was up the China Sea to my destination in Hong Kong. This city left me gasping. I had never visualised a place bursting with so much energy. The huge harbour was a seething mass of shipping with everything from 30,000-ton liners to tramp steamers and coasters as well as Naval ships, with an incessant movement of junks and sampans. Many ships were unloading and loading at anchor with lighters alongside and every time these left to return ashore there was a great deal of noise and exploding fire-crackers. I was told that this was to frighten away the devils that would have been collected from a white man's ship.

There was no sign of *Eagle*, so I hadn't a clue where to go.

I found that the Naval headquarters were in an old monitor, so wended my way there to cry 'Help'. They told me that *Eagle* was at Wei Hai Wei, another treaty port further north; she would be returning shortly and, meanwhile, I should go to Kai Tak aerodrome and ask the RAF to look after me. They arranged transport, and bodies to carry my gear, and we crossed the harbour to the Kowloon side in the ferries that gave a continuous service. Kai Tak was a grass field with wooden hangars lashed to the ground with massive steel cables to avoid their being blown away by typhoon winds. There were very fine permanent living quarters. The RAF were most hospitable and I was soon comfortably settled.

They knew quite a lot about *Eagle*'s work and told me that her principal job had been anti-piracy patrols. Small coasters and trading junks on the China coasts were in continual danger from pirates who boarded them, removed the cargo and murdered the crew, then either abandoned or sank the vessels. *Eagle*'s aircraft, appearing anywhere at any time, were an effective means of discouraging them.

When I reviewed the situation, I found that there had been some definite shortcomings in school geography. The city was not, in fact, Hong Kong, which was only the island.

The city on the island was called Victoria and most of the business and residential side of the colony was there. On the mainland side of the harbour was the smaller town of Kowloon, where most of the industry was situated. Behind Kowloon were the New Territories which had been leased some time after the original colony and were largely barren, but a little agriculture had been achieved. The railway line to China terminated there. Kai Tak airfield was immediately beside the water, and today is Hong Kong Airport, the runways having been built out into the sea on reclaimed land.

On my first day the RAF took me into town and I had my first lesson in Pidjin English, which I had always assumed to be a sort of ungrammatical English. However, I found it was virtually a new language and that a working knowledge of it was necessary to have any hope of success when dealing with the Chinese workers. The first time that I became conscious of this was when we were about to climb up the steps of the very imposing Hong Kong Club. Two distinguished-looking Europeans of the ambassadorial type appeared at the doors and walked in a dignified manner to the top of the steps where they stopped; one raised his face to the sky and screamed 'Two Piecee Cooli'. I demanded an explanation and was told that they wanted a sedan chair, which by then had arrived, and they continued their dignified progress into it.

Much of this language I found to be hilarious, particularly when connected with aircraft. At the airfield the mundane tasks such as refuelling were carried out by 'coolies' and, after taxying in from a flight, one stood up in the cockpit and screamed 'Steam chicken gone thirsty', which immediately attracted a petrol bowser. Another surprising system was that, in clubs, hotels and reastaurants, one never used cash, all transactions being done on the 'chit' system by signing one's name and adding the name of one's ship or station. At the end of each month these were sent to the paymaster of the ship, who paid them and added the cost to mess bills. I imagine that this system was wide open to 'fiddling', but it appeared to work perfectly.

I liked the Chinese people who were cheerful and hard-working and also incredibly clean; even the rags worn by the most decrepit coolie were always spotless. Another thing I learned about was 'The Great Chinese Squeeze', an arrangement by which everyone involved in any transaction earned 'commission'. A good example was buying a suit, which it was most unwise to do oneself, the correct method being to approach one's Boy, who always had a distant relative who was the best tailor in Hong Kong.

He brought patterns of first-class English material and, after a choice was made, disappeared with a well fitting example already owned. The following day he reappeared with a perfect copy. The cost was unbelievably low but, despite this, the Boy would have received his rake-off.

'Loss of face' was a terror to them all. If, for instance, anyone ran out of soap, this would be a loss of face for his boy and so someone else lost his soap, the result being that the loser's boy lost face while the original boy saved face. Fear of 'devils' also haunted the less educated Chinese, who were convinced that they were continuously followed by a tribe of them and that the best way to be rid of them was to leave them on a white man. One method of achieving this was to dash across in front of the white man's car so that it just scraped past. Unfortunately, their judgement was often below the necessary standard and they came to an untimely end. The fine for killing an unlucky one was 100 dollars – slightly more than £5 – as it was hardly the fault of the driver.

For a week I lived at Kai Tak with no particular duties, so spent the time exploring this fascinating new world both on the ground and from the air. The RAF had very kindly lent me an Avro Tutor.

Seen from above, the coastline was an intricate lacework of islands and bays one of which, known as 'Junk Bay', contained some 100 moored junks; another bay contained a sampan city where thousands of families spent their lives in small boats. Another interesting place was the Portuguese colony of Macao, 40 miles from our colony, which was the Monte Carlo of the area with many casinos and gambling dens, as well as being the headquarters of the Tongs, who ran a protection racket on many Hong Kong businesses. The Chinese are inveterate gamblers and it was impossible to go far without seeing a group of coolies playing Mah Jong at incredible speed and losing their paltry wages.

At the end of this week I was told that *Eagle's* aircraft would be arriving early the following morning, and the ship soon after. Her two squadrons of Swordfish landed at breakfast time and I helped to shepherd them to their parking lot. The squadrons were Nos. 813 and 824, the latter being the one to which I had been appointed, so I searched out the CO, Lieut-Cdr. Debenham, who was an observer. Some of the pilots accompanied me to a vantage point to see the ship's arrival.

Chapter 5

China Fleet Carrier

HMS *Eagle* was an impressive sight as she steamed through Lei Yue Mun Pass into Hong Kong harbour. She was due to recommission on this visit and so was wearing a paying off pennant: an enormous length of white bunting with a red cross that flew from the mainmast right down the flight deck and far astern, where it was held out of the sea by two large balloons scrounged from the meteorology department.

Studying the ship's history, I had found out that she had been laid down before the First World War to be a Chilean battleship called *Almirante Cochrane* but had not been completed until much later when the Admiralty bought her and converted her into an aircraft carrier and finally commissioned her in 1922. She had many unusual features, one being that she was the only carrier in the Royal Navy with the affectation of two funnels. Having been in China for some years, she displayed numerous signs of local workmanship such as the teak quarterdeck rail, which was beautifully carved with Chinese dragons. Her hull had retained the battleship design of her day so that her bows curved forward at the water-line to form a ram like the prow of a Roman war galley.

The flight deck followed the shape of her main deck, narrowing to a point at the forward end. This was a rather stupid piece of design as it shortened the take-off area, every inch of which was useful when an aircraft was heavily loaded.

She had no crash barriers, which greatly increased the time taken for a squadron to land on. After catching a wire, each aircraft had to taxi on to the lift, have the wings folded, and be lowered to the hangar deck and pushed off; the lift had to return to flight deck level before the next aircraft could land. The handling party actually did their job at remarkable speed and the pilots timed their approaches to touch down at the instant the lift reached deck level. Nevertheless, it took four times longer than the barrier method.

In later years, using barriers, the RN landed aircraft at 15-second intervals, which was three times as fast as our US allies could achieve and the difference was noticeably maintained at night. In combined fleet tasks it was usually necessary to steam into wind for longer than was desirable while waiting for US carriers to recover all their brood.

In the afternoon some of the squadron officers took me on board: a simple process, as she was lying alongside to ease the recommissioning task.

I toured the ship, and found the cabin which was to be my home for two years. I was a poor little Sub-Lieut. at that time so was only entitled to a double cabin, but in fact I was to be on my own for most of the time. All the stewards and others with menial tasks were Chinese, and very good at their jobs: they even staffed the NAAFI, and all the catering side was handled by a perfectly spherical gentleman called, appropriately, Wing Fat. I found that even that job was covered by the 'squeeze' as it was considered so lucrative that it had to be bought for many thousands of dollars when the person currently holding the office was prepared to relinquish it.

Eagle remained in Hong Kong for ten days, so the squadrons lived in and worked from Kai Tak. I was quickly absorbed into squadron routine and was allocated my crew. My observer was Petty Officer Wilks. Apart from the TAGs (Telegraphist Air Gunners), he was the only non-commissioned aircrew in the ship. The RAF always had a fairly large proportion of Sergeant Pilots but there were few of their equivalent in the RN. PO Wilks was a very competent observer and we worked well together, but I felt that mixing commissioned and non-commissioned pilots and observers was awkward. It was not possible to know each other really well, as there was little opportunity to socialize when off duty.

At Kai Tek I practised some deck landings. On 12th August 1939 the ship sailed with me on board, because there was a lack of confidence in my ability to put a Swordfish on deck without breaking it. When we cleared the channel into open water the ship turned into wind and the eighteen aircraft of the two squadrons landed on without incident. In the afternoon we again turned into wind, this time entirely for my benefit, so that I could get on and off the ship with a reasonable chance of remaining in one piece. I made three deck landings without causing undue excitement, which no doubt was a relief to my crew.

Before leaving Hong Kong we had been briefed that we were to go to Singapore, where *Eagle* was to be dry-docked for routine scraping off of barnacles and other minor dockyard jobs. During this trip we were busy every day with flying exercises, which included dummy torpedo attacks, navigation, and dive-bombing with practice bombs on a target towed astern of the ship.

When carrying out practices with 824 Squadron, particularly torpedo and dive-bombing attacks, I was struck by the dedication of their aircrews compared with those of the training squadrons. After every flight there was a detailed analysis of successes and failures; new ideas were discussed with great seriousness and tried in the next exercise, the slightest fault being corrected, not only by the pilots but also by the ground crews. At first I assumed this was simply the different attitude of a front line squadron, but I soon realised that these exercises were, in fact, training for imminent, real operations.

Recently I had been so overpowered by this new world of the Orient that I had glossed over the happenings on the opposite side of the earth. For this I had no excuse, as world news was broadcast daily on long wave W/T (Morse) by organisations such as Reuter, and this was published in the press and on the local radio news broadcasts. Even at sea it was read by the telegraphists, typed, and pinned to notice boards throughout the ship. Had I paid more attention to these reports I would have realised that war clouds were building rapidly over Europe, blacker and lower each day. The situation was continually under discussion in the wardroom.

The headline in these discussions was the incredible naivety of our politicians, who accepted Hitler's statements and promises despite his every action belying his words.

Most of us had read, in full or in part, translations of *Mein Kampf* and excerpts from Hitler's speeches and those of his cronies, Himmler, Goebbels and von Ribbentrop. It appeared from these that Hitler could not understand why we always seemed to be against him, when he regarded the British as the only other great Aryan race, who should be his allies. If we would not join him voluntarily we must be forced to do so. He was convinced that, with his leadership, Germany would be a Great Power (*Grossmacht*) but that, allied to us, it would be a World Power (*Weltmacht*). There was some logic in this: in 1939 Great Britain ruled, directly or indirectly, one third of the earth's land mass and controlled much of its oceans. It was not until later that it became known that one of Hitler's visions was a third Reich ruled by him with Edward VIII as puppet emperor.

In all our discussions there was complete acceptance of the imminence of war and, with our usual gross overconfidence, we assumed that we would rapidly defeat Germany. We were hoping war would come quickly, to end the period of indecision. It was difficult to understand why the older members of the ship's company, who had fought in that earlier 'War To End All Wars', did not share our enthusiasm.

We spent five days exercising. Then, when only twenty minutes' flying time from Singapore, both squadrons took off in the early morning and landed at RAF Seletar in time for breakfast. While disembarked we flew a great deal, sometimes three or four times a day. We concentrated on dive-bombing and night flying, which included night ADDLs on a dummy deck laid out to conform to a ship's flight deck lighting. I had always enjoyed night flying and found no difficulty in mastering the deck landing system; in fact, I don't believe any of us found a major problem. However, there was a great tendency to show off to the RAF, who were impressed by our skill in landing on a narrow strip, delineated by two rows of tiny white lights that were only visible on the final approach. We were guided in by the DLCO (Deck Landing Control Officer) using illuminated white wands to replace the 'bats' used by day.

Singapore is virtually on the Equator, with a hot, sticky climate, so the routine was to fly from early morning to lunch time, after which we normally went into the city, which I found fascinating. The magnificent and very busy harbour was surrounded by docks and warehouses, while in the city centre were imposing buildings housing the Government Offices, banks and headquarters of large companies. The many hotels and restaurants were overshadowed by the famous Raffles Hotel where we often had dinner. The food was first class almost everywhere, with luxuries available which one would not have expected to find. Fresh strawberries were common, delivered daily from the hills farther north in Malaya. Although prices were not so low as in Hong Kong, everything seemed remarkably cheap.

The British community numbered thousands and included complete families with children of all ages. Many of these families, I found, had no intention of ever returning to the UK, where they could not hope to live to the same standard. To most of them the only thing of any importance was the social scene, which was covered by a strict, out-of-date etiquette.

Dress was very formal: during the day most men wore white or khaki shorts but, by seven o'clock each evening, one had to be wearing a white dinner-jacket or 'bum-freezer' – similar to a tropical mess jacket – if appearing in a hotel, club or restaurant. I found that I could not be invited into anyone's home until I had 'called' officially, leaving two visiting cards in a box at the gate. However, I think that most of us found plenty of enjoyment when off duty provided that we obeyed the rules carefully. On most days we spent a good deal of time at the swimming club, where we had been made honorary members and which was a magnificent affair with a large pool, bars and restaurant.

Very few people seemed concerned about the news in Europe. They obviously felt that nothing would affect Singapore, which they regarded as a fortress. This faith was based on some batteries of 16-inch naval guns sited to repel any seaborne invasion. The future would show how misplaced was this faith.

In our last few days at Seletar the news showed that our politicans were, at last, waking up and preparing for war. Poland, with whom we had a treaty, had rushed troops to her borders. In England, art treasures were being moved to safety and preparations for mobilisation were in hand.

On August 28th we flew on board *Eagle* and continued the concentrated exercises. On August 29th Hitler demanded Danzig and the Polish Corridor and issued an ultimatum to Poland. On August 31st we heard that he had offered Britain a pact to defend the British Empire, if we would help him gain the Polish Corridor and give back to Germany the colonies that she had forfeited in 1919. This was, of course, rejected and the Royal Navy was mobilized and Army and RAF reserves called up. Our Government confirmed that we would honour our pact with Poland. On 1st September Germany invaded Poland and we issued an ultimatum to Hitler which had absolutely no effect. In the evening of the 3rd September there was a signal to 'General' from the Admiralty: 'Commence hostilities against Germany.' This was received with almost a sense of relief.

Our Captain (Captain A.R.M. Bridge) broadcast to the ship's company. We darkened ship, and ready-use ammunition was brought up from the magazine, including shells for our 6-inch guns which were all of 1914 vintage and clearly stamped to prove it. We went to Action Stations at dawn and took off armed with bombs and depth charges to search the area far and wide. We found numerous merchant ships, which our observers called up by Aldis lamp demanding name and destination.

This had little effect beside annoying the Merchant Navy. We could not find anyone with whom to be warlike and it was all rather an anticlimax.

When we returned from this first war-time flight we heard the news that the liner *Athenia* had been torpedoed and sunk on the first day of hostilities. We had all been quite convinced that, as soon as we declared war, there would be immediate British successes, and it was something of a shock to find that first blood had been to the enemy. However, another general signal from the Admiralty cheered us; it simply said: 'Winnie's back.' This meant that Winston Churchill had been appointed First Lord of the Admiralty. The news was hailed with enthusiasm by the Navy as we all felt that we now had someone with a more realistic attitude in the Government.

During the next few weeks we continued to search the seas in all directions; the coast of Sumatra and the Andaman Islands, then across to Ceylon and beyond to the Maldive Islands. We called at Colombo on occasions to refuel, pick up mail and stores and give the crew a break ashore.

In the first few days of these searches our briefing had been vague and we were not clear about our targets, but this was clarified and we found that the major panic at that time was over German surface raiders. In particular, it was known that the pocket battleship *Graf Spee* was somewhere at sea and a terror to all merchant ships. In fact, we had no real excitement. There were a number of reports of U-Boats which turned out to be quite harmless and friendly whales and dolphins.

News from home was not encouraging: on 17th September we heard that Stalin had also invaded Poland, but the worst was on 18th September when we were horrified to find that HMS *Courageous* had been sunk. We had felt that a carrier, with its aircraft and surface escort, was virtually immune to submarine attack. There were serious faces in the wardroom when the untruth of this sank in.

Some other information came trickling through which left us absolutely incredulous. Our relatively small RAF bomber force had been risked, and the aircrew's lives endangered, by being sent over Germany to drop 6,000,000 leaflets.

We were even more incredulous on hearing that reconnaissance and intelligence reports had shown that Hitler was massing troops and tanks in the Black Forest, providing an obvious target for our bombers, but the War Minister had refused to allow them to be bombed because the area was 'private property'. Were we being governed by fools? The effect this would have on the fighting forces and their morale could not have been realised. We had thought that this would be a short and lively war but now began to see that it was likely to be a much longer one.

More bad news on October 16th: HMS *Royal Oak* had been sunk in the 'impregnable' Scapa Flow.

During the month of October we continued to search the seas for someone upon whom to wage war, but all the shipping we met was either friendly or neutral. Our main base was Colombo, but we often called to refuel at other places. The Seychelle Islands were unusual and pleasant; in Madagascar the climate was appalling and the ship was attacked by myriads of flies.

By early November we had found our way back to Singapore,

44

where the naval base possessed the only dry dock in the East large enough to take *Eagle*, while her bottom was being scraped and her boilers cleaned.

We had all been wondering what effect the war might have had on Singapore during our absence. It did not appear to have changed very much. The most important part of life was still the social round. The only obvious difference was that the RN, Army and RAF now wore uniform all the time; even the local Territorial Army unit wore a form of uniform and walked around saluting one another. The advantage to us was that we could enjoy a short rest period in peace-time surroundings. After a week on the island we re-embarked and sailed west to continue our searching of the Indian Ocean.

Every so often we spent a few days with our aircraft at Trincomali, a huge, protected anchorage big enough to take a large fleet and having an RAF airfield called China Bay. I was to come to know this place well. My only excitements were caused by engine trouble when, for a few days, we suffered from shaky fuel which must have been supplied to us at some refuelling stop. One aircraft was forced to land in the sea but, after an air search, we found the crew safe and well, in their dinghy. In my case I twice suffered very severe engine trouble, but my good old Pegasus ground on for a sufficient time to allow me to make emergency landings on the ship. I felt that my friendly devil who had looked after me in the crash in 50 Squadron, still had my well-being in hand. I had become on very friendly terms with him and now called him 'Joey'.

Aircrew were a superstitious crowd and nearly all of us had some form of lucky charm. One of my friends had a teddy bear called Rupert without which he would not fly; another always wore a Chinese medallion on a gold chain around his neck which had been a prized possession of his kid brother but which the boy had insisted on his having when he became a pilot. Both of those friends survived the war. A few put their trust in their religion to protect them; I never heard of this being very reliable.

During November, December and January, the news from Europe did not improve. Both merchant shipping and the Royal Navy had sustained a number of losses. We were heartened, though, in December when we heard that the cruisers *Exeter*, *Ajax* and *Achilles* had engaged the *Graf Spee* and driven her into Monte Video, later to be scuttled. This removed our principal target.

In this same month my promotion to Lieutenant came through, not because of any particular merit, but based on the seniority that I had carried with me from the RAF. My achievement of this auspicious rank while still at the age of twenty resulted in a certain amount of tooth-sucking by the ex-Dartmouth officers.

We spent Christmas Day at sea. The start was not very festive for me, as it was my turn to do the dawn anti-submarine patrol ahead of the ship. However, we had quite a lively time during the remainder of the day which included the old naval tradition that the officers act as waiters to serve their men with their Christmas dinners. I found that it went down very well with the men and there was much hilarity.

January brought depressing news about convoy losses in the North Atlantic and a number of RN ships being lost. On the other hand, we were pleased to hear that Stalin's invasion of Finland was going badly and his forces had suffered high casualties from the unexpectedly spirited defence from the Finns.

At last, on 1st February, we were detailed for a more interesting job: we were to escort the Australian Expeditionary Force across to the entrance to the Red Sea in a convoy designated US1.

We flew ahead of the ship to the rendezvous and met a most stirring sight: a convoy of eleven troopships and passenger liners, many with famous names, steaming fast in immaculate formation with a covering force consisting of the elderly battleship HMS *Ramillies*, and the cruisers *Sussex* and *Hobart*, screened by destroyers led by *Westcott*. I often thought with nostalgia of this fast convoy, when I was rolling across the Atlantic in an escort carrier covering a six-knot convoy of elderly freighters. We crossed to Aden without any alarms and lay in this ghastly port for a day.

Also there to refuel was the liner SS *Andes*, bound for Singapore with the 2nd Battalion Argyll and Sutherland Highlanders. Their fate would be to suffer high casualties fighting the Japanese, the survivors spending years of misery in prisoner of war camps. From Aden we steamed down to South Africa and called for a week at Durban to 'show the flag' and give leave. I shall never forget the wonderful hospitality received in that city, which exceeded anything I would experience in future years in the Navy. From South Africa we wended our way back to our old home in Singapore, where we disembarked all our aircraft to RAF Sembawang, an airfield near the naval base.

We spent almost two months in Singapore, presumably because no one could decide what to do with us, living in what was virtually peacetime. Very little seemed to be happening in the land war in Europe, which was being called 'the Phoney War'. In the war at sea, however, the Royal and Merchant Navies were suffering. We were disastrously short of escort vessels, and the few available were being flogged to death.

One piece of news cheered us: despite having declared neutrality, Norway had allowed the German ship *Altmark* to take refuge in her fjords while some three hundred British seamen from ships sunk by the *Graf Spee* were imprisoned in her. The destroyer HMS *Cossack* steamed straight into the fjord, lay alongside *Altmark*, took off our people and steamed out again. This was, to us, a really typical RN operation.

When at Sembawang, we worked Tropical Routine, not flying in the afternoons. It was the monsoon season and watches could be set by the rain. It started at 1330 and stopped very conveniently at 1600, so that we could easily arrange to reach the swimming club at exactly that time. We were all given a week's leave and I spent mine in Kuala Lumpur, the capital of the Federated Malay States. This was a very fine city, largely run by the British although we had no legal right to do so. Another diversion that I found was motor racing, having been recruited in to the team of a Chinese gentleman called Lim Peng Hong, who ran a successful car business but also built racing cars. It was good experience but I don't recall winning any races.

Being a Scot I naturally migrated towards the Argyll and Sutherland Highlanders, the second battalion of which had come out in the *Andes*, and became very friendly with a subaltern called Dick Webber who was later captured by the Japanese and spent years of horror working on the Burma Road. Fortunately, he survived and we met soon after the war. He attended my wedding and I attended his.

The situation in Europe became progressively worse with Germany invading Norway and Denmark, but we were wildly enthusiastic when we heard that the FAA had attacked and sunk the cruiser *Konigsberg* in Norway. This was a tremendous boost to our morale, which shows how out of proportion one's reaction can be to an event simply because it is dear to the heart.

On 9th May, having had virtually no warning, we re-embarked all the aircraft and *Eagle* sailed to join the Mediterranean Fleet. Having at last a definite object in view resulted in a wave of enthusiasm on board. I think that we had all felt rather embarrassed about our sheltered existence.

We steamed at our best speed across the Indian Ocean, only doing what flying was necessary for essential anti-submarine patrols. By this time a shuffle of aircrews had given me a new observer, Lieut. Pat Humphreys who was very experienced and probably the best observer with whom I ever flew. He had already distinguished himself during the Spanish Civil War, when he had been awarded the Empire Gallantry Medal (later to become the George Cross).

We passed through the Straits of Bab-el-Mandeb, up the Red Sea and through the Suez Canal, then turned westward to join the fleet in Alexandria. I was looking forward to our arrival for reasons quite unconnected with the war. I have always been fascinated by Greek and Roman history, and felt a thrill at the idea of seeing the city founded by Alexander the Great some 2,300 years ago. Unfortunately, the great Pharos which was one of the Seven Wonders of the World had long disappeared and there was only a normal lighthouse at the harbour entrance.

The harbour, however, could not have been more impressive; on our port side, as we entered, was a long line of destroyers and light cruisers, two of which were very modern French ones. One destroyer was Polish. Beyond these were the merchant ships and the steam yacht of King Farouk, the dissolute young monarch. Behind this shipping was the palace of Ras-el-Tin, taken over by the RN as the HQ of the Rear Admiral, Alexandria. In front of the warehouse and dockyard buildings were a dry dock, a submarine depot ship with its brood alongside and an old passenger liner acting as accommodation ship for the RAF Sunderland Squadron; near them were the oilers of the Royal Fleet Auxiliary. On our starboard side was a line of battleships including HMS *Malaya*, and HMS *Warspite* wearing the flag of Admiral Andrew Cunningham, the C-in-C. At the nearer end of this line was a ship which appeared to date from the earliest days of the dreadnought and was the French battleship *Lorraine*. All the ships were immaculate apart from the three French ones, whose rigging was festooned with washing. After a deal of pushing and shoving by tugs we moored fore and aft about 50 yards from *Lorraine*. Then we took a closer look at our new home, which was a hive of activity.

Pinnaces and tenders were tearing around in all directions, while amongst them were dozens of fellucas – small open boats with huge lug-sails – which provided a 24-hour taxi service between ships and the shore and proved both useful and cheap.

The news from home was appalling. On 10th May, Hitler's troops had swept through the neutral countries of Holland and Belgium then on into France, where the British Army was trying to slow them down with little help from the demoralised French troops. In the next few days we heard about the amazing operation of the 'Little Ships' which rescued a large proportion of our army and many of the French who were still prepared to fight. Despite our admiration for this very British operation we were, of course, all worried sick about our country now being alone with an army which had lost its equipment, standing by to defend the island against an apparently unstoppable German horde. It was strange to find, in these circumstances, that the morale of the FAA remained as high as ever. This inability of our nation to accept defeat has saved us many times in history, despite its illogicality.

· During the first few days in Alexandria we did our homework about the Italian Navy and Regia Aeronautica, since it was clear that they were the reason for our presence. Mussolini was only waiting to see 'which way the wind blew' to decide which side to join and it must seem likely that the most loot would follow joining the Nazis. Our studies showed that the Italians had many excellent ships including modern, fast battleships: between the wars they had designed and built some very fine aircraft. We had little knowledge of the abilities or morale of the crews.

Between bouts of homework we had the opportunity to see something of the city, a surprising mixture of up-market shopping and hotel areas surrounded by appalling squalor. It was very cosmopolitan; all the catering and restaurant businesses were owned and competently run by Greeks; the major industries were run by Jewish families; there were many Italians, the majority of whom filled the role of house-maids and shop assistants; most of the Egyptians seen around carried out the more menial tasks but also provided the Police and Army lower ranks. They had virtually no middle class but only a wealthy and well-educated aristocracy and the 'fellaheen' or peasants, who were treated virtually as slaves.

We were warned that, should we have any dealings with the police, we must insist on their finding an officer of at least Inspector's rank, who could write Arabic, as the policeman would probably be illiterate! An Egyptian Army major, who had been at an English public school and then Sandhurst once said to me: 'The Egyptian Askari (Private) is the worst bloody soldier in the world.' Later in the war my experiences confirmed this fully. Language was most complicated; most business and conversation amongst the upper classes was conducted in French, although a good deal of English could be heard: the aristocratic Egyptian could usually speak fluently in Classical Arabic, French, English and Italian and often German, while the felaheen only spoke a crude Arabic. We felt rather like the latter, most of us having only a smattering of schoolboy French apart from our own language.

We had very little time to settle down in our new situation before the C-in-C, who was always bursting with energy, had the whole fleet at sea to practise every maritime exercise.

Tension was building up. Something must happen soon. It did on the 10th June. Mussolini finally decided that it was safe to join Hitler and declared war on the Allies. We viewed the future with excitement tempered with some trepidation.

On that same day we heard that the FAA had suffered another blow. HMS *Glorious* had been sunk by the German battlecruisers *Scharnhorst* and *Gneisenau*. We had a horrible feeling of vulnerability. Already we had lost *Courageous*, which left us with one modern carrier *Ark Royal*, the elderly *Furious* and *Eagle*, the small *Hermes* and the converted merchant ship *Argus*. The new *Illustrious* class was not yet in full commission. We would be the main target for the Italian Navy and Air Force. It was not long before this fear was proved to be justified.

Chapter 6

We go to War

After spending a week steaming around the Eastern Mediterranean looking for the enemy, we learned from RAF reconnaissance that the Italian fleet was lying comfortably in Taranto, so we returned to Alexandria.

We had been given some fighters: three Sea Gladiators had been delivered to El Dekheila for us. This place was Alexandria Airport, where the Egyptian Airline, MISR Airways, ran a vague service, and there were a few small private aircraft. Dekheila was later to become the headquarters of the FAA in Egypt. The pilots went out in groups to have experience on the type, as we did not yet know who should fly them and it was likely that any of us could find ourselves 'fighter boys'. The Gloster Gladiator was a delightful aircraft to fly, with a top-speed of 250mph and smooth, responsive controls, and superbly manoeuverable; it was one of the most satisfying aircraft that I have ever flown. It was decided that the flight should be led by our Commander (Flying), Commander C.L. Keighley-Peach, who had been a pilot in FAA Fighter Squadrons flying Nimrods and Ospreys. Four Air Branch officers who had served in RAF fighters before transferring to the RN made up the flight.

On our next trip to sea we were shadowed by Cant flying boats, which were quickly destroyed by our Gladiators but not before they had given warning of our position. Soon a formation of Italian SM79 three-engined bombers appeared, flying at about 14,000 feet, and dropped sticks of bombs which seemed to be aimed mainly at us. As soon as they approached the fleet, every ship opened up with its high-angle guns, providing quite a barrage, and the enemy aircraft departed at high speed, some before they had released their load. Our gunfire did not appear to have hit any of them nor had their bombs hit us, although some had exploded in the sea quite close to us. This was the first time that we had been under fire and we had not particularly enjoyed having things dropped on us from above.

Our first time in action caused an unexpected incident: we had a mutiny! The next afternoon we found our whole complement of

Chinese assembled on the flight deck abreast the island, chanting 'Too long this flucken shlip'. I suppose they had some justification, because we had left Singapore without giving them any warning of our destination and dumped them in the middle of a war. They were pacified by a promise of repatriation to Hong Kong when we returned to harbour, which we did. They were replaced by Royal Marines, Naval Stewards and Maltese who did an admirable job, but we missed our cheerful Chinese 'boys'.

On June 22nd, four of us were sitting around a table at the Alexandria Sporting Club enjoying our very British afternoon tea, when some French officers came rushing in waving papers, throwing their caps on the ground and shouting 'La France a capitulée.' Other Frenchmen present leapt up and lamented loudly. We continued to sip our tea and look terribly British, so that no one could think that we had anything to do with these noisy people – anyway, we had been expecting it to happen for at least two weeks.

Two days later we awoke to find that the French Admiral had informed our C-in-C that he intended to sail back to France. Admiral Cunningham had replied 'No Way'; he was certainly not going to give the ships of their fleet to the Germans. Their reaction was to make the signal 'Lorraine has her main armament trained on Eagle.' A quick look in her direction left us with no doubts. To anyone who has not had the opportunity to look straight up the barrels of very large and fully loaded guns, at a range of 50 yards, I cannot recommend the experience. However, our Admiral immediately replied 'Warspite's main armament is trained on Lorraine.' Looking around, we could see that other British ships had their guns trained on the French cruisers.

We spent the day in a condition of severe twitch while the impasse continued. In late afternoon an agreement was reached, everyone pointed their guns in less offensive directions and our knees stopped knocking. The French had accepted the offer to repatriate those who wished to go home, while the others remained in their ships 'on parole', after all ammunition had been removed with their oil fuel, other than the small amount necessary to run the ships' auxiliaries.

Some members of the press came on board to ask their fatuous questions. One of our stokers was asked how he had felt with all those big guns pointed at him and had replied: 'How would you feel, Mate? I was fuckin' shittin' masel'.' I think he spoke for all of us.

Naturally, part of our minds was always occupied with what was happening further north. It seemed obvious that Hitler's next move must be an attempted invasion of England. Already the Luftwaffe had started to build up its bombing raids and the RAF was doing yeoman work shooting down far more of the enemy than they were losing themselves. We gave the RAF full marks for this but were less enthusiastic about certain stories filtering through on the 'grape vine'.

Some of our FAA Skuas and Rocs helping to cover the beaches for the evacuation at Dunkirk had been shot down by the RAF, whose aircraft recognition course had only, apparently, covered Spitfires and Hurricanes. We sincerely hoped that fighter pilots in the Middle East could recognise a Swordfish. More cheering was news that FAA squadrons, some operating from Hatston in the Orkneys, had been doing great work attacking German shipping around Norway.

In early July first blood to *Eagle*'s aircraft came for 813 Squadron which had disembarked and, operating from Sidi Barani, had attacked the important Italian port of Tobruk with torpedoes, sinking the destroyer *Zeffiro* and the liner *Liguria*, as well as damaging another destroyer and a freighter. In addition, Lieut. Collins had attacked and probably sunk a submarine, then machine-gunned the airfield. We were full of congratulations, but wondered if 824 Squadron would have the chance to prevent our colleagues developing superiority complexes. It was not to be long.

On 8th July we were at sea again with all aircraft embarked and a fleet of three battleships, cruisers and destroyers.

The sun had not ascended far before the Regia Aeronautica decided to have a field day. Waves of SM79s came over at high level to rain bombs on us, having selected *Eagle* as their target. High level bombing is notoriously inaccurate but we had to give full marks to the Italians, who were getting much too close for comfort. We felt that we would rather be somewhere else. There was unusual enthusiasm for flying the normally unpopular anti-submarine patrols. I did two during the day, which took me away from the ship for over five hours. When on patrol we could see the splashes from bombs falling around *Eagle*, but she always steamed safely through them.

Much of the credit for our charmed life must go to our Commanding Officer, Captain A.R.M. Bridge, who had made a study of ballistics and would stand all day on the bridge watching the SM79s through his binoculars and, as the bombs were released, would give calm wheel orders. As he swung the ship to starboard a stick of bombs would fall near our port side, and vice versa. This elicited the signal from the Admiral: 'I have watched with fascination your handling of your unwieldy vessel.'

We returned from our second patrol just as a raid was ending, only to find that trigger-happy HMS *Malaya* couldn't recognise a Swordfish and opened up on us with her AA guns. Fortunately, she wasn't very good and nothing came near us before someone told her to stop. We landed on without any further problem and at dusk the raids stopped.

The Italian Fleet was at sea. Dawn searches, flown by 813 Squadron, had found it in the Gulf of Calabria, shadowed, and reported four battleships with cruisers and destroyers. Our ships altered course to converge with them and increased to maximum speed, which was restricted by the old *Ramillies*, although she did her best, and by *Malaya* which was suffering condenser trouble.

Excitement was rising, as we knew that we must soon be ordered to send off a striking force. It was the turn of 824 Squadron, and the torpedomen worked flat-out to check and set their babies and hook them on to our aircraft. The Italian Air Force arrived again, causing volleys of curses from our men trying to handle the heavy torpedoes on their trolleys while the ship heeled in violent turns to avoid the bombs.

We had chosen our tactics and were continually re-briefed on the position and formation of the enemy fleet. Midday was the time agreed to take off, as it would coincide with the change-over of shadowing aircraft and patrols and thus avoid delaying our ships more often than absolutely necessary to allow *Eagle* to turn into wind. Tension was building up and it was difficult to keep still. Soon after 11.30 we were told to man our aircraft so I climbed into the cockpit while my observer, Petty Officer Mears on this occasion, clambered in behind, loaded with his chartboard and instruments. My rigger helped to fix my harness then, with a pat on the head and a 'Good luck, Sir', dropped down to join the mechanic and help to wind up the inertia starter on my engine. We started up, I made the cockpit checks, then sat back to await my turn to take off. I found that much of the tension had disappeared and it had become the normal routine that we had repeated so often. My turn came and I opened the throttle to accelerate down the deck, passed the island where some of our people were waving, and rose into the air. One circuit of the ship gave time for all aircraft to be airborne and we edged into formation, climbing slowly on course for the enemy fleet.

Struggling up to 7000 feet, we cruised along in bright sunshine which seemed to belie our war-like errand. After flying for nearly an hour we saw the Italian fleet on the horizon. It gradually took shape until it covered a vast expanse of sea, then individual ships became clearly defined. The three sub-flights broke away and we aimed for position to make a copy-book attack. Suddenly we saw puffs of brown smoke breaking out above and ahead of us; they were firing their high angle guns, but most of it seemed to be bursting well above us. Our sub-flight leader chose the largest ship nearest to our side and we began to dive. The ships were steaming at very high speed with great, white wakes streaming astern; I estimated that they were doing over 30kts, giving a very difficult target, so I aimed my dive to reach water level as far ahead of the enemy ship as possible. As our height was lost, she opened up with close range weapons throwing multi-coloured tracer into the air which seemed to approach incredibly slowly, then pass at tremendous speed. As I manoeuvred for position the ship started to turn to starboard, providing me with the worst possible angle of attack; the best that I could do was to fire at an angle that might hit her port quarter. The air was full of tracer as I dived down until I pulled out just above the water, swung to starboard, flattened out and held the aircraft straight and level until, in the best position that I could manage, I pressed the button on the top of my throttle.

I then felt the jerk as the torpedo dropped, and fought to hold her down against the loss of weight while making a vertical turn to the right and zig-zagging away towards safety in the hope that this would confuse the gunners.

In a few seconds PO Mears called that we were out of range, so I eased the throttle back and began to climb slowly on a course for home, which I hoped was still afloat. I asked if all was well in the rear cockpit and was assured that it was. I wanted to know if he had seen any hits, but he hadn't. Another Swordfish appeared to our right so I edged into formation and was shortly joined by another. I asked for a count of those in sight and only seven could be seen; it looked as though we had lost two but, within a few minutes they appeared below us. We had not lost a single aircraft.

A surprising feeling of relaxation came over me and I realised that for the last fifteen minutes my heart had been thumping like a hammer. As we came within sight of our fleet we found them ready for us, *Eagle* already turning into wind so that we could go straight in to land.

We all thumped down on to the deck and were struck down below to the hangar, where we were greeted by demands to know how successful we had been; unfortunately, none of us could confirm a definite hit. The instant that we were pushed off the lift, the crews fell upon the aircraft with refuelling lines while the torpedomen pushed trolleys with fresh torpedoes under the fuselages. It looked as though we were going to do it again. We were: we were told to grab a quick bite of lunch, then stand by to take off.

By 1600 all aircraft had been refuelled and re-armed and, sitting in our cockpits waiting for the ship to turn into wind, we saw the most wildly encouraging sight: the fleet was charging along with great, white bow-waves breaking at the blunt stems of the battleships, the huge 15-inch guns of *Warspite*'s A and B turrets were rising to maximum elevation and, on the masts of every ship, huge battle ensigns streamed out – a sight not seen since the Battle of Jutland in 1916 – and gave the effect that cavalrymen must have felt before a charge. In a rush of adrenalin, I wanted to stand up and shout 'Let's get at them!'

One after another we streamed into the air, edging into formation and climbing towards the enemy fleet, which became visible immediately, little more than twenty miles away.

I felt a bump and my Swordfish rocked as though I had hit a patch of rough air; I called to my observer 'What on earth was that?'. He said, '*Warspite* has opened fire; that was a 15-inch salvo passing underneath.' Having been modernised, unlike the other battleships, her guns were the only ones yet within range.

In minutes we were close enough for the sub-flights to split away so as to attack from different directions. My position was again to port of the target and I dived, making every effort to reach a good angle for a drop. As I almost reached the water, I pointed ahead of the bows of a huge ship which had already started to turn away: the air was full of tracer; they seemed to be firing every gun that they possessed at us: I pressed my throttle button, felt the fish drop, then repeated the break-away tactics of the earlier attack. We were clear, once again without a scratch. I thought that I might have gained a hit on my target's port quarter but she didn't appear to be losing speed.

In a matter of minutes we were circling our own fleet to find that, once again, we had not lost a single aircraft. *Warspite* was still firing salvo after salvo and we could see the splash of her shells landing around the Italian vessels. Amazed, we saw the whole enemy fleet turn away and steam flat out on a diverging course from our ships.

This larger and more modern Navy was in full flight. What a débacle! We wondered which had frightened them most – the shell fire or the FAA.

Eagle, with some attendant destroyers, broke away from the other ships and turned into wind for us. As we were pushed off the lift we found our ground crews cheering and waving and, as we climbed down, they were offering us 'sippers' from their coveted rum ration, which they had kept for our benefit. This was the greatest honour that an officer could receive from his men in the Royal Navy: it was an emotional experience and an offer that the most rabid tee-totaller could not refuse.

We went to be de-briefed and found that we had made history! This was the first time that aircraft had made a torpedo attack during a fleet battle, and we had done it twice in four hours. We were pleased with ourselves, but disappointed in gaining so few, if any, confirmed hits.

In the two hours before dusk we were air-raided eight times with no hits, then it stopped and we assembled in the wardroom with the usual waving of arms and cries of 'There I was. . . . .'

A report was picked up from Italian radio and luckily we had an officer who could translate it. The Italians reported an engagement with the British Fleet and admitted the loss of a destroyer and a submarine, which rather surprised us, giving their casualties as 29 killed and 69 injured. *Warspite's* salvos had, in fact, badly damaged their flagship. Their Air Force claimed to have sunk *Eagle* and one battleship. Actually, no ship of ours had been damaged, nor had we suffered a single casualty during the actual battle although *Gloucester* had been hit and her captain killed in one of the air raids.

The next day we were surprised and relieved to have no air raids at all. We started the day with a discussion about what we had learned: firstly, relatively few aircraft attacking a fast-moving ship taking avoiding action had little chance of success, despite many months of practice. The answer seemed to be a large force of aircraft coming on to the target from different directions and dropping so many torpedoes that some must be bound to hit. This was proved true in the Pacific in years to come. More encouraging was the fact that not a single aircraft had been hit, despite the very heavy AA fire that we had met. As it was our first experience of this type of opposition, it was a great relief.

In future I was often to have the unpleasant experience of being in a ship under attack from low-flying aircraft which appeared to be invulnerable to an intense AA barrage.

We went back to our old routine and two A/S patrols fell to my lot, this time with my usual crew of Pat Humphries and Naval Airman Smith as TAG. On the way back from the second one, my good old Pegasus engine decided that I had asked too much of it on the previous day, and cut dead. I thought that we were surely about to ditch but managed to coax it into giving a few unenthusiastic bursts which were just sufficient to let me make a rather hairy deck landing.

When we reached the hangar we found that the excitement for the day was not over. The Italian Fleet was reported to be in the port of Augusta and 813 Squadron was arming up with torpedoes to make a dusk attack on the harbour. With the targets at anchor we had great hopes of doing more damage than we had when they were steaming fast.

Some hours later they all returned and we were disgusted to find that the majority were still armed with torpedoes. The birds had flown, probably to Taranto, and they had had to be content with sinking the destroyer *Leone Pancaldo* and damaging an oiler.

Admiral Cunningham decided that little could be achieved by

remaining at sea and turned for Alexandria, accompanied by the Regia Aeronautica which had re-awakened and made fifteen raids, again without hitting anyone. When things died down the C-in-C made a signal addressed to *Eagle* and repeated to all the Med. Fleet:

I wish to congratulate your officers and ship's company most sincerely on the fine work carried out during the last week's operations, often under the most exacting conditions. On Tuesday 9th with only 17 Swordfish embarked and after two days flying your aircraft kept touch with the enemy fleet, flew off two striking forces of 9 TB's within a space of four hours both of which attacked the enemy and returned. I consider this a performance unsurpassed in carrier history. I sympathise with you that more hits were not obtained and that the Augusta operation on the night of the 10th did not yield better targets. The work of the two Gladiators on the return trip has been excellent and the results most satisfactory and highly creditable to the pilots concerned. I wish to congratulate you personally on the way that you have handled and worked *Eagle* throughout. I watched with amazement the skill and ability with which you dodged the many bombs directed at *Eagle*.

It was nice to be appreciated.

One more A/S Patrol on the 12th was my last flight for the trip so I had time to analyse my feelings on my first operation against an enemy. I wondered if 'Joey' had been helping but, as no one else had been hit, I couldn't give him special credit. However I had been sure that I was going to ditch when my engine cut out but I had managed to limp to the ship and land safely, so perhaps he was due some thanks. I toasted him at the wardroom bar.

Had I been scared? It seemed to me that the tension had gone as soon as we had taken off because we were carrying out the routine that we had practised so often, admittedly without the target shooting at us. I don't remember feeling particularly frightened: I think that I was more alarmed on the next day when I thought I was going to ditch.

As we approached Alexandria the Squadron disembarked to Dekheila, where we were used for anti-submarine patrols around the entrance to the harbour and also for Army Co-operation work, largely helping the 'brown jobs' to test and improve the camouflage of the city's anti-aircraft defences. On one of these flights I gave my two Army passengers a fright because my engine cut out three times. When we landed I demanded a new engine. The Pegasus in my dear old Stringbag K8419 (E5B) had given continuous trouble since I had flogged it to death at the Battle of Calabria, and many hours of work by our fitters had failed to put it right. Flying over the sea with an engine in which one has lost faith is bad for the nerves. She was left at Dekheila to be rejuvenated when we next went to sea and I flew other aircraft. This foray with the fleet only lasted a few days, as we made lengthy searches of the Aegean Sea but could find no trace of the Italian Fleet.

When in range, we flew ashore to collect my aircraft, which had been given a new lease of life. The next day I took it ashore again with the rest of the Squadron aircraft.

Chapter 7

Four for the Price of Three

We spent a few days doing practices and patrols until we received a cry for help from 202 Group RAF. They were short of suitable aircraft to cover ships steaming up and down the coast, principally to Mersa Matruh, to deliver supplies to the Army. To meet this *cri de coeur* we flew to the RAF landing ground at Ma'aten Bagush, which was my first real experience of the Western Desert, being some 100 miles west of Alexandria.

My idea of a desert had been gleaned from *Beau Geste* and stories of the French Foreign Legion and had produced a vision of miles of rolling sand inhabited by Bedouin Arabs riding horses and camels, brandishing swords and muskets and led by a handsome sheik. I found that the nomadic Bedouin in the Western Desert were normally scruffy people who reserved water for drinking only. They travelled on their feet in most cases, led by a decrepit sheik who, if he was lucky, rode on a mangey donkey. The only ones that bordered on the novelist's type were some that I met in Cairo, who were dressed in immaculate European suits and spoke fluent French and English.

The coastal plain was hard, stony ground with a thin layer of sand although, further inland, there were areas of dunes, in particular the Quattara Depression. Following the coast westward was a reasonable tarmac road stretching as far as Algeria, and alongside this was a railway line, in full operation, which continued as far as the Egyptian border at Solum. The running of the trains had been taken over by the Royal Engineers.

Hoping that we might find some targets, we took with us a Torpedo Flight of which I was a member. The RAF welcomed us warmly and helped us to be as comfortable as possible although we quickly appreciated that, by comparison, we had enjoyed absolute luxury on board ship. We lived in tents, sleeping on camp beds, but the thing we found most unpleasant, after the cleanliness of ship life, was that everything touched seemed covered with grit. The slightest movement, particularly of transport or aircraft, caused clouds of fine, dusty sand. The worst of these conditions arose during a khamseen (sand storm). This starts with the atmosphere becoming sullen and heavy, then a brownish pall appears which becomes a tan-coloured curtain rising thousands of feet into the air. A whispering begins as the wind increases; grains of sand tumble over one another as if possessed until the whole surface of the desert has become a flowing sea. The whispering becomes a hissing as the full fury of the storm strikes.

Hair, ears, mouth, uniform and boots instantly fill with sand. The heat grows, sweat dries instantly and skin cracks. The Arabs say that after two days of khamseen murder is justifiable. I must fully agree with them. The effect on aircraft engines can be imagined and the skill of our mechanics in keeping them running was beyond praise.

Close to the railway line, supplies were reasonably plentiful and food was quite palatable, together with adequate bar stocks. There was always an acute shortage of glasses and I learned a cunning trick to overcome this, one that I was to use often over the years. An empty bottle was filled with old engine oil to a height of three or four inches; a metal rod or poker was then heated and plunged through the oil to touch the bottom of the bottle, which split neatly around the level of the liquid; a little use of sandpaper produced a reasonable container. At the back of my mind came a vague school memory of the Coefficient of Volumetric Expansion, which must have had something to do with it.

The desert was a place that lent itself to thought and soliloquy. It was impossible to avoid feeling that our little world was a separate entity from the remainder of the universe. It was so different from the luscious green fields of Europe. Everywhere that the eye could wander there was the same dull hue. Each day was the same as its predecessor; the sun blazed down from a cloudless sky which gave little contrast to the land. Out of range of the sound of moving transport or the revving of aircraft engines there was total silence; no birds sang. After night-fall the noiselessness became almost formidable. Usually, when talking of silence, one accepts the background murmuring, the crackling and creaking of a cooling building, the soughing of wind in a tree and the cry of a night bird.

The RAF asked us to search along the coast and provide cover for shipping, particularly around Mersa Matruh, but we found no enemy activity.

We had only been there a short time when it was decided that 824 Squadron should move up to Sidi Barani and from there make a torpedo attack on Tobruk. I was not involved in this operation because of aircraft unserviceability problems. The remainder of the torpedo flight flew off to Tobruk on a moonlight night and attacked the shipping in the harbour. They succeeded in sinking the destroyers *Ostro* and *Nembo* but were greeted by a violent, intense AA barrage which hit many of their Swordfish and resulted in our first casualties. Lieutenant George Brown, our Senior Pilot, was severely wounded but managed to fly home, but the observer, Petty Officer Wynne, died from his wounds the following day. This was a considerable blow to us and I think we lost any feeling of invulnerability that we might still have held.

RAF Blenheims made regular reconnaissance flights along the coast of Libya, and on 21st August they reported a submarine depot ship in An-el-Gazala, a small Italian port and airfield in Bomba Bay, and a submarine coming in from sea. This seemed the perfect FAA target and the RAF expected us to send all our aircraft armed with torpedoes and every other missile we possessed. However, with our usual gross over-confidence, we decided that three torpedo aircraft would be adequate.

At this news there were cries of 'Where the hell is An-el-Gazala?' The observers rushed off to examine a chart and pointed with their fingers, to give the impression that they had known all along. It was clear that we would need to pass Tobruk, which we knew to be heavily guarded, as well as other fighter airfields. The chart also showed a distance of some 300 miles, and there was no doubt that, even if we refuelled at Sidi Barani, the 155 gallons in a Swordfish main tank would not get us there and back. Long-range tanks would be needed.

We had been screaming for these tanks for months and had been promised them when suitable transport from the UK could become available. Meanwhile our fitters had, with great engineering cunning, designed a tank which looked like, and probably was, a 44-gallon petrol drum, to which they had welded supply lines on the bottom and a little vent pipe on top. This was secured in the observer's cockpit with straps; there was no room for the TAG, as the observer had to move aft into his cockpit to navigate, work the radio and, if necessary, fire the Lewis gun, all this while breathing high octane vapour from the air vent in the extra tank. I was happy that I was a pilot.

Another snag cropped up; the leader of our torpedo sub flight was suffering from bronchitis and the medical fraternity utterly forbade him to fly. A cry to Dekheila resulted in the arrival of Captain 'Ollie' Patch, our only Royal Marine and now our Senior Pilot, first thing next morning.

We took off for Sidi Barani at 7.00 am, Ollie leading, with Midshipman (A) C.J. Woodley as his observer, Lieutenant (A) N.A.F. Cheeseman with Sub-Lieut. (A) Freddie Stovin-Bradford as observer on his starboard side; I was on his port side with Petty Officer A.H. Marsh as observer. Woodley was suffering from tonsilitis and should not have been flying but was determined not to be left out, and insisted with a dreadful croak that he was fully fit.

After more than one hour's flying over the desert we reached the airfield at Sidi Barani and flew around to have a careful look. We had been warned that, being on the border between Egypt and Libya, it had been repeatedly bombed by the Italian Air Force and the surface was like a ploughed field. We selected an area that seemed less rugged than the rest and landed without breaking anything.

Some RAF were waving their arms about on one side of the field so we assumed that that was where we were expected and taxied over, stopping our engines as quickly as possible to avoid creating a sand storm. They were all very welcoming, and immediately put men on to fuelling our aircraft. This was a thankless task, as the fuel had to be pumped by hand from drums, every little drop through a muslin cloth to avoid any sand sneaking into the tank. They took us to their Mess-cum-Ops Room, which was cunningly constructed of petrol tins filled with sand, roofed by a tarpaulin and containing two wooden benches and a collection of camp stools round a trestle table.

We felt very sorry for the RAF detachment that had been exiled to this dismal place, with only the most basic facilities. They were close to the Libyan border so were bombed fairly frequently and had little with which to defend themselves. It seemed a recipe for insanity.

We fought our way in through an atmosphere of dust and tobacco-smoke and they gave us breakfast of tinned sausages with the inevitable baked beans followed by bread, with marmalade dug out of a tin with a bread knife. While we were enjoying this magnificent repast the RAF's ancient Bombay transport arrived with our maintenance crews, their tools and sundry bits and pieces that might be needed. With them arrived Leading Torpedoman Arthey, who always did a superb job. The desert is no place for delicate instruments such as torpedoes but he nursed them with loving care until the very last minute before take-off so that on this occasion, as always in the past, they were to run impeccably.

Delivering our people to us was typical of the co-operation we always received from the RAF in the desert. This may have been partly due to the enthusiasm for the FAA held by Air Commodore Collishaw, the Air Officer Commanding in the Western Desert who had been a pilot in the RNAS during the first war and later Wing Commander (Flying) in HMS *Courageous*.

The report from the Blenheim reconnaissance arrived shortly before 1000. It confirmed the ships were still at Bomba, so we quickly conferred on our 'plan of action'. We decided to fly out to sea for about 50 miles, then turn west, flying no higher than 50 feet above the water, which would make it impossible for the Italian sound detection system to pick us up, and would certainly put us out of visual range from the shore. Hopefully, this would give us some protection from patrolling fighters, which were our greatest worry. A Swordfish, although wonderful in many ways, was not an ideal platform from which to have a scrap with a fighter.

We took off just after 1000, slipping into a very loose 'Vic' formation just above the surface of the sea. This was to avoid using more fuel than absolutely essential; flying in close formation needs continual throttle adjustments which tend to swallow fuel. On the other side of the coin, flying so low is very uneconomical, as an engine won't accept any attempt to lean out the mixture with the mixture control lever.

Bearing in mind the old adage that you can't win them all, we adopted the motto 'Forge on regardless' as we turned westward. The next two hours were boring. There is so little to occupy the mind on the way to an attack. Too much thought about the possible amount of flak and the nearness of enemy fighters tends to engender large amounts of twitch.

Despite the fact that little effort was required to keep station in such loose formation, it was unwise to slip into a daydream as, at 30 feet above the water, it would only need a slight nudge on the stick to hit the sea. Apart from this small effort there was little to do but admire the limited scenery. The sky was an unbroken pale blue fading to almost white on the horizon on our right. On our left the sky merged into the sand-coloured haze over the desert. Below us the sea showed a calm, blue surface dappled with light from the sun blazing overhead and showing clearly the almost black reflection of our three Swordfish. There was no life other than the occasional irate sea-gull fluttering away from our disturbing presence.

After nearly two hours, Ollie's gesticulating arm indicated that we should turn to the left. We turned some 90° on to a course that should take us into Bomba Bay, assuming that young Woodley had got his arithmetic right. Clearly he had, as we saw, in a few minutes, the land ahead and some tiny ships in the far distance. Marsh suddenly shouted 'Submarine dead ahead', at the same moment that I myself saw a large submarine on the surface, moving very slowly, and presumably charging its batteries. Washing festooned it from stem to stern and I immediately thought 'That would not be allowed in the Royal Navy.' Many of the crew were sunbathing on deck and, seeing a torpedo bomber coming straight towards them, jumped over the side and swam madly away, for which they could hardly be blamed. I couldn't help feeling that it was a bit hard to disturb their lunch-time break, but what a target! Some intrepid character, however, opened up with a machine-gun from the conning tower but didn't do any damage. We saw Ollie's torpedo drop a few hundred yards from the target while I swung to port and Cheeseman to starboard to go for the depot ship from opposite sides. Within a few seconds we saw a huge explosion amidships on the submarine, which split in two, the bows quickly disappearing, while the stern stuck up into the air before also sliding below the surface.

I continued my sweep round to port, closer and closer to the depot ship, whose huge bulk now seemed almost to cover the horizon, when I saw that she was not just one ship: a destroyer and another submarine were tied alongside her. I shouted 'Bloody hell, we can't miss them all.' Ollie's efforts had woken them up: the destroyer opened fire with fully depressed guns but most of it went over my head; the depot ship was firing much more dangerous tracer, the familiar red, yellow and green coming straight at me in the usual slow curve, then flashing past as though suddenly accelerating – I prayed that it would continue to flash past. Closer, yet closer we came to the ships until, convinced that I couldn't miss, I let my torpedo go, holding straight for a few seconds then pulling into a vertical turn to port, holding the nose down to counteract the rise due to losing the weight of the fish, and knocking in the automatic boost override. We were much closer to the ship than I had intended and almost scraped down her starboard side. Marsh was hammering away with his Lewis gun, which was probably good for his morale but would not have done much damage to the Italians as, in our steep turn, his gun was pointing to the sky. We were flying over the desert and out of range of the flak. I took a deep breath, which seemed the first time that I had exercised this function for some minutes, and eased the rate of turn, knocking out the auto boost override to stop the Pegasus guzzling fuel. Out of the corner of my eye I could see a cloud of black smoke issuing from the far side of the ship. Cheeseman must have hit. Within a second there was a tremendous explosion on our side of the target. A vast cloud of black smoke tinged with flame shot hundreds of feet into the air while great lumps of debris were falling out of it. I must have hit the depot ship's magazine. My turn was swinging me back towards the bay so I gave a thought to my job and turned back to the sea. Petty Officer Marsh was dancing up and down in the rear cockpit and shouting but, of course, I couldn't hear a word in the slipstream. Finally he appreciated that conversation would be improved over the intercom and told me that all three ships seemed to have blown up into little pieces and the remains were sinking. This looked like a good day's work.

Marsh and I and our aeroplane were still in one piece so all we had to do was to fly back to Sidi Barani in the same condition, enemy fighters and fuel consumption permitting.

As we passed seaward over the coast I saw Ollie Patch circling ahead and goofing at the activity in An-el-Gazala, so closed into tight formation on him. I asked Marsh if he could see Lieut. Cheeseman and he said that he was coming up astern. Great! We hadn't lost anyone. As we all came together there was much waving and 'thumbs upping'.

We eased out into open formation again, heading seaward for some fifteen miles, then turned east on to a steady course. About 40 miles from Bomba we saw a Cant Z501 above and to seaward of us. It paid us no attention; the crew's eyes were no doubt fixed on the explosions in the bay. I doubt if a little flying boat could have done us very much harm anyway.

As we repeated our wave-skimming journey back to Sidi Barani I felt my left ankle itching so put my hand down to scratch it: there was a spot of blood on my sock; I must have knocked my heels together some time, I thought.

After flying for over one-and-a-half hours I began to be concerned about fuel because the indicator was showing singularly little. I could not understand why, since I calculated that I should have enough for another hour. I tried easing the mixture control lever a little forward but the engine did not like it and the revs started to drop: I instantly pulled it back into rich. Despite the fact that we were following the leader my observer should have been keeping a plot, so I asked him for our ETA. He said, 'About fifteen minutes,' and this was confirmed by Ollie starting a gentle turn to starboard. Almost immediately we could see the shoreline ahead. I was somewhat relieved, as it would have been a horrible débacle to have completed an apparently successful attack, then fallen into the sea within a few miles of home. I edged over towards the leader, pointed to my engine then downward; he raised his hand in approval so I eased up to about 200 feet, saw the landing ground ahead and, with no attention to circuit drill, throttled back and went straight in to land, hoping that I had not chosen a part of the field mottled with bomb holes. It was reasonably smooth, so I came to a halt in good order.

The other two landed behind me and we taxied towards the ground crews, who were waving beside the tents. As we cut our engines they came rushing up, led by Leading Torpedoman Arthey demanding to know if his beloved fish had run properly. We assured him that he had done a grand job and that they had all run perfectly and had probably sunk four ships. He was overjoyed and almost speechless with pride. He certainly deserved all possible praise. The fitters and riggers were shouting to know if the aircraft had been alright and if we had any problems. They were as pleased as Arthey when we were able to tell them that there had not even been a backfire from an engine. These men did a wonderful job, particularly in desert conditions in these days before engines had been modified to protect them against the blowing sand. I often felt that they did not receive the credit due. When their aircraft were away on an operation they were more worried than the aircrew. I was often very touched, when a crew failed to return, by the distress on the faces of the ground crews. I recall a petty officer saying to me 'You know, Sir, it's like losing some of your own family.' Although full of congratulations, they were all, including the RAF, quite reasonably dubious about our claim to have sunk four ships.

While the aircraft were being refuelled, we crept out of the blazing sun into the Ops. room, where the RAF provided huge pots of hot, sweet tea which they offered to lace with their limited supply of spirits. Much as we would have liked to accept, we felt it would be unwise as we had still to fly back to Ma'aten Bagush. We sent a signal to report that the operation had been successful, roughly what we had done, and asked for Blenheim photo-reconnaissance as soon as possible.

Cheeseman told us that he had nearly had a catastrophe: he had been about to drop his fish when Freddie Stovin-Bradford had seen that they were over shoal water and just stopped him in time; to reach deeper water he had to get very close to the target but had seen the torpedo hit the submarine amidships and explode before finding himself over the airfield at about 50 feet. No aircraft seemed ready to take off but there were men running around to whom they waved but did not get the courtesy of a reply.

When we stolled back to our Swordfish, I was horrified to see that some of the cowlings behind the engine had been removed. My fitter came to me and said: 'You ain't flyin' that there kite anywhere today, Sir.' He showed me where a bullet had come through the cowling, smashed the extension to the main spar, scraped across the bottom of the main fuel tank, fortunately a self-sealing tank, passed over the rudder bar and exited through the other side. The scratch on my ankle came from the bullet on its way out. Had its path been a fraction to one side it would have hit my ankle bone and the chance of my being able to fly home would have been remote. When I had finished gasping, I immediately thought: 'Good old Joey, he's done it again.' I felt that he was entitled to some display of gratitude but it is difficult to know what to offer a friendly devil; he probably wouldn't appreciate a bottle of scotch or a box of chocolates; I could only hope that he would accept my kindly thoughts.

The only way to travel back to Bagush was for me to pack into the back of Ollie's aircraft with Woodley while Marsh did the same sardine act with Freddie. We arrived safely and were, once again, greeted with congratulations, but scepticism of our claims. After a scrub and a change into clean khaki shorts and shirts we had a fair meal and propped up the bar while waiting for the results of the reconnaissance. It arrived during the evening and we found that their photographs, when developed and analysed, had proved that all four ships had sunk and the harbour was littered with oil and debris. We maintained that it had all been very easy but, in truth, I think we had rather swollen heads.

At 0311 the following morning a signal was received from the Admiralty, marked 'IMMEDIATE' and addressed to C-in-C Mediterranean and repeated to HQ Middle East, which said: 'Submarine broke in two. Some of the crew jumped overboard when air torpedo was running. Depot ship fired 4 inch AA, destroyer fired Pom Poms and multiple MG's. Three successive explosions occurred in these ships alongside each other. Subsequent Recce. confirms two submarines, one destroyer and one depot ship destroyed. Wreckage and heavy oil smear visible on sea. Photographic analysis follows.' Long afterwards we learned that there had been an additional bonus. Ollie's sub. had been modified to carry the Italian 'Chariots', two-man torpedoes intended to attack our fleet in Alexandria, and also some of the trained crews.

Surprisingly the Italians had, on their radio, admitted the loss of four ships. They maintained, however, that it was the result of an attack by an overwhelming force of torpedo bombers and motor torpedo boats. I imagine that their local CO would have felt a little silly if he had admitted that it had only been three Swordfish.

The Commander-in-Chief Mediterranean Fleet, Sir Andrew Cunningham KCB, DSO, was enthusiastic about these results, which confirmed his views that torpedo bombers were the answer to destroying an enemy fleet in harbour. It was one pace nearer the Battle of Taranto. In his despatch to the Admiralty he wrote: 'This attack which achieved the phenomenal result of the destruction of four enemy ships with three torpedoes, was brilliantly conceived and most gallantly executed. The dash, initiative and co-operation displayed by the sub-flight concerned are typical of the spirit which animates the Fleet Air Arm Squadrons of HMS *Eagle* under the inspired leadership of her Commanding Officer.' As he would have been the first to appreciate, a few words like these do much for the morale of aircrews. He confirmed his views by recommending the DSO for Ollie Patch, the DSC for the other officers and the DSM for Petty Officer Marsh. Their Lordships duly agreed and we were able to buy our pieces of ribbon from Messrs Gieves's representative in Alexandria.

For a few days after the Bomba Raid, my poor old Stringbag was still at Sidi Barani awaiting spares and I had few squadron duties to keep me occupied. This gave me time to think about events in the rest of the world.

Force H from Gibraltar, with *Ark Royal*, had virtually destroyed the French Fleet in Oran to avoid its falling into Nazi hands. In France itself Petain was turning it into a Fascist state. As might have been expected, the Channel Islands had been occupied and Hitler was massing troops in France to invade England. It had been clear to the German High Command that, before laying on a full-scale invasion, it would be necessary to destroy British air power. With this in view they had used over 1,000 aircraft to bomb our towns and airfields in the South of England and industrial cities in the Midlands and on the East Coast. This had done considerable damage and had brought our civilian population into the front line, causing a horrifying number of casualties. However, the RAF had also bombed Berlin, which Goering had assured Hitler the Luftwaffe would never allow to happen.

The newspapers claimed that, with their Hurricanes and Spitfires, our colleagues of the RAF had destroyed 694 German aircraft for the loss of only 150 of their own. We pilots were hesitant to accept these claims and were to be proved right, but nevertheless they had obviously done incredibly well. This terrific fight had already been named 'The Battle of Britain' and Winston Churchill had made his famous speech in Parliament in which he said: 'Never in the field of human conflict was so much owed by so many to so few.' Perhaps we would never be invaded after all.

Our convoys were still being slaughtered in the North Atlantic and food was very strictly rationed. It looked as if things might begin to improve when Winston made a deal with Roosevelt to lease to him bases in Newfoundland and the West Indies in return for 50 over-age destroyers. These would be little use to the fleet but could be a godsend for our convoy protection.

On 29th August we flew back to Dekheila then, on the following day, embarked again in *Eagle*. A spare aircraft had been found for me so I no longer had any excuse for being lazy.

Chapter 8

No Longer Alone

On 31st August we were at sea with the greater part of the Eastern Med. Fleet, and steaming to the south of Crete in the hope of finding the Italians. It seemed that I must compensate for my days of rest, as on that day I was detailed for three flights, two searches and one A/S patrol, and flew for over eight hours. We searched the area around Crete and along the Greek coast but found no sign of the enemy.

What had happened was that, during the last few weeks, the Italian Fleet had been reinforced by the arrival of two new battleships, *Vittoria Veneto* and *Littorio*, whose guns could outrange those of all our ships except *Warspite*. Admiral Inigo Campioni, the C-in-C of the Italian Fleet, had taken a squadron of 5 battleships, 10 cruisers and 34 destroyers to intercept our force of 2 battleships, *Eagle*, 5 light cruisers and 9 destroyers. A severe storm had blown up, preventing the use of reconnaissance aircraft, and his destroyers were not riding it well. As a result, the Italian High Command, Super Marina, had ordered a return to base. Campioni had therefore reversed course and retired to Taranto.

One object of our trip was to cover a convoy from Alexandria to Malta, which arrived safely. There was, however, a second purpose which gave us much joy. For a long time we had known that the new armoured aircraft-carrier HMS *Illustrious* was to join us. We had been promised this for so long that she had been christened 'HMS *Illusive*'. At last she was on her way from Gibraltar to meet us. She was equipped with two squadrons of Swordfish, Nos. 815 and 819, and 806 with the new FAA Fighter, the Fairey Fulmar. None of us had yet seen that aircraft and could only recognise it from photographs. *Illustrious* was commanded by Captain Dennis Boyd, whom we knew to be very pro-FAA and who had even learnt to fly at his own expense. She wore the flag of Rear Admiral Lumley Lyster, who had been appointed Rear Admiral Aircraft Carriers Mediterranean. This appointment was to have considerable effect on our future, since he had been Captain of HMS *Glorious* in 1938 and had worked out a plan to attack the Italian Fleet in Taranto, which had been abandoned when the Munich Crisis had faded. This great addition to our strength was accompanied by the modernised battleship HMS *Valiant*, which was virtually a sister-ship of *Warspite*, plus a number of cruisers and destroyers.

During one of our searches we met a Swordfish from *Illustrious* and exchanged welcoming signals. It was encouraging that we were no longer alone.

Much less cheering, however, was to find that a few of the Luftwaffe had arrived to bolster the Regia Aeronautica. We were attacked by JU87s, known as Stukas. This was a very different kettle of fish from high level bombing by SM79s, as the Stuka was one of the best dive-bombers of World War II and the pilots were highly trained and experienced, having accompanied the Panzer advance through France. They were horribly accurate and were fitted to make an unnerving banshee scream when diving. There were no direct hits, though, probably due to the amazing ability of Captain Bridge to make *Eagle* dodge like an MTB.

During the early evening four Fulmars suddenly appeared and we immediately opened fire with every AA gun that we possessed; meanwhile our pilots ran around screaming that they were friendly. Eventually this sank in and firing ceased, having fortunately failed to hit any of them. It was established that they had been driving off bombers with some success, but in the process had become hopelessly lost and unable to find *Illustrious* until, greatly relieved, they saw our fleet with *Eagle*. We turned into wind and took them on board.

Naturally our pilots were keen to examine the Fulmars, after which we took charge of the visitors.

One of them, Sub-Lieut. Graham Angus Hogg RNVR, always known as Angus, was a Scot from Edinburgh. Being a fellow countryman, I naturally looked after him and found him some gear and a bed. We chatted during the evening and I found that he had had a remarkable career in the Navy: by the age of twenty he had been awarded the DSC and had been three times Mentioned in Despatches.

He had suffered a very unpleasant experience when returning from a patrol over the evacuation beaches at Dunkirk, when the RAF shot him down. He had been flying a Roc and, although it had been badly shot about, he had managed to land it in England, himself unhurt but his TAG dead. Taking his parachute, as these were in short supply, he had gone off to find transport. However, being fair and rather Teutonic-looking, wearing no cap and carrying a parachute, he was arrested; a volley of good English oaths in a Scottish accent eventually put the matter right. Having returned to his base, he recorded his opinion of the RAF in somewhat derogatory terms.

We hit it off remarkably well and later, in Alexandria, often went ashore together and visited each other in our respective ships. The following year we found ourselves both instructing at RNAS Abroath, shared a cabin and became close friends.

Our much augmented fleet now turned towards the east and we continued patrols and searches for the enemy, without finding him on the sea, though aircraft continued to attack us. The Fulmars frequently broke up these attacks and made unnecessary our previous reliance on the poor Gladiators, which had done such noble work.

Now that we had twice the number of aircraft that *Eagle* alone could supply, Admiral Cunningham felt that it was time something was done about the airfields on the island of Rhodes, which were the source of many of the enemy air raids. It was decided that Swordfish from both ships would attack the two airfields concerned on the morning of 4th September.

The plan was that *Illustrious*'s aircraft would attack Calato while we dive-bombed Maritsa, the two events being co-ordinated so that we all arrived just as dawn was breaking. This was a perfectly good plan and none of us in *Eagle* was particularly worried, as we expected to achieve complete surprise and did not anticipate that an airfield would have very heavy anti-aircraft defences.

Unfortunately, as our Scottish poet Burns, whose work I loathe, said in one of his more memorable remarks, the best laid plans 'Gang aft agley.' It is extraordinary how often, when a large gaggle of aircraft is involved, an operation which has had long and careful planning ends in chaos, while one that is arranged on the spur of the moment runs like clockwork. We had a jam-up on deck and, although we did not know this until later, *Illustrious* also had some confusion which took time to correct. The effect was that the timing became slightly out of phase. Having no knowledge of anyone else's difficulties, we eventually took off with seven aircraft of 813 Squadron and six of 824. On this occasion I had my own observer, Pat Humphries, with Naval Airman Williams as TAG.

In pitch darkness we set course for Rhodes, a flight of nearly two hours. I never liked long journeys before an attack because I found that tension built up during the period of preparation, but as soon as I was settled in my aircraft and involved in the routine of flying in formation, it ebbed away, leaving my mind free to wander.

I would dwell on the coming attack and visualise the target and the probable amount of flak, so that by the time I arrived, my nerves were twittering, skill was obliterated by excitement and a little man was banging at the back of my head crying 'Let's get at the bastards.' The effect might be to pull out of the dive much too low and either be hit by debris or actually fly into the target. There were cases where fighter pilots straffing railway lines passed only a few feet over the locomotive and were blown to pieces by the exploding boiler. I tried to put my brain in cold storage for the duration of the flight. This is not good flying practice, as a pilot should always be fully alert to any emergency. I would not much enjoy a passage in an air liner if I knew that the captain's mind was in limbo.

On this occasion the system seemed to work reasonably well and I was still in a calm state when the shores of Rhodes came in sight. Unfortunately, the operative word was 'sight' as it was becoming obvious that the plan of arriving at first light was failing and we would reach the target in broad daylight. To make matters worse we could see explosions and smoke rising from *Illustrious*'s target so they were awakening the island's defences and, probably, the fighters.

Nevertheless, 813 Squadron moved into bombing formation and dived down on to Maritza airfield, followed by my squadron.

We were met by a surprising amount of high angle and tracer AA fire, but nothing hit us so I aimed at the hangars and dispersal areas, letting my bombs go and pulling out of the dive at about 500 feet. Buildings were already blazing and covered with black smoke. As I pulled away and dived towards the surface of the nearest piece of sea, we had time to notice that the sky seemed full of CR42s – there were probably four or five of them – so I felt 'Here it comes; this isn't my day.' As we neared the surface of the water, Pat Humphries called in his usual calm way: 'There are two CR52's on our tail.' I had often practised fighter evasion tactics but had no great faith in them, but there was nothing better that I could do, so I held the aircraft down at a few feet above the sea, zig-zagging, while Pat gave me a running commentary on the fighters' movements. As they approached from our quarter our TAG opened up with his Lewis gun, while Pat fired Very lights at them as fast as he could reload his pistol: this may appear rather pointless, but was based on a rumour that the Italians had heard of something they had christened 'Churchill's secret weapon', about which we knew nothing.

Continuing his commentary, Pat reported that the fighter was within range and opening fire. I closed my throttle and made a vertical, tight turn towards the CR42 while we were still almost on the surface of the water – any aircraft other than a Swordfish would have spun into the sea – at which the fighter pulled away while his colleague, having left it too late, flew straight into the water. I expected another attack but he had either run out of ammunition or lost his nerve, and turned for home. This was all very satisfactory and the excitement appeared to be over.

I aimed towards the west until Pat had done his arithmetic and given me a course to steer for the fleet. When we seemed to be out of range of unfriendly aircraft, I climbed to a more reasonable height for the journey. We could see various other Swordfish in the distance but they were too far away to bother about getting into formation. After flying for over an hour we saw the fleet in the distance but, at that point, my Pegasus engine started to make very expensive noises, so Pat flashed his Aldis lamp to ask for an emergency landing. With a deal of grunting and groaning the engine kept running until we thumped down safely on *Eagle's* deck.

As we were struck down into the hangar I noticed a number of bullet holes in the wings and one in the engine cowling, although none near the cockpits. I thought 'Good old Joey, he's done it again.'

When we had accounted for all our aircraft we found that 824 Squadron had suffered no losses, but four of 813 had failed to return. This was the first time we had suffered appreciable casualties. I was distressed, because the observer of one of the missing ones had been Alan Todd, a friend of mine. This upset me particularly because I felt, probably unjustly, that his loss might have been avoided. I knew that he and his pilot had been totally different personalities and heartily disliked each other. I feel that a crew in which the members do not have complete confidence in each other is a prescription for disaster. We hoped that some of those missing might be prisoners of war: an unfounded hope.

A few weeks later I found that, for some reason, I had been Mentioned in Despatches.

With only a few A/S patrols to amuse us we returned to Alexandria, where we were able to join the aircrew from *Illustrious* and find out about the work of the FAA in other parts of the world.

We had been starved of such news and had never been able to understand the apparent secrecy campaign covering everything that naval aircraft did. Particularly when we were operating from shore bases, our raids were frequently reported in the press as RAF operations. In later years they were sometimes credited to the US Air Force. This was rather discouraging. However, we heard from our colleagues that our squadrons, working from the Orkneys, had been doing noble things in Norway and that *Ark Royal's* Swordfish had made successful attacks on airfields in Algeria as well as getting a torpedo hit on the battleship *Dunkerque* during the unpleasant business with the French fleet. In the same incident 814 Squadron in HMS *Hermes* had obtained a hit on the new French battleship *Richelieu* and put her out of action.

The FAA was expanding rapidly and pilots and observers were being recruited for the RNVR Air Branch. Arrangements had been made for the pilots to be trained at the US air base at Pensecola. This seemed an excellent system, as it allowed them to be trained without disturbance from air raids.

One disadvantage of the system, which I was to learn to my cost, was that night flying was carried out over brightly lit towns, and on airfields that were a blaze of lights with brilliantly lit runways: there were problems when they returned to the UK for operational training and were obliged to fly over a blacked-out countryside and land at an airfield, if they managed to find it, with only a row of tiny lights.

We also learned the encouraging news that a number of new armoured fleet carriers were building and light fleet carriers were on the stocks. Some merchant ships, too, had been converted, including the liner *Nairana*. For these ships and the general expansion, many new squadrons had been formed.

While in harbour we had time to think about the happenings at home. The Battle of Britain was continuing and the Luftwaffe was suffering much higher casualties than the RAF. A number of cities, London in particular, were being very heavily bombed, with high civilian casualties.

The morale of everyone was still high and it was very much 'business as usual': the King and Queen were not leaving the capital, which was remaining as the seat of government. It looked as though Hitler had no hope of invading England this year.

At sea there had been horrifying losses. The Germans now had the use of French ports for their U-Boats to attack our vital convoys in the Atlantic. To make things worse, they were converting merchant ships to surface raiders and these were more heavily armed than our rather ineffectual Armed Merchant Cruisers. This looked like an ideal job for the FAA, if we could spare the carriers.

In our own part of the world, the Italians had invaded British Somaliland and then Greece. Our government had promised to support the Greeks, although we could not see what could be done, as our army was itself short of men and equipment. After some initial success our forces were in retreat in the Western Desert and the Italians had invaded Egypt but had stopped and dug in at Sidi Barani.

For the next few weeks we spent much of the time in harbour while *Eagle* patched up some damage from near misses during bombing raids. On one occasion 309 bombs had been dropped on us in two days.

We did some flying from Dekheila but had a rather quiet time in general. *Illustrious*, however, went to sea with the fleet and 15 of her Swordfish made a successful attack on Benghasi, where they sank two destroyers and damaged some other ships. During October we ferried some aircraft to Malta and did routine A/S patrols and searches for the enemy fleet which, once again, were fruitless.

One day I flew with our Senior Observer, Lieut. David Goodwin, to take a film of the cruiser HMS *Liverpool* returning after having been hit by a torpedo from an SM79. She was an extraordinary sight, having lost most of her fo'c'sle, but appeared to be on an even keel; her bulkheads must have been extremely efficient.

The only warlike activity on this occasion was providing a diversion for *Illustrious*'s squadrons, which were mining the entrance to Tobruk harbour.

When we are still at Dekheila bad news arrives: *Eagle* is definitely out of action for some time. Shaking from near misses has made a mess of her avgas supply lines. *Illustrious* has just suffered a hangar fire and lost a number of her Swordfish. The buzz is that we are to lend her some of our aircraft. We are unenthusiastic about this, as it would seem that her pilots will be flying our aircraft while we sit around on our bottoms doing ship duties. Rumour is later amended and we find that the true story is that some of us are to join *Illustrious* and fly our own aircraft.

This looks interesting.

Chapter 9

The Famous Victory

On 6th November three of our crews joined *Illustrious* in harbour together with the maintenance crews, bringing with them the personal gear of the five of us who were to take our aircraft on board. The following day the ship went to sea and we flew out to join her. I had never before landed on a deck fitted with crash barriers and felt that I must come in low to avoid any danger of missing the wires, which didn't matter much in *Eagle* as you just took off again and had another attempt. The DLCO greeted me with furious 'Too Low' signals so I rose slightly and just slid over the round-down. I was signalled rapidly ahead over the lowered barriers and, as I was parked with folded wings in the forward corner of the deck, I looked around to see another Swordfish coming up beside me and a third already touching down. The landing rate was at least four times better than we could achieve in Eagle, where each aircraft had to be struck down into the hangar before the next could be landed.

The ship's people were very welcoming and we were shown to what appeared to be comfortable cabins. Later we found that they were over the propellor shafts, so that the vibration was appalling and it was almost impossible to sleep. We had to use camp beds in the corridors or on the quarter deck, which was reasonably comfortable with plenty of bedclothes.

We were in a different world from that of *Eagle*. *Illustrious* was huge, and full of equipment that we had never seen or even heard of. Apart from the fittings, radio and radar, etc., she had a formidable armament of AA guns. We also appreciated the atmosphere on board. Every member of the ship's company was dedicated to the operation of the aircraft and proud and enthusiastic about her as a carrier. This was so different from *Eagle*, where we had tended to be regarded as inconvenient passengers.

During the following days we shared with 815 and 819 Squadrons the routine of searches and A/S patrols. However, there was also time to brief us on the 'object of the exercise'. We were engaged upon a series of operations covering virtually the whole of the

Mediterranean. It was named MB8, involved a vast number of ships going in many directions, and was dependant upon most accurate timing. With our usual lack of faith in the staff we felt that there was little chance of it all working out as planned. We were to be proved wrong.

We had been at war with Italy for five months, during which the fleet had made sixteen sorties to sea. On only three occasions had the Italian fleet also been at sea and only one of these, the encounter off Calabria on the 9th July in which we had taken part, had resulted in a very brief action between the battle fleets. Even this had been too much for the Italians, who had slunk into their base at Taranto and stayed there. Mussolini had only the Adriatic and Tyrrhenian sea where he might feel that he had some command by virtue of air power and numerous submarines. Apparently he wanted his battleships to dominate the Greek campaign from Taranto until they could take part in his hoped-for triumphant entry into Athens. The object of MB8 was to reinforce the Eastern Med. Fleet, cover convoys to and from Malta, take supplies and troops to Greece and set up a base for refuelling in Crete. Finally, something had to be done about the Italian battle fleet in Taranto.

Practically every serviceable ship of the Royal Navy in the Med. was to be involved in these operations. We had 5 Battleships, 10 Cruisers, 2 Anti-Aircraft Cruisers, 30 Destroyers, the old monitor *Terror* and various trawlers and minesweepers and 2 aircraft carriers.

There were four convoys to be covered: MW3 from Alexandria to Malta consisting of 5 merchant ships carrying stores and petrol and to be joined by 2 ships for Suda Bay, in Crete, carrying fuel, petrol, AA Guns and Motor Transport; AN6 consisting of 3 ships carrying petrol and fuel from Egypt to Greece; ME3 consisting of 4 large, fast (15 kts or more) empty ships from Malta to Alexandria; AS5 was an unspecified number of ships from Greece to Egypt. There was also the monitor *Terror* with the destroyer *Vendetta* waiting in Malta for passage to Suda Bay, where *Terror* was to be harbour defence ship.

Combined with this complicated movement of merchant ships the Royal Navy intended to discomfort the enemy with a number of other operations. Force H from Gibraltar, being the *Ark Royal* (Flag of Vice Admiral Sir James Somerville), the cruiser *Sheffield* and the destroyers *Duncan, Isis, Foxhound, Forester* and *Firedrake*, was to act as covering force for Force F, consisting of the battleship *Barham* with the cruisers *Berwick* and *Glasgow* and the destroyers *Giffin, Greyhound* and *Gallant*, which was carrying troops (a total of 2,000) to Malta, then reinforcing the Eastern Med. Fleet. This was named 'Operation Coat'. On the way, aircraft from *Ark Royal* were to bomb Cagliari.

Vice Admiral Pridham-Wippell (Vice Admiral Light Forces) with the cruisers *Orion* (Flag), *Ajax* and *Sydney* and the destroyers *Nubian* and *Mohawk*, was to proceed to Piraeus to discuss the Greek situation with their people, then steam to Suda Bay to organise the construction of the base, where there was much to be done, including a boom to be laid, AA guns to be mounted and an airfield to be set up. Added to these, arrangements had to be made for fuelling, handling equipment and stores, accommodation for the troops, administration and medical facilities. Having ensured that all this was in hand he was to proceed to the Straits of Otranto, where he was to attack the Italian convoy which ran nightly across the Adriatic from Otranto, Brindisi and Bari.

Numerous other minor operations were also included but the culminating grand slam was to be Operation Judgement, an attack by the Fleet Air Arm on the Italian naval base at Taranto, intended to cripple their battle fleet.

So, this was where we came in! The rumours, guesses and, perhaps, fears had been well founded. Now we must do our homework.

An attack on Taranto was not a new idea, so we looked firstly at the history of the project. It had been considered as early as 1934, but more as an exercise than an actual operation. However, in 1938 it had reared its head again when the Munich crisis had been at its peak and Mussolini had been visualising himself as a modern-day Roman emperor. He had already carried out an entirely unprovoked invasion of Abyssinia. At that time HMS *Glorious* had been the carrier in the Med. Fleet and had been commanded by Captain Lyster, who was with us now as Rear Admiral Aircraft Carriers. The Munich panic had died down, but by then her aircrews had been trained; many of them were now with us.

For some time Admiral Cunningham had been considering the possibility of attacking Taranto with torpedo bombers and had been particularly impressed by the damage that *Eagle*'s aircraft had done to ships in harbour, as in our attack on Bomba. Unfortunately there were problems: firstly, the Swordfish would require long range tanks, as it would be most unwise for a carrier to put itself sufficiently close to the target to be in normal range; sufficient long range tanks had not been available until *Illustrious* had brought them. Up to the last minute, aerial reconnaissance of the harbour would be essential, but the RAF had no suitable aircraft to provide this; the arrival of Glenn Martin Marylands in Malta had now solved that problem; the aircrews needed practice in night torpedo dropping and the use of flares; this was achieved by mid-October. The operation was now feasible, so an attack was planned for 21st October. A hangar fire in *Illustrious* which destroyed some of her aircraft, caused a postponement. The next date chosen was the 30th October but this, too, was cancelled as there would be no moon, and a moon was thought to be essential. Finally, the night of 11th November was chosen.

The original plan of attack had been to use 30 aircraft from *Illustrious* and *Eagle* in two waves of 15. Nine of each range were to be armed with torpedoes, 5 with bombs and flares and one was to attack with bombs from the east as a diversion. Again the plan had to be changed, as *Eagle* was out of action, reducing the number of aircraft available. Five of her aircraft had transferred to *Illustrious*. On 9th and 10th we suffered a further reduction in numbers, as 3 of her Swordfish had ditched due to contaminated petrol taken from the oiler *Toneline*. This left only 21 aircraft, so the plan had to be: 12 in the first strike and 9 in the second, only 6 in each group to be armed with torpedoes.

However, the various delays had done some good. The photo recce had shown balloons and anti-torpedo nets. One of our staff officers had been flown ashore daily to get these pictures, had become very excited on seeing the balloons and, of course, wanted to show us the photos. Despite the fact that they had been taken entirely for our benefit, he was forbidden to do this, because they were 'Top Secret'. This was typical of the attitude we suffered from during the war, when little specialised units thought that they were, in themselves, the means to the end. Luckily the staff officer was a man of some ingenuity and had sneaked the prints from the RAF files, taken them to *Illustrious* to be copied, then returned them the following morning.

Obtaining this knowledge was vital if rather alarming. However, the situation was not as bad as it seemed. The 'cloak and dagger' boys (Intelligence) informed us that part of the balloon barrage had blown away in a recent storm and had not been replaced since the Italians had insufficient hydrogen, either because their stores had failed to order it or because someone had flogged it on the black market; furthermore the net defences had not been completed. The shipping using the harbour had found it an inconvenience!

The next thing to be studied was the layout of the harbour and its defences: the position of the targets and the route in and, hopefully, out to avoid the balloons and nets. There were, in fact, two harbours: the main, outer harbour, called the Mar Grande, contained the battleships which were moored on the eastern side and protected by a breakwater called Diga di Tarantola, lines of balloons and AA gun batteries; they were about three quarters of a mile from the shore. The most recent photos from the RAF Marylands showed six battleships and, further out, three heavy cruisers and eight destroyers. The smaller, inner harbour called the Mar Piccolo contained cruisers and destroyers and other small ships and tenders. On the land were oil storages and a seaplane base with hangars. The obvious plan was for the torpedo aircraft to attack the battleships, while the bombers and flare-droppers went for the ships in Mar Piccolo, the seaplane base and the oil storage depot. There was much discussion about angles of approach and final attack with the usual amount of argument, but we were all in general agreement.

We looked at the known AA defences. The Italians had long appreciated that Taranto would be a prime target for torpedo bombers and had surrounded the harbour with a formidable array of high angle and closer range batteries of guns and to this had to be added the massive number of guns from the ships. Our staff, sitting in comfortable chairs, had decided that the anti-aircraft fire could be discounted! It was fortunate that we did not know until later that they had also accepted 50% casualties! Nobody asked us if we accepted these odds.

From where and how far would we have to fly? The answer was that *Illustrious* would leave the main fleet at dusk and steam at high speed to a position 40 miles west of Kabbo Point on Cephalonia, giving us a distance of some 170 miles to fly to the target. Having flown-off the aircraft, she would cruise around until taking up a position 20 miles from Kabbo to be ready to take on any aircraft that returned, the first being likely at about 0100.

The next point was of prime importance to those of us who had transferred from *Eagle*. We had brought 8 crews but only 5 Swordfish – who was to go? We found that the first strike was to be led by Lieut-Cdr. K. Williamson, the CO of 815 Squadron from *Illustrious*. Our Captain Ollie Patch, Royal Marines, who had led us at Bomba, was to be in charge of the bombers and flare droppers, with Lieut. D. G. Goodwin as his observer. Lieut. K. C. Grieve of 813 Squadron would be observer to Lieut. C. B. Lamb, a pilot from *Illustrious*. Lieut. Maund of 813 Squadron with Sub.-Lt. W. A. Bull as observer would man a torpedo aircraft. The second strike was to be led by Lieut-Cdr. J. W. Hale, the CO of 819 Squadron, with Lieut. G.A. Carline as observer. Lieut. Bayley of 813 with Lieut. H. J. Slaughter would be a torpedo dropper; finally 824 Squadron would provide me with my usual observer, Pat Humphreys, to try to torpedo one of the battleships.

So now I knew. Ever since the idea of Taranto had been mooted I had had a premonition that the burden of torpedo dropping would fall upon me. This was probably due to my having, over the last few months, thrown a few fish at ships with a certain amount of success such as in our attack at Bomba. My feelings were mixed. Certainly, it was a boost to the ego to have been chosen but, on the other hand, it looked a pretty hairy operation, with less chance of returning in one piece than on earlier ventures. There was nothing to be done about it but put my faith in my friendly little devil 'Joey' who had looked after me since I had first learned to fly. I had a drink and tried to look enthusiastic.

During the few days before 'judgement' we had not been overworked but I did have a trip which became a little dicey on the 8th November. Pat Humphreys and I with Ldg. Airman Ferrigan as TAG were sent off to search for the ever-elusive Italians. As usual we didn't find them, but we found the cruiser *Ajax* looking for our fleet. We gave them the position by Aldis lamp. After leaving the cruiser we found a Cant Z 501 flying boat sitting in the sea with two perfectly healthy looking men in it: it was one that the Fulmars had shot down earlier. Having completed the search, we returned to the position where we expected to find the fleet. There was nothing but water in any direction. I had every faith in Pat's navigation, so was sure that it was not his fault. We started a square search but dusk was falling and, the fleet not showing any lights, we were afraid of passing by without seeing it. We were relieved when we got a D/F bearing from *Illustrious* and soon found her. By that time it was pitch dark but I managed to make one of my better night deck landings. There had nearly been one aircraft and crew short for the raid.

We were only required to do one more routine A/S Patrol on the morning of the 10th. After landing we found that we were to rest until the following evening. We attended some updating briefings, studied the weather reports and kept an eye on our aircraft. In fact, we had the utmost faith in the ground crews who checked and re-checked everything. The people working hardest were the unfortunate fitters of 819 Squadron who, after the disastrous loss of three aircraft, had to drain and completely flush out the tanks and engines of all the squadron aircraft, then refuel them from a different ship's tank. They worked all night at that job.

It was now the morning of 11th November, so we had time on our hands to find out how our huge operation, MB8, was faring. Our force, termed Force 'A', comprised almost the whole of the Med. Fleet. It was an impressive sight, and we flying people probably had a better view than those in ships. With us in *Illustrious* (Flag of RAA) were the battleships *Warspite* (Flag C-in-C), *Malaya* (Flag of Rear Adml. Rawlings), *Valiant* and *Ramillies*. We had 3rd Cruiser Squdn. *Gloucester* (Flag of Rear Adml. Renouf) and *York*. We were covered by 3 groups of destroyers; the 2nd D/F *Hyperion, Havoc, Hero, Hereward, Hasty* and *Ilex*; the 20th Div. *Decoy* and *Defender*; the 14th D/F, *Nubian, Mohawk, Janus, Juno* and *Jervis*. However, we kept growing and shrinking as units left to carry out jobs and others joined us from other duties. On 7th and 8th *Ajax* and *Sydney*, cruisers, had joined us after taking HQ 14th Infantry Brigade and equipment from Port Said to Suda Bay. On 9th *Ramillies* and 3 destroyers had been detached to cover the convoy from Alexandria to Malta, then to cover the fast (15kts) convoy ME3 to Alex. Today *Orion* joined us after her dash to the Piraeus and Crete. Yesterday we steamed westward to a position 40 miles west of Malta to make our rendezvous with the reinforcements for our fleet and were joined by the battleship *Barham*, the cruisers *Berwick* and *Glasgow* and the destroyers *Griffin*, *Greyhound* and *Gallant*. These ships immediately left us to disembark the 2,000 troops they were carrying in Malta before rejoining us.

Apart from our diversion to meet *Barham*'s party, we in *Illustrious* had spent our time in a more or less central position between Malta and Crete, to give general cover to the various groups against any foray by Italian surface forces and, as far as possible, to provide some fighter cover with our Fulmars. The only other fighters available in that part of the sea were three Gladiators – small biplanes – which were beautiful aircraft to fly but hardly a match for modern, low-wing monoplanes. They were based in Malta, and for some months were to be the island's only protection against daily air raids from the Italian fields in Sicily, which were in easy range. They christened them 'Faith, Hope and Charity'. Malta was in a most vulnerable position and was to put up a marvellous resistance that became one of the epic defensive actions in history (resulting in its being awarded the George Cross by King George VI). Despite its defensive role it was to remain a base for offensive operations and its Swordfish were to be a major factor in the disruption of supply convoys to the Axis forces in North Africa.

We had thought that all these ships scattered over the Mediterranean would have given the Regia Aeronautica a series of field days. However, we had suffered very little from enemy activity. At lunch time on the 8th a reconnaissance aircraft had spotted us and been driven off by our fighters, but obviously had reported us because, in the afternoon, another appeared and was again driven off. Within the hour, seven SM79s materialised. These were attacked by three Fulmars which shot down two of them and made the others jettison their bombs and leave the scene hurriedly. Yesterday, the 10th, when we were west of Malta to meet *Barham*, we were again shadowed and the Fulmars shot down a Cant Z501. This was followed, about an hour later, by the arrival of ten SM79s. They were flying at about 14,000 feet and were again attacked by our Fulmars and dropped their bombs at random doing no damage.

Their submarines had not had any greater success. *Warspite* had heard two under-water explosions which must have been torpedoes self-destructing and *Ramillies,* covering convoy ME3, heard three such explosions. No ship was hit, although Italian radio claimed a successful attack.

I joined most of the other pilots in the hangar to see our aircraft being armed for our jaunt that night. The bombers and flare-droppers were being loaded with 250lb SAP (Semi Armour Piercing) bombs. These aircraft carried a different type of long-range tank from those carrying torpedoes. This tank was cigar shaped and strapped to the torpedo rack. Our aircraft were to carry a new type of torpedo which we had not used before. It carried a Duplex contact/magnetic pistol designed to pass under the battleship and explode below its soft underbelly: it would also explode on contact with the target. We had agreed that these would be set to run at 27kts and at a depth of 33ft. A device consisting of a cable unwinding from a spool had been designed to avoid the weapon porpoising, or diving too deeply and sticking on the bottom of the harbour. They had been set to a low safety range of only 300 yards. We hoped that they would work better than the Italian ones; our torpedomen lavished care on them and we had never suffered a failure in the past. There was little else to do but have some food and wait.

Most of us filled in the time by walking around the quarter deck to watch the other ships – always a sight worth viewing. As dusk was falling and presaging the friendly anonymity of darkness, we broke away from the main fleet and, accompanied by the 3rd Cruiser Squadron *Gloucester, Berwick, Glasgow* and *York* and four destroyers, we turned at high speed to the north to take up our flying-off position 40 miles west of Cephalonia.

We watched the cruisers and destroyers building up speed. The sea was calm and its deep blue was broken by great curving swathes of water scattered into spray almost at the level of their fore-decks. I was reminded of a sharp knife slicing through the soft cream on the top of a cake. Our ship, too, was rapidly increasing speed; on the quarter deck, near the stern, my teeth began to grate from the shuddering vibration; astern, the wash from our propellors was rising in a foaming mass well above our heads. The sight thrilled me and I could have watched it for hours but the shaking became too much for comfort, so I escaped to the wardroom and tried to read a magazine.

Zero hour was fast approaching. By 1930 the first strike was being ranged at the after end of the flight deck. By 2015 all was ready and the twelve pilots manned their aircraft, followed by their observers armed with chart boards and their other paraphernalia. Most of us of the second strike took up vantage points to watch the performance.

We soon heard the familiar whine of inertia starters being wound up, the spit and cough as the engines fired, then the increasing roar as the pilots warmed them, then ran them to full throttle. *Illustrious* began to gather speed as she increased to 30kts, to give the maximum possible wind speed over the deck to lift the heavily laden aircraft into the air; the natural wind was light and variable and gave little help. At 2030 the first Swordfish went roaring down the deck and lifted easily before it reached the bows. The other nine followed without incident and disappeared towards the north west. It was all very routine and unexciting. As the last aircraft left the deck the ship rapidly lost speed, to give reasonable conditions to the handlers who were ready to range our strike; it isn't easy to push Swordfish around with 30kts of wind howling over the deck.

In three quarters of an hour it would be our turn, so we went below to collect our flying gear and personal items to take with us such as lucky Teddy bears. I did not have anything of that sort, but put my faith in 'Joey'.

At 2115 we were told to man our aircraft. I climbed on to the flight deck to find E5H; my faithful E5B was languishing at Dekheila. I climbed in, settling myself on the parachute. My fitter and rigger strapped me in, gave me a pat on the helmet and said 'Good luck, Sir, see you in the morning.' I hoped that they would. Pat Humphreys struggled into his cramped cockpit behind me. In a few minutes the FDO's illuminated wand started to circle with the signal to start up our engines. The crew wound the inertia starter: as the revs. were building I set the throttle, then knocked on the two magneto switches as the clutch was engaged. With a cough, splutter and a cloud of exhaust the engine fired and I caught it on the throttle, setting it for warming up. I checked the engine instruments, which all read what they should, then ran the engine to full throttle, switching off and on each magneto switch. The old Pegasus was running perfectly so I reduced to a tick-over and waited.

I could feel the ship building up speed and turning slightly into the fitful wind. I heard the leader's aircraft open up and roar down the deck. The aircraft handlers were doing their usual hair-raising act of ducking round the whirling propellors to pull chocks away. When my turn came I followed the FDO's signals to taxi into the centre line of the deck, held on the brakes while the wings were spread and locked, then, opening the throttle fully and easing in the boost override, I let the brakes go and started my take-off run. With the ship's speed of 30kts, air speed rose rapidly; as we passed the island a quick glance at the ASI showed it rising to 70kts. We rose smoothly into the air and I climbed away in a gentle turn to port and reduced the revs. to normal climbing power. I looked above for the other aircraft and Pat and I saw them at the same time. I slid into my slot in the formation as we continued to circle the ship. I asked Pat if he knew the reason for the delay. He said that he could only count seven of us, then corrected this to eight. As we passed again through north the leader, Lieut-Çdr. Hale, straightened up and set course to the north west. Later we found that L5F and L5Q had started to taxi at the same time and had collided; the latter had not been damaged and had taken off to join us but L5F with Lieuts. Clifford and Going had suffered broken ribs and torn fabric and had to be struck down for repair. Herculean efforts by the riggers had made it serviceable in a quarter of an hour and the crew, who had begged permission to be allowed to go on their own, took off only 24 minutes after us.

We gradually climbed to 8,000ft, passing through a layer of filmy cloud. Pat told me that we now seemed to be another aircraft short. We did not know at the time, but L5Q had lost its long range tank which, as she was one of the bombers, had been strapped to her torpedo rack. The engine had cut, but her pilot, Lieut. Morford, had managed to restart it. He now had insufficient fuel to fly to Taranto and back so had returned to *Illustrious* where, not expecting a friendly aircraft, they had opened fire on him, stopping, luckily, before he was hit.

So now we were only seven. It was a beautiful picture-postcard evening: there were only a few wisps of cloud below us, otherwise the sky was clear, and littered with a blaze of stars; to the south a three-quarter moon was throwing a golden pathway across the calm sea; the air was smooth giving hardly a judder. It would have been the most perfect evening to enjoy flying, had it not been for the reason for our flight.

It had become quite cold, but that could be expected in an open cockpit at 8,000ft. I asked Pat if he was comfortable and he replied: 'As far as might be expected'. I didn't envy him, jammed into the aftermost cockpit with vapour from the tank wafting around him while I was in reasonable comfort sitting on my parachute cushion, with an acceptable amount of space and surrounded by the familiar instruments.

Once again I found myself with very little to do. My old trick of putting my mind into cold storage didn't work this time. It seemed like riding through Egypt on a camel while pretending that the pyramids didn't exist.

After flying for more than an hour I noticed that the dark blue fabric of the horizon ahead was torn by a patch of light. I pointed it out to Pat, who looked through his binoculars and said that it must be Taranto, but neither of us knew why it appeared to be flood-lit. As we closed the land, the light seemed to flicker and pulse until, when we were closer still, it began to look like a major firework display. With some horror I realised what it was: AA fire. What were they shooting at? The first strike should have been well clear long ago.

The loom of the land began to clarify and our two remaining flare droppers broke away to our right, heading for their zone over the oil storage depot. There was a healthy fire burning over there, so someone in the first strike must have achieved a hit.

We were still some ten miles from the harbour but, at a height of 8,000 feet, it was becoming clearly delineated in the bright moonlight and the glare from the tracer. Although partly obscured by smoke and gunfire it was a copy of the excellent photos given to us by the Marylands. Hale altered course slightly to port and we could see, to our right, the breakwater, Diga Di San Vito, and dead ahead the little Isoletto San Paolo with the larger island, San Pietro, just to the left of it. We began to open out the formation and slide into a well spaced line astern.

Our plan was to pass around and to seaward of the submerged breakwater, then to turn towards the east after passing Cape Rondinella, cross the land, then dive down behind the balloon barrage, turning south as we came over the harbour so that the battleships would be broadside on to us and actually overlap so that, if we missed our chosen targets, there would be a chance of hitting the next in line. It was a good plan on paper.

The northern shore of the basin was lit by flashes from gun batteries there and, now falling behind us, the island of San Pietro was spurting flames.

I could imagine Pat at that moment; he would be stowing his chart board and navigation gear in some relatively safe place, and checking that his 'G-string' was firmly secured and that his parachute pack was easily accessible, although there would not be much chance to use it during a torpedo attack. His usual calm voice came down the Gosport tubes: 'The course for *Illustrious*, incidentally, should be about 135°. You might like to set it now.'

He was being very thoughtful; if he were to be knocked out while I was still in one piece, I might be able to find my own way home.

We passed Cape Rondinella, starting to lose height and turn in over the land. The harbour was partly obscured by smoke from the guns and the burning oil depot, and also from another blaze to the north – the seaplane base or a crashed Swordfish? The ground was clear below in the moonlight. I could see streets of houses like a town plan with open spaces of parks or playing fields. I hoped that the residents were all in air raid shelters, as spent bullets and shrapnel must be raining down like lethal hail stones.

I followed the leader as he gradually lost height. Suddenly there was a burst of light to the eastward as the first flare ignited, followed by others until they hung in the sky like a necklace of sparkling diamonds. This seemed to drive the Italians to even greater fury – the flak doubled in intensity and the curtain of barrage below us now rose into a cone like a feathered head-dress: above us high-angle AA was bursting in crackling puffs of smoke. If the tracer was one in five there must be more metal than air. 'My God! No one can fly through that – shades of Balaclava!'; in the increasing chaos I lost sight of the other aircraft; no matter, a coordinated torpedo attack was not so important, as the targets were stationary; we must simply get amidst the battleships and do our own thing.

Ahead there seemed to be a partial hole in the flak just where I wanted to be – I aimed for it calling to Pat: 'Hang on, I'm going down.' 'OK. Do your worst. Good luck.'

I pushed the nose down, easing back the throttle to avoid over-revving the engine. The speed built up – 140kts, 150kts, 155kts – I wanted to dive as steeply as possible, knowing that a gentle angle would only give me more time in the barrage. We were in it – the familiar red, green and yellow lines of tracer were crawling up towards us then hurtling past; ahead they appeared as a tangle of colour. The slip-stream was screaming through the struts and bracing-wires, and past my ears; my nose was filled with the stench of cordite; there was tracer above us, tracer below us and tracer seemingly passing between the wings. The dive was steepening and the speed building up – 160kts, 170kts – we met a barrage balloon! No self-respecting balloon should have been at that height; its cable must have been shot away. I hauled the stick over to the left – I missed it. There was a tremendous jar, the whole aircraft juddered and the stick flew out of my hand. 'Christ! I've hit the balloon cable' – but the wings were still there. I grabbed the stick – it wouldn't move – we were completely out of control. It was no time for finesse. I applied brute force and ignorance. It moved most of its travel to the right but only partially to the left – was it working the ailerons? – No idea! I looked ahead. 'Bloody Hell!' We were diving almost vertically into the centre of the City of Taranto! I hauled the stick back into my stomach – were the elevators working? They were; an elephant seemed to be sitting in my lap but slowly we began to level out, but still curving round to the right. Were we going to make it? Buildings, cranes and factory chimneys were streaking past below us then we shot over the eastern shore of the harbour and were level over a black mirror speckled with the reflection of flames and bursting shells. I stirred the stick around and found that I had, at least, some sloppy lateral control. Air speed? Far too fast to ditch if we had to and too fast to drop a torpedo. I was determined to aim it at something after carrying the bloody thing all that way and having a rather hairy dive – I'd be damned if I didn't do something with it.

A quick glance around: to my right and slightly behind me was a massive black object covering most of the horizon and having a vast castle towering above it – a battleship. I heaved the stick over to the right putting us into a near vertical turn towards the target. I thought: 'That was a damned stupid thing to do; she might not go back.' She did. I levelled out after turning 180° and pointing towards the great black hulk of the ship. Height OK, judging from the level of her deck – air speed dropping nicely – angle of attack not ideal but the best that I could do – aircraft attitude for dropping a torpedo rotten. The only way that I could achieve a straight line was skidding with some left rudder and the right wing slightly down. Torpedoes don't like being dropped when not perfectly level. There was surprisingly little flak around us. I was forced to revise this opinion. She was awake and had seen us. Strings of lights prickled along her decks and multiple bridges and grew into long, coloured pencil lines drawn across the dark sky above us. She was giving us everything except her 15-inch guns but, thankfully, she seemed unable to depress her other guns low enough to hit us. Closer and closer we came, her decks ablaze with muzzle flashes, the superstructure towering above us. 'Look out! Don't get too close, these things have a safety range.' I pressed the button on my throttle lever, felt the torpedo release, held straight for a couple of seconds then threw the stick over into a vertical turn to starboard.

Inevitably, after dropping a nearly 2,000lb load an aircraft rises and E5H was no exception. We rose right into the ship's gunfire. I fought the sloppy controls to force her down, crying: 'Fly, you bitch' – poor thing, she was doing her best. There was another jar and shudder – we had been hit again – 'Hell's teeth! Leave me something to take home.' Finally, I managed to push her down to skim the glassy surface, opened the throttle wide and knocked in the override. 'Careful; don't hit the water.' It's difficult to judge height over a smooth surface, particularly at night.

Ahead was the Diga Di Tarantola with its balloons. I must avoid that if I could but mustn't get too far to the right as there were more balloons over there. I edged over to pass slightly to the right of the Diga which, I hoped, would take me clear of balloons on each side. I could see San Pietro about three miles ahead; its batteries and those on the floating pontoons across the harbour entrance were still firing but were aiming towards the centre of the basin. Tracer from the battleship was passing over from astern of us and disappearing ahead. Scraping the surface of the sea we shot past the island into the wonderful, welcoming anonymity of the darkness. We were in clear air and still flying, although hardly in the approved flying school manner. Would she keep on flying long enough to get home?

I eased the nose gently upwards, took out the boost override and adjusted the throttle to give me normal climbing revs and boost. She started to climb. I moved the stick gently in all directions and applied a little rudder in both directions. Everything seemed to be working, at least to some extent but I could only keep a straight course with the starboard wing a few degrees down and by applying some left rudder. She was behaving much the same as she had when I was trying to attack the ship. No well behaved Swordfish should fly like that but, if she was prepared to fly at all, I would not criticise too much.

I swept my eyes over the dashboard. The engine instruments were showing no problems; revs steady; boost OK; oil pressure correct; oil temperature a little high but that was reasonable with the way that I had been treating the poor engine. Flight instruments were all over the place showing wing down, skidding and a general lack of keenness for the aircraft attitude. This, at least, showed that they were working.

It felt as though we had been over Taranto for hours, but in fact it could not have been more than a few minutes. Since Pat was always the perfect observer who never interrupted when I was involved with things that needed my full attention, I had not worried about his silence but I now felt a bit concerned, as I hadn't heard a word since we had left the coast. I lifted the Gosport tube and called rather tentatively:

'Are you alright, Pat?'

There was a sound like the heavy breathing at the beginning of an obscene telephone call, then:

'Yes – physically. What is your condition?'

I assured him that I seemed to be functioning normally and he said:

'Oh, that's good. I thought that you might be damaged as you have bent the aeroplane a bit'.

'It wasn't my fault. It was the bloody Eyeties.'

He assured me that he had not intended to imply any criticism of my flying which he felt must have been fairly competent, as I had got in and out and we were still flying, and he had had some doubts about that happening when we had entered the barrage. I explained what had happened during the dive and the attack. This caused silence for few moments: he had not appreciated that we had been completely out of control and nearly in a nasty mess in the centre of Taranto, nor that I had had only partial control during the attack. He had not noticed, either, that we were not able to fly straight even now. Eventually he said:

'I see. I suppose we should consider ourselves fortunate. Do you think that you can get what's left of this machine back to *Illustrious*?'

I replied that there was a fair chance and I was going to try, as I did not fancy eating spaghetti for the rest of the war. He quite agreed and said he left it entirely to me. I suggested that we would be more likely to find the fleet if he would give me a course to steer, and his reply was that I would have to wait a few minutes as all his navigation gear was somewhere in the bottom of the cockpit; meanwhile, I should steer roughly south east. I was already pointing more or less in that direction so left him to do some hunting around the floor.

After a remarkably short time he gave me a course. I set it on my compass but was not entirely happy about it, as magnetic compasses have a dislike of being skidded sideways. We compared it with the two observers' bearing compasses in the back, achieved a reasonable average and set it on my gyro. I had levelled out at 2,000 feet, which I felt was high enough since I had no wish to suffer from the cold as we had on the way in. The engine instruments were still reading healthy levels but the flight instruments were all over the place, which was not surprising in the attitude in which I was forced to fly. At a greater height I could have saved fuel and made more use of the mixture control but as, by my calculations, we had sufficient petrol for at least three hours, I felt that it should be enough to find the fleet or a piece of dry land.

Having done everything we could for our own preservation, we had time to discuss the attack. I had been rather too busy when over Taranto to think about things other than my own problems, so hoped that Pat could tell me something. He could not clearly tell what had happened to the battleships because with torpex torpedoes which explode underneath the target, hits are not immediately clear; he had, though, seen an explosion alongside one of the ships, the *Littorio* he thought, which had looked like a torpedo exploding on contact. He said that it had looked to be down by the bows. Another which he could not identify had seemed very low in the water. He had recognised our ship, which he said had been *Vittoria Veneto*, but I had to admit that I was doubtful of having hit it as our aircraft had been virtually out of control when I dropped. He was able to confirm that the seaplane hangars and the oil depot had been blazing. It seemed that we had done some damage.

I asked him about the health of our radio. He told me it was thriving and he could hear a great deal of chatter on the Italian naval channel, mostly in plain language; the word 'Taranto' kept cropping up but he couldn't understand the rest of it. He was able to get Radio Milan, which was playing gramophone records of Verdi operas. As my helmet was only fitted with Gosport tubes, I was not able to hear any of it. I just shut up and let him amuse himself.

My mind began to dwell on how I was to land this thing on deck – assuming that we found the ship – when there was no way that I could keep her level; furthermore, I had no idea whether we still had any wheels, or even undercarriage. I thought that I might be able to level out and kick her straight as I cut the engine then, even if she fell to pieces at that point I might, with any luck, manage to slither into the barrier.

When we had been flying for well over an hour since our hurried departure from Taranto, I began to feel that we should know something shortly. I was suffering from a very stiff and rather painful left leg from having to hold on left rudder all the time. I asked Pat if he had any idea of our ETA. In an incredibly calm and confident voice he replied: 'Oh Yes. About 25 minutes. I was just going to tell you that, I have picked up the ship's beacon.' My spirits rose about 200%. I asked for the change of course. He told me to carry on as I was. It took a few moments to accept this. We had been flying over the sea, at night, for well over 100 miles; there had been nothing with which to check dead reckoning navigation other than, perhaps, a back bearing of Taranto in the early stages, but he had brought us back to a moving fleet without a single alteration of course. I had always known that he was a good navigator but this was phenomenal. I didn't hurt his feelings by suggesting that there might have been an element of luck.

Fifteen minutes later I saw the foaming, phosphorescent swirl of a destroyer's wake as we passed over the screen then, directly ahead, the bulk of *Illustrious* loomed and became a familiar shape in the bright moonlight. I switched on the navigation lights and then, behind my left ear, came the flicker of Pat's Aldis lamp as he gave the recognition signal. A pinpoint of light from the ship's island acknowledged. I eased the throttle slightly back to lose height, then, as we passed over her flight deck, banked as far as possible into a left-hand turn to make a very wide circuit. Poor old E5H refused to turn to the left any more steeply. I pulled the little lever that should release the arrestor hook and hoped that it had worked. We were losing height at the desired rate and my gentle circuit seemed about right to bring me in line with the flight deck. As I turned on to the final approach the lines of lights delineating the landing area and the DLCO's illuminated bats became clear. Good. I eased back the speed to that approved for deck landing a Swordfish. The damned thing was immediately out of control. I banged the throttle open and at once achieved the old skidding but controllable attitude. The DLCO was giving me furious 'Too Fast' signals: hard luck. Fortunately, he was very experienced and good at his job, realised that there must be some reason for my wild progress and gave me a very early 'Cut' signal as I slid up to the round-down. We hurtled over the first arrestor wires, missing them all; the left wing started to drop – here we go – a terrific jerk – we had caught a wire while still airborne – a resounding thud as the wheels hit the deck – then we were stopped. I couldn't believe it: we were home with both of us unhurt. I sat like an idiot holding the brakes on, then suddenly woke up to the furious 'Come On' signals from the FDO. Releasing the brakes I taxied forward on to the lift, where the handlers instantly folded the wings while I cut the ignition switches. The faithful Pegasus gave a final splutter and cough, then subsided into glorious silence.

I said to Pat: 'Sorry about the landing.' His reply was: 'I thought it was quite good in the circumstances.' Praise indeed.

The lift dropped to hangar level and we were rapidly pushed into the brilliant lights. I was absolutely astonished at the scene. The hangar was full of Swordfish! Nearly everyone must have returned safely. I had expected that we would have been one of the few to survive. Pulling off my helmet, I heard cries from the fitters and riggers: 'Fookenell, mate; look at 'im!' 'Look at that ruddy wing!' 'See them bleedin' ailerons!' I followed their eyes: the rod connecting the ailerons on the port upper and lower wings was smashed with the jagged ends grinding together, resulting in one aileron being slightly up and the other slightly down – not surprising that I had suffered a loss of lateral control: the port, lower main plane had a hole about a yard long by half a yard wide. How on earth could any aircraft fly in that state? I did not think that anything but a Swordfish could have done it. At that point I would have happily subscribed towards a statue to the designer.

I felt that I had to give 'Joey' some credit, but couldn't help thinking, albeit somewhat unfairly, that if he had concentrated a bit harder we might not have been hit at all.

The lads climbed on to the stub-planes: 'Are you OK, Sir?' 'How did you fly it back in that state?' 'Did the fish run alright?' 'Did you hit anything?' I told them that I was fine, it must have been their good maintenance that kept it flying, the torpedo dropped alright, but I had not got a clue about hits. I promised to tell them all about it when we found the true results.

At debriefing we found that all aircraft had returned except two. Lieut-Cdr. Williamson with Lieut. Scarlett of 815 Squadron and Lieuts. Bayley and Slaughter of our own 824 from Eagle were missing. We were distressed about the losses, but amazed at the low percentage of them. We hoped that our colleagues might be prisoners of war.

With the flak, smoke and general chaos over Taranto, no one could be clear about what had been achieved. It looked as though there had been torpedo hits on the battleships; the seaplane base and the oil depot, everyone agreed, had been burning merrily and there had been confusion in the Mar Piccolo. We would have to await the Maryland's photographs to know the truth. There was one great disappointment: a high percentage of bombs had failed to explode. No particular reason for this had as yet been found;* it was most unusual. Especially furious were Clifford and Going, who had made such efforts to get their aircraft repaired and then attacked on their own; not one of their bombs had exploded.

We trooped down to the wardroom to find that the catering staff had been doing their bit. Apart from drinks they had laid on masses of grub and even a huge cake. The room was full of aircrew, all nattering at once, the pilots waving their arms with cries of 'There I was, nothing on the clock, flak hurtling past my ears. . . . .' It was not long, however, before the crowd began to thin. A veil of fatigue was falling over everyone. I staggered off to the cubby-hole where I had rigged my camp bed, stripped off and fell into my sleeping bag. As soon as I closed my eyes it seemed that a film screen had been implanted inside my lids, and long, coloured pencil lines of tracer were flashing past me. Eventually I must have dozed for a time, for I awoke just before 7 o'clock to feel the ship shaking like a leaf as she steamed at high speed to rejoin the main fleet. There seemed little chance of any more sleep, so I dressed and climbed to the quarter deck where I found a number of others who were suffering from the same problem.

It was a grey day. The Mediterranean sun had crept behind a curtain of grey cloud, the sea was grey and, as far as the eye could see, there were grey ships. We were rejoining the fleet when suddenly the dismal scene was brightened by a splash of colour as a hoist of signal flags climbed up the mainmast of the flagship. Someone who could understand these things without the aid of a book, translated. I am sure we all felt a surge of euphoria. It was one of the greatest compliments that a ship can be paid in the Royal Navy. With typical understatement it read:

'Illustrious manoeuvre well executed.'

Feeling no little pride, we went down to enjoy a huge breakfast. There was much more chatter than usual. It is an accepted procedure in the Navy to remain silent at breakfast, possibly for the benefit of any hangovers, and one expects to hear only the rustle of a newspaper or a sotto voce request for the salt.

* Later found to be due to faulty manufacture.

After the meal we moved into the ante-room, where we received a shock: it was planned that we should repeat our performance that night! There were a few gasps and a general silence. An observer broke it and brought back to me that I was thinking of Balaclava as we entered Taranto. 'They only asked the Light Brigade to do it once.'

It appeared that, in view of the success of our night's effort, a plan had been passed to the C-in-C that it should be repeated with twelve aircraft. Admiral Cunningham had queried the fairness of expecting the pilots and observers to do it again so soon, but agreed to leave the decision to the Rear Admiral Aircraft Carriers. The tentative plan had been worked out that an attack could be made from the same position as on the previous night.

Usually, when an operation is projected there is enthusiasm and a great deal of discussion, but this time it was sadly lacking. I went into the hangar, as I had promised my crew that I would give them more details. They had already heard a buzz about another operation and were horrified. 'They aren't going to make you do it again, are they, Sir?' I told them that it might happen. Old E5H was looking very depressed, lying like a plucked turkey with her port mainplanes on the deck beside her, the ailerons removed and much of the fabric stripped: the engine cowlings were off and piled in a heap beneath her. They told me that she would need many new ribs, new ailerons and control rods and then re-covering with fabric. The engine which had served me so well needed a complete check and a run on deck as, on my own admission, I had grossly mistreated it, using the boost override for far longer than the maximum time approved in the book. They said that there was no hope of her being ready to fly that night. I wondered if that would preclude my being in the crews for the next operation but thought not as, being one of the torpedo pilots, I could easily be given another aircraft. Everything was still in the melting-pot.

For the next few hours we wandered desultorily round the ship waiting for a decision. In the end we were told the idea had been cancelled as the weather report was completely unsuitable. I think that the Meteorological Officer was the most popular officer in the ship!

The fleet spent that day steaming south of Crete but, finding nothing interesting, the C-in-C gradually altered course towards the south-east and headed home. On the way to Alexandria we were virtually unmolested. On three occasions, Cant Z501s attempted to shadow us but were all shot down by our Fulmars before they could make enemy reports. Those of us who had been at Taranto were allowed a rest, and I did not fly again.

News of the convoys and the cruiser action began to trickle in. To our astonishment the whole complex MB8 operation had run like clockwork. All the convoys had reached their destinations on time, the Merchant Navy had co-operated magnificently and their cargoes had been unloaded and the ships on their ways again exactly according to schedule. There had not been a single ship lost or even damaged. There had been one piece of stupidity which, fortunately, had not resulted in disaster. Convoy AN6, carrying vital petrol and stores, had left Port Said for Greece on 4th November. It was escorted by a mine-sweeper and armed trawlers which had a maximum speed of 7kts. It was an 8½kt convoy! Later it had been joined by more ships with the AA Cruiser HMS *Calcutta* whose Captain later was to make a scurrilous but highly justified criticism of those who had provided an escort slower than the ships it was supposed to protect!

On the night of 11th November, while we had been having fun over Taranto, Vice Admiral Pridham-Wippel in *Orion*, with the cruisers *Sydney* and *Ajax* and the destroyers *Nubian* and *Mohawk*, had dashed into the Straits of Otranto, where they had found a convoy of four ships escorted by a destroyer and a torpedo-boat. They had destroyed the convoy and driven off the escorts, which had done little to defend their charges. While our ships were mopping up the Admiral had ordered a withdrawal to the South at 28kts. He had received a signal from the Naval Attaché in Ankara that the Italian fleet intended to bombard Corfu that night. There was little future in taking on a fleet of battleships with his three cruisers, and he had wisely decided to withdraw. It had been a very successful operation, had done appreciable damage to the enemy, and no doubt had raised the morale of the Greeks.

Analysis of the Maryland's photographs of Taranto harbour on the morning after our attack reached us. We were astonished. We had done far more damage than we had realised. The *Littorio* was badly down by the bows and partly awash, with auxiliaries alongside, presumably trying to keep her afloat. The *Cavour* had been beached and abandoned with her decks below water. The *Duilio* had also been beached. In the Mar Piccolo there were ships lying around and the water covered with oil and debris. The seaplane hangars had been completely burnt out and the oil depot was still smouldering. It was an amazing result from 21 elderly bi-planes with the loss of only two. In fact, we also heard that Lieut-Cdr. Wiliamson and Lieut. Scarlett had been picked up unhurt and were now POW's, so we had really suffered only two casualties.

Admiral Cunningham was over the moon. With the loss of three battleships the Italian fleet was, for the first time, far inferior in

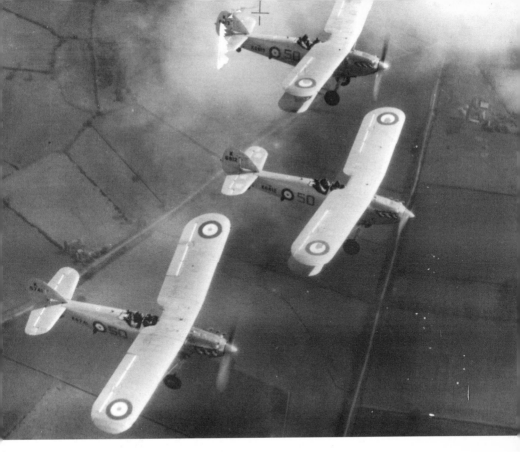

Hawker Hinds of 50 (Bomber) Squadron RAF Waddington 1938

Nearly the author's last flight

The New Air Branch shows off. Fairey Swordfish of TTU Gosport 1938

Learning how to do it. TTU Gosport 1938

Wildcat – The end for enemy convoy shadowers

Flying conditions were sometimes difficult

Some Seafire landings were exciting

HMS Biter "working up"

Repairing the author's aircraft after the Bomba raid

A little too close to the AA Guns!

Taranto – The Mar Grande the morning after. Battleship Conte di Cavour sunk by the stern

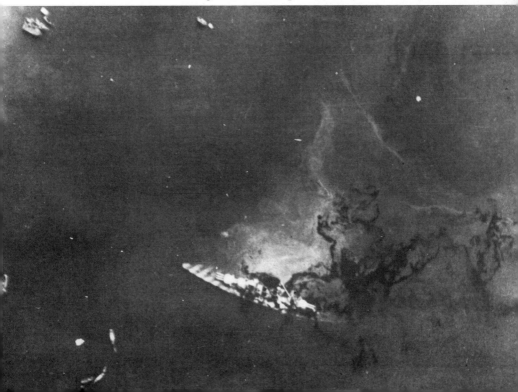

(Left): Taranto – The Mar Picco[lo]
the morning after,
12 November 1940

(Below): HMS Eagle

(Bottom): HMS Illustrious

A Postage Stamp to land on

Hellcat of 896 Squadron. HMS Empress, East Indies 1945

Catapulting Avenger in Trincomali Harbour. HMS Empress 1945

striking power to ours. In addition, the two serviceable battleships, *Vittorio Veneto* and *Guilio Cesare* had been moved to Naples and a division of heavy cruisers had moved to Messina. This put the main Italian sea power, with its notoriously short range, too far away from our shipping routes to be a major menace.

It was a very happy fleet that entered Alexandria.

As we picked up our mooring it was easy to make comparison between the Italian fleet as it now existed and the Naval might assembled in our British base. Side by side in the centre of the harbour lay *Warspite, Valiant, Malaya, Ramillies* and *Barham*, the aircraft carriers *Illustrious* and *Eagle*, submarines alongside their depot ship and rows of cruisers and destroyers. Further in were oil tankers, fleet auxiliaries and merchant ships, while in the water between, pinnaces and tenders tore around dodging the feluccas with their off-white sails. It was a hive of activity and a most impressive sight. We pilots, however, could not help thinking 'What a superb target.'

Although many considered us biased, we of the Fleet Air Arm thought that the day of the great capital ship was over, when it could be menaced from the air at sea and was so vulnerable in harbour that it had to be based far away from the area where it was most needed. We could not know it then, but we were to be proved right when the Japanese copied us at Pearl Harbor. The Pacific War was virtually to be controlled by superior carrier air power. We had broken through history to open a new era in sea warfare.

Taranto was to become a very famous victory.

YEAR 1940.		AIRCRAFT		PILOT, OR 1ST PILOT	2ND PILOT, PUPIL OR PASSENGER	DUTY (INCLUDING RESULTS AND REMARKS)
MONTH	DATE	Type	No.			
Nov.	—	—	—	—	—	— TOTALS BROUGHT FORWARD
"	2	SWORDFISH	K8419	SELF.	LT. HUMANABYS. L/A. WILLS.	A/S PATROL.
		"EAGLE SQUADRON", H.M.S. ILLUSTRIOUS.				
"	7	SWORDFISH	P4070	SELF.	LT. HUMPHREYS. L/A. FERRIGAN,	A/S PATROL: 1ST LANDING WITH BARRIER: 16 KNTS. OVER DECK: DAMAGED, TAIL WHEEL.
"	8	SWORDFISH	P4070	SELF.	LT. HUMPHREYS. L/A. FERRIKAN.	SEARCH: FOUND ATAK: GAVE POS. OF FLEET. FOUND CONT. 2501, IN SQR: (CUST DOWN BY FULMARS EARLIER), 2 MEN ALIVE: PROC. WITH SEARCH. FAILED TO FIND FLEET. SQUARE SEARCH: N.R.: A/S. RET. SAFELY. LANDED IN DARK
"	10	SWORDFISH.	P4206	SELF.	LT. HUMPHREYS. N/A. BALDWIN.	A/S. PATROL: N/A.
"	11 /12	SWORDFISH	P3999	SELF.	LT. HUMPHREYS.	ATTACK ON ITALIAN BATTLE FLEET IN TARANTO HARBOUR: ARRIVED TARGET MIDNIGHT. FLEW OVER TOWN AND BASE. N.R. POOR, MET BARRAGE BALLOON AT 7000' (PROB. ADRIFT): DIVED THRO' INTENSE L.A. BARRAGE. HIT BY M.G. BULLETS, PETROL PIPE, STRUT SMASHED, FORM. LT. BLOWN OFF. INT.-AIR.-AOD. DAMAGED. OUT OF CONTROL FOR 500'. DROPPED FISH ON PT. QNTR. OF "LITTORIO" PROB. HIT. TURNED TO STBD. HIT BY EXPL. CANON BULLETS IN PT. MN.-PLN. S PARE SMASHED GOT AWAY SAFELY. RET. TO "ILLUST." LANDED, O.K. RESULTS OF RAID:- 3 BATTLE-SHIPS OUT OF ACTION, 2 CRUISERS & 2 FLEET AUXLRS. SINKING. SEAPLANE HANGAR AND DOCKS DAMAGED.— NOT BAD!
		Awarded Mentn. in Despatches (3:1)				
		FLT. 824 (E.) SQUDN. DISEMBARKED H.M.S. NILE II. DEKHEILA.				
"	20	SWORDFISH	P4206	SELF.	LT. HUMPHIEYS. PILT. (A) WOOGLEY.	BEACON TEST. ABSOLUTELY NO RESULTS.
"	23	SWORDFISH	K8419	SELF.	L/A. WILLS.	TO EAGLE. OUTER. A/S. HAPPENING.

Extract from my log book showing the Taranto raid 11-12 November 1940.

Chapter 10

The Aftermath

We arrived in harbour to be greeted with an acclaim which became quite embarrassing. Apart from sundry pats on the backs from other ships in the fleet, signals came in from flag officers all around the Mediterranean and from the RAF. There were congratulatory messages from Durban in South Africa and even from the United States, which was still a neutral country.

The First Lord of the Admiralty, Mr (later Viscount) A.V. Alexander, broadcast to the nation a glowing tribute to the FAA. The Prime Minister, Winston Churchill, very relieved to have a success to announce at last, indulged in some exaggeration when he rose in the House of Commons to say 'The result affects decisively the balance of naval power in the Mediterranean and carries with it reactions upon the naval situation in every quarter of the globe. I feel sure that the house will regard these results as highly satisfactory and as reflecting the greatest credit upon the Admiralty and upon Admiral Cunningham, the C-in-C in the Mediterranean and, above all, on our pilots of the Fleet Air Arm.'

Everyone was particularly gratified by a message to Admiral Cunningham from the King, who said 'The recent successful operations of the fleet under your command have been a source of pride and gratification to all at home. Please convey my warm congratulations to the Mediterranean Fleet and, in particular, to the Fleet Air Arm on their brilliant exploit against the Italian warships at Taranto.'

The press clutched at the opportunity to report something better than continual defeats and losses, and excelled themselves with headlines and photographs of *Illustrious* and of Italian ships. Some newspapers were carried away by more enthusiasm than accuracy, such as the one that explained how we had been escorted by Fulmars to protect us from night fighters. The *Times* stuck to facts and said: 'The congratulations and gratitude of the nation are due in their fullest measure to the FAA, who have won a great victory in the largest operation in which they have yet been engaged against enemy ships and to Sir Andrew Cunningham who is the first Flag Officer to handle the new weapon on such a scale and has used it triumphantly'.

It was not difficult for us to believe that our attack had been worth the effort.

When we from *Eagle* returned to our own ship, most of its company were glad to see us and pleased that their ship had played a small part in the battle, even if she had not been able to be there herself. Captain Bridge was most enthusiastic and the majority of the ship's officers welcomed us warmly. However, there was, as always, one jarring note. Amongst the executive officers there were some who had left the service after World War I, either because of the Geddes axe or for some personal reason, and had now been called back. To them it seemed that the aircrews and aircraft were inconveniences cluttering up their ship. They showed their feelings by childish and derogatory behaviour. A typical example occured on the day that the local Gieves representative had managed to obtain a few yards of medal ribbon and a number of us had assembled to go ashore wearing the blue and white of the DSC. A particularly unpleasant Lieut-Commander said in a loud voice: 'Oh, look at all the little boys with their Good Conduct Medals'. There was a noticeable silence, and other officers within hearing had the grace to look embarrassed.

Eagle was a reasonably happy ship but those of us who had spent some time in *Illustrious* could not help noticing the different atmosphere there. In *Illustrious* everyone on board was prepared to work himself to the bone to keep the aircraft flying and to give the pilots and observers all the backing that they needed. I think that this difference may well have been because *Eagle* had enjoyed a peacetime existence until Italy entered the war, whereas *Illustrious* had been built in a wartorn country with the sole object of operating aircraft, and all her crew had already suffered the exigencies of war.

After a day in harbour all the Taranto crews received an invitation from the C-in-C, amounting to a summons, to repair on board *Warspite* to have drinks with him. He greeted us all most cordially, spoke to us individually about our parts in the attack and other operations in which we had taken part and made us all sign his visitors' book adding 'Taranto' against our names.

I had never met Admiral Sir Andrew Cunningham before and found that he was not a particularly large or impressive man, but he radiated personality. Enthusiasm hung like an aura around him and he was obviously born to be a leader.

He spoke of the effect that the attack would have on the Mediterranean theatre, releasing ships for duty in other parts of the world where they were much needed. He also said that we could all expect some solid awards for our efforts.

The list of 'solid awards' arrived shortly. It had been assumed that *Illustrious* would be deluged in a shower of 'gongs' after the publicity and acclaim. The list contained the names of the two Squadron Commanders, who both received DSO's and their observers DSC's; Olly Patch and his observer, David Goodwin, each received a DSC. That was all. There was no mention of those who had worked so hard in the ship and on the staff.

The fleet was amazed; the people of *Illustrious* were appalled and almost mutinous. We felt somewhat personally slighted, but the principal reaction of all aircrew was that it was a calculated and blatant insult to the FAA and we laid the blame on their Lordships of the Admiralty, to many of whom Taranto must have sounded the death knell of their image of naval warfare with battleships pounding each other with 15-inch shells.

Admiral Cunningham was furious, as he had recommended that all engaged should receive decorations, and other very senior people made clear their disgust.

As a result of this reaction a further list was published, many months later, which bestowed DSC's on those who had achieved confirmed hits. The remainder, which included Pat Humphries and myself, were Mentioned in Despatches. There was still no recognition for the ship's company of *Illustrious*. This list was a slight improvement, but had arrived so late that many on it had already lost their lives. It was clear that anyone who wished to be covered with glory should not have joined the FAA.

The effects of MB8 on the overall strategy in the Middle East, and the Italian reaction to their dismal failures, only reached us in spasms and it was not until many years later, when I was attending the Staff Course at the RN College, Greenwich, that I learned the complete story.

Count Ciano, the Italian Foreign Secretary and Mussolini's son-in-law, kept a comprehensive diary in which he recorded largely unbiased views on the shortcomings of their High Command, comparing them with the apparently efficient organisation of the British Commander-in-Chief. After Taranto he wrote of his surprise at Mussolini's calm reaction to the disaster:

'A black day, the British, without warning, have attacked the Italian fleet at anchor in Taranto and have sunk the dreadnought *Cavour* and seriously damaged the battleships *Littorio* and *Duilio*. These ships will remain out of the fight for many months. I thought I would find the Duce downhearted. Instead he took the blow quite well and does not at the moment seem to have fully realised its gravity.'

Many criticisms in Ciano's diary were backed by senior officers in the Italian navy. They complained bitterly about the divided control of the Regia Aeronautica, the lack of maritime aircraft generally and, in particular, inadequate reconnaissance aircraft and torpedo bombers. Admiral Inigo Campioni, the C-in-C of their fleet, was always most critical of their air force, complaining particularly of its inability to provide him with adequate information about the movements of British ships, and its mistakes in bombing his own fleet. For this latter complaint we had some sympathy for their pilots, as we were not entirely blameless in this respect. At a height of some 10,000 feet it is difficult to distinguish between one grey warship steaming over a grey sea, and another. If one expects to meet an enemy in a particular position and has not been warned that similar friendly forces are somewhere near, one tends to attack without waiting to lose the element of surprise.

Admiral Campioni had also come to appreciate the advantages of a fleet with an aircraft carrier, whose fighters could shoot down reconnaissance and bomber aircraft and whose torpedo planes could cause confusion in a fleet even if they failed to obtain hits.

Lack of competent reconnaissance was blamed as the principal cause of their disaster at Taranto. They had taken for granted that, if British forces came within 180 miles of it, their fleet would sortie to engage them and prevent them launching torpedo bombers, but no-one told them when the British fleet arrived! Fulmars had shot down almost all the Cant Z501 flying boats that attempted to shadow us. Conflicting and often inaccurate reports of the various units of MB8 scattered all over the Mediterranean had utterly confused them. On their own admission they were unable to clarify the situation until after the war.

Illustrious and her aircraft had proved that the vital element of any offensive operation in modern warfare was the achievement of air superiority; this fact was brought painfully to our notice in the very near future.

The security of Taranto had been in the hands of Admiral Arturo Riccardi, who was quite clear about the reasons for the failure of the base defences. The torpedo nets had been rigged at a depth of 8 metres, while our weapons had been set for 10 metres. Furthermore, they had not yet laid enough of them. The balloon barrage had been quite inadequate and many balloons destroyed in the gale had not been replaced, as they had no hydrogen with which to fill them. He considered that the anti-aircraft defence had been chaotic, since some 14,000 rounds of various calibres had been fired from the shores in addition to a considerable unspecified amount from the ships and yet they had only managed to shoot down two slow bi-planes out of all those that had been obliged to fly low and level to drop their torpedoes. This wild firing had also caused much damage to their own ships and shore establishments.

As a result of this débacle, we had assumed that heads would roll in the Supermarina, as they would certainly have done in our Navy. There did occur a shuffle around of Admirals, but it was not clear whether it involved promotions or demotions.

Admiral Inigo Campioni became Deputy Chief of Staff, being relieved by Admiral Angelo Iachino who had prevously commanded a squadron of 8-inch gun cruisers. Admiral Arturo Riccardo took over the job of Chief of Staff from Admiral Domenico Cavagnari, although he lacked sea experience. This might have been a case of having the right politics or the right friends.

Listening to these stories and reading the diaries and reports, I gained the impression that Count Ciano and senior Italian officers had great respect and admiration for the British Navy. They often gave more credit and praise to our operations than to those of their own forces. They were strange enemies.

Chapter 11

Return to Routine

Alexandria always amazed me. Although the Army was waging a war in the desert and we were playing the same games at sea, and there was even an occasional, ineffective air raid, it could have been a town in peace time. There were first-class restaurants and well stocked bars; the shops were filled with clothing, watches and jewellery, at very reasonable prices. To anyone recently arrived from England, the sight of the windows in the patisseries and confisseries, stocked with cakes and luscious chocolates, made his mouth hang open in disbelief.

The hotels, bars and clubs were usually packed with uniforms of the allied countries. Apart from the British there were Frenchmen, Poles, Greeks, Jugoslavs and Czechs as well as many wearing the flashes of other parts of the British Empire: Canadians, Australians, New Zealanders and citizens of the smaller colonies. Those men from all over the world who had joined us to fight the common enemy were an encouraging sight.

In a number of places of entertainment there were notices reading: 'In bounds to officers only of his Brittanic Majesty's Forces'. This was not, as it may appear, a piece of snobbery but quite a sensible idea. Both officers and men could let their hair down without the feeling of being watched or the danger of unpleasant scenes arising when too many pints had gurgled down too many throats.

One place that bore this notice was a large house wearing the sign 'Chez Marie'. This establishment was, quite blatantly, an up-market brothel, staffed by not-unattractive Syrian girls. It also contained a bar and restaurant which we were welcome to use without taking advantage of the other facilities. The whole character of the place stemmed from Mary herself, who was a cultured, middle-aged lady of unspecified nationality, although rumoured to be a White Russian Countess. She was extremely kind-hearted and mothered the midshipmen and junior officers, unhesitatingly lending them a few pounds when they were hard up. She was often seen at the race course, immaculately dressed, with admirals and other senior officers raising their hats to her. Mary's was a popular meeting place.

One of the most eagerly awaited events in any ship was the arrival of mail. Every effort was made to ensure that it reached the forces overseas as often as possible but this was dependent upon shipping and aircraft space being available, and consequently reached us spasmodically. On arrival it was instantly snatched and read avidly although it was weeks out of date. This time in harbour a large batch was delivered, carried out by the grace of HMS *Barham* and the cruisers. It was natural that all news should be shared and discussed and it was illuminating to see the reactions of people living in different parts of the country. From those in cities that had been heavily bombed, typical remarks were 'You will remember Mrs So-and-So who lived across the road. Her house was destroyed by a bomb the other night but they are OK. Grandad has joined the Home Guard.' Completely dissimilar were some of those from people living in the country, in complete safety, with eggs and milk readily available from local farms. These were often long diatribes about the horrors of rationing, the hardships they were suffering and the inconvenience of the village being invaded by evacuee children from the cities.

Some of the most instructive letters came from teen-age brothers who had the technical knowledge to give lyrical descriptions of raids, with the types of aircraft involved and the size of bombs dropped. The Censors often found them too knowledgeable, and mutilated them.

Censorship was a vexed subject and we all loathed the duty imposed on us to read the letters written by other ranks and stamp the envelopes 'Passed by Censor'. We tried to pick them by a lucky dip system so that, as far as possible, we could avoid reading those of our own men. Nevertheless, it was impossible not to be embarrassed when reading the private letters of a man to his wife or girl-friend.

With the mail came out-of-date copies of the newspapers. We were, in fact, usually reasonably up to date with world news from the radio and local papers like the *Egyptian Mail*, which simply translated the radio reports into journalese. We knew that Coventry had suffered a devastating attack by the Luftwaffe which had destroyed much of the city and caused over 1,000 casualties.

Horrifying stories were published about Nazi atrocities in Poland: it appeared that they were conducting wholesale excutions and that, if any member of a family was considered to be guilty of anti-Nazi activities, all his immediate relatives were shot or hanged. Hitler was said to have decreed that the Jewish race was to be exterminated, and to have disposed of tens of thousands of them, herding half a million into ghettos. We found this hard to believe in modern times and felt that many of these reports must be propaganda similar to the atrocity stories of German activities in World War I, which had been proved quite unfounded. Later we were to find that there was no doubt about their truth. Hitler had also annexed Hungary and Czechoslovakia, but we knew it was not a case of them joining him voluntarily, as he liked to imply, because we had a number of Czech units with our army in Egypt.

The RAF were giving back to the Germans some of their own medicine: on one night 2,000 bombs had been dropped on Hamburg. The Greeks were doing well and had driven back the Italian invasion force at their borders. This had not pleased Mussolini, who had sacked Marshall Badoglio, his C-in-C.

Our colleagues from *Ark Royal*, operating with Force H from Gibraltar, had destroyed a number of warships and merchant ships in Sardinia and, a few days later, had encountered an Italian fleet consisting of the two serviceable battleships, *Vittorio Veneto* and *Guilio Cesare*, with six cruisers and a number of destroyers. Eleven of her Swordfish had made two torpedo attacks on these ships without achieving any hits. Although this result was disappointing, we could not help feeling some satisfaction, being only human, after our similar lack of success in July.

By the time we had enjoyed a week's rest in harbour, Admiral Cunningham had become restless again and took us all back to sea. We embarked in *Eagle*, as she was sufficiently serviceable to operate aircraft again. The plumbers had been hard at work patching up our pipe systems and now considered that there was a fair chance that the avgas lines would supply aircraft fuel and not the effluent from the Royal Marines' heads. A week was spent at sea giving cover to convoys to the west and steaming as far as Malta. Apart from some ineffectual air raids, there was little excitement.

Returning to Alexandria, we disembarked to Dekheila where we found some new arrivals. Camped around the airfield was a Polish cavalry regiment.

They called themselves 'Le Premier Régiment de l'Infanterie Polonaise'. No-one knew why a cavalry regiment should be called 'Infantry' and why it should have a French name. They had escaped from Poland, complete with horses, and found their way overland to Egypt. Their officers were very friendly and all spoke fluent French but little English. We took some of them flying and, in return, they insisted that we ride their horses. I found this most alarming: I have always been very fond of the horse as an animal but have had little experience of riding him, always feeling that there had been an oversight in his design, there being no brakes or throttle. However, by hanging on like grim death and clutching the poor beast's mane, I remained in the saddle long enough to satisfy honour.

Many things about the Poles were difficult to understand. Why did their unit consist almost entirely of officers? They seemed to have simply abandoned their men and fled. Although we had been told that there had been fierce resistance to the invasion of their country, they gave little evidence of any battle experience. We learned more of the story from a British naval officer who had acted as liaison to a Polish destroyer in our fleet. Apparently there were two political factions in Poland with diametrically opposed views, which had resulted in the followers of one side making a spirited defence while the others kept out of danger as far as possible. In fact, the government had fled from Warsaw to safety before the city became dangerous.

The destroyer which had joined us certainly did her share, but we were horrified by the Polish interpretation of discipline, which was barbaric. On one occasion a seaman had over-enjoyed himself ashore, missed the last boat to the ship and been absent overnight. He was immediately tried on the accusation of 'desertion in the face of the enemy' and sentenced to death! Fortunately for him, serious sentences had to be approved by the C-in-C, who reduced the death sentence to one week's stoppage of leave.

We spent the next two weeks at Dekheila doing odd jobs and providing A/S patrols across the entrance to the harbour, on one of which I caused some alarm. My observer, a young midshipman on this occasion, asked me to drop a smoke float so that he could find the wind for navigational purposes. I selected the appropriate switch and pressed the bomb release button. The aircraft gave a surprising jerk, then there was a cry from the back seat that there had been a huge explosion in the sea astern of us.

Some electrician with his mind on higher things had crossed some wires in the bomb selector circuit so that, instead of dropping a smoke float, I had dropped four depth charges. Fortunately no ships had been underneath me.

One night I was hauled out of bed at 3.00am to fly two naval gunnery officers to Ma'aten Bagush, where they were to liaise with the Army, who had asked the battleships to bombard Italian positions on the Libyan border. General Wavell had decided to launch an attack to drive the Italians away from Egypt. I would have expected a project like this to be Top Secret, but it had become a general topic of conversation. A few days after this flight the Army pushed forward with great effect, taking thousands of prisoners.

We were moved to Fuka Satellite after a short time and there we remained for a month. At least we were employed constructively. We flew almost every night, providing cover for convoys carrying troops and supplies to the Army and shiploads of Italian prisoners going the other way.

Some of these operations involved flights of over four hours, much of which could become boring, but often it was interesting, such as when we 'spotted' for our ships shelling the enemy positions; on one sortie we watched the old monitor HMS *Terror* firing at shore targets. She was an extraordinary ship, almost as wide as she was long, flat bottomed with very little draught and fitted with a gun turret having one huge 15-inch gun. I had last seen her at Singapore.

Other very long night flights were simply designed to keep the Italians short of sleep prior to an army advance. Over towns like Bardia, we flew around for an hour dropping one bomb every two minutes; it must have been infuriating for them. There was seldom any appreciable AA fire and no one was ever hit.

On two occasions we were detailed to lay magnetic mines outside Tobruk harbour. This did not cause any particular difficulty once we had taken off, but our first attempt started with a period of complete chaos as, having no previous experience of a whole squadron taxying over the desert at night, we had not realised that our slipstream would cause a sandstorm. No one could see where he was going and it was providential that we all had the sense to stop and switch off our engines before there were any collisions.

When visibility improved we pushed all the aircraft into a position from which they could taxi to the take-off end of the field without blowing sand over the ones following. By the time the problem was overcome everyone was in a foul temper, but we eventually got into the air and then into formation.

We flew out to sea for a few miles, then roughly followed the coastline for nearly two hours. It was not necessary to keep out of range of Italian listening posts as, to the best of our knowledge, the enemy had no night fighters. We laid our mines, which we had been carrying on our torpedo racks, in the channel leading to Tobruk harbour. Exactly where to lay them was a problem. The object, of course, was to sink supply ships entering or leaving the port. However, the Army hoped to capture Tobruk in the near future and use the port for their own purposes and, if our mines were successful, the entrance would be blocked by sunken ships. It was a 'can't win' situation, and we had to arrive at a compromise. Laying mines was an unsatisfactory job for aircrew because there could be no bangs and flashes to show that the effort had been worthwhile. Reports received later suggested that some merchant ships had hit our mines, so perhaps our time had not been wasted.

Our living conditions at Fuka were not exactly five-star. We were accommodated in wooden huts on the opposite side of the airfield to the RAF unit and slept on camp beds in a dormitory system. Cooking was done on paraffin stoves by a Palestinian 'chef' who was hardly cordon bleu standard. Shortly after we settled in we found, in the galley, an enormous number of open tins, whose contents had not been required for the day's menu. Our cook soon provided the explanation: rations were supplied in large tins without any brightly coloured labels showing the contents, but only printed stickers; he had hoped to disguise his total illiteracy. We impressed upon him that the simple solution was to ask the nearest member of the squadron to translate the labels for him, as there was a fair chance that one of us would be able to read.

We learned more about the desert during the month that we spent there. On our earlier, short visits it had been summer time and the problem had always been to keep cool, but now it was winter and, although the day temperature would have been regarded as mild in England, it could be intensely cold at night. Instead of khaki shorts and shirts we needed army-style battle dress and heavy sweaters.

During the summer we had spent much of our off-duty time swimming in the warm sea, so baths and showers were not essential; it was different in the winter, when we had to make do with our very limited water ration. Fortunately, an air squadron had the advantage of fast transport – even if equipped with Swordfish. Frequent trips to Dekheila were needed, for aircraft to receive their routine maintenance inspections and to collect essential spares, so we took turns on these flights, which gave us opportunities for baths and a sight of civilisation.

We found some unexpected conditions in the desert at night. When travelling even a short distance, when there was no moon and the camps were blacked out, it was essential to navigate carefully. Once, four pilots left in a van to visit our RAF colleagues, about a mile away on the other side of the airfield. They returned over an hour later having been completely lost.

As most of our operations were at night we were often up and about at dawn and were fascinated to find how fertile the desert ground would be if properly irrigated. At first light the sand was covered with tiny, pink flowers; half an hour later, at sunrise, they had all disappeared.

We were fated to spend Christmas at Fuka and were not very pleased. In fact, it proved to be good fun. With rations arriving regularly by road and rail and augmented by air transport, we stocked up with turkeys, Christmas puddings and wines. The problem of how to roast the turkeys was overcome by some brilliant civil engineering. With stones and old tin cans we constructed an oven, heated by wood soaked in discarded engine oil. It proved most efficient and, allowing our Palestinian to boil the vegetables and puddings, we dressed in the most respectable pieces of uniform that we could find and enjoyed an excellent dinner with stupid, childish games afterwards.

This year the festive season was cheered in our part of the world by the success of the Army. We were given daily the estimated position of the front line, in the hope that we would avoid dropping missiles on our own troops but, by the time that we received the information, they were much further advanced. The Italians were dropping their guns and running. More than 200,000 prisoners had been taken, many of them overjoyed to have been captured. They admitted that they were looking forward to being taken to a place of safety, decently fed and given a bed in which to sleep.

We occasionally saw some of them and were astonished at their condition: they were clothed in decrepit remnants of uniform, half-starved and filthy, many being verminous. The ships used to tranport them to Alexandria had to be disinfected before being used for any other purpose. The arrival of so many prisoners needing to be accommodated and fed caused problems to our Headquarters staff.

During December we put in a great many flying hours. I found that my log book showed nearly 70 hours, half of them at night, which is a high total for a single-engined aircraft in the FAA.

While we were doing our land-based act, *Eagle* had been ferrying aircraft to Malta: *Illustrious*'s squadrons had made attacks on Italian bases and airfields in the Dodecanese Islands: the battleships had bombarded various points along the coast in support of the Army.

By early January we were getting restive and feeling it was hgh time we returned to our own element, although we knew that the Mediterranean was about to become a much more dangerous place for an aircraft carrier than it had been to date.

We were now to meet the Luftwaffe, an opponent very different from the Regia Aeronautica.

After Taranto, Hitler had written to Mussolini suggesting the 'transfer of German Air Forces to the Mediterranean mainly to act in co-operation with those of Italy against the British Fleet'. Realising that there was no hope of invading England at that time, he was left with a stock of surplus aircraft with experienced crews. He therefore decreed that a unit of the Luftwaffe was to be sent to Sicily.

Fleigerkorps X, commanded by General Geisler, was already beginning to reach the Sicilian airfields. This unit of 350 aircraft comprised 150 JU 87 and 88 dive bombers, 40 twin-engined ME 110 fighters and 20 Dornier and Arado reconnaissance aircraft. The thought of our ships being attacked by the Stukas (JU 87s) gave much cause for concern, as this was a deadly machine carrying a 500kg bomb, which it released from an almost vertical dive with considerable accuracy. This was clearly going to affect our fleet's virtually free use of the Mediterranean Sea.

Perhaps we should have been glad that these reinforcements had not been sent earlier. Admiral Bernotti wrote 'The cooperation of the Axis powers in the Mediterranean might have produced decisive results for the general conduct of the war had it eventuated quickly and in a timely manner, immediately after the fall of France. Instead it was invoked to deal with a disastrous situation. Objectives which could have been realised relatively easily during the first months of hostilities became more difficult as the conflict progressed because Britain had the free use of the oceans.' The late arrival of the Fleigerkorps may have saved us so far, but it didn't make the future less bleak.

One week into January 1941 we were suddenly recalled to Dekheila and, the following day, flew on to *Eagle*. There was, we found, furious activity all over the Mediterranean. A complicated series of shipping movements was taking place which bore a strong resemblance to MB8 at the time of Taranto. Force H was covering a convoy of ships from Gibraltar, loaded with supplies for the army in Greece and destined for the Piraeus. It included a ship carrying stores to Malta. Combined with this operation, which had been given the code name 'Operation Excess', there was a small convoy of fast ships to be covered from Alexandria to Malta and a fast and a slow convoy from Malta to Alexandria and Port Said.

After passing through the dangerous 'Narrows' between Sicily and Tunisia, *Warspite* and *Valiant*, with *Illustrious*, were to provide the cover for the eastern part of the route of 'Excess', and for the other merchant ships from Malta. Admiral Cunningham was uneasy about the situation because he felt that, particularly in the area of narrow seas, the ships were open to attack by the Regia Aeronautica, much reinforced by the Luftwaffe, and to submarines and MTB's. Furthermore he was unsure of the position of Italian surface forces as these had been scattered far and wide after Taranto and the Marylands, excellent as they had proved to be, could not possibly cover all the harbours from which the enemy might sortie.

These involved movements progressed without any hitch until Force H had delivered her convoy to the west of the narrows and turned back for home; at that point she was attacked by two motor torpedo boats, but repelled them without difficulty, sinking one of them. SM79 bombers then attacked, but were driven off by *Ark Royal*'s fighters. Force H returned safely to Gibraltar.

On the eastern side of the channel, Admiral Cunningham's force rendezvoused with 'Excess', as arranged, on the morning of 10th January. Then the trouble started.

The first casualty was the destroyer *Gallant*, which hit a mine, her bows being blown off. While she was being taken in tow two SM79s, armed with torpedoes, attacked the battleships, followed some two hours later by two more. They were not very experienced in this type of bombing; they dropped their torpedoes a mile and a half from their targets and the battleships had no difficulty in avoiding them. The flight of Fulmars from *Illustrious*, which had been covering the fleet, was engaged in driving off the Italians some 30 miles away when the fun started. This resulted in our hurried embarkation and old *Eagle*'s dash to sea.

We landed-on, to be greeted with the news that *Illustrious* had been attacked by Stukas and put completely out of action as far as operating aircraft was concerned. Our fears about circumstances changing after the arrival of the Luftwaffe had not been unfounded. Some two weeks later, when *Illustrious* reached Alexandria, we learned the details of that disastrous day.

While the Fulmars had been some miles away, a large enemy formation had been reported to be closing on the fleet, resulting in the fighters being recalled to patrol overhead.

Unfortunately, they had expended most of their ammunition, so the ship had to turn into wind to fly off four reliefs, using the opportunity to relieve the Swordfish A/S patrol. As this manoeuvre was being completed, two formations of Stukas appeared at 12,000 feet and took up position astern of the fleet, where they split into sub-flights of threes and made an expert and brilliantly co-ordinated attack on the carrier. One flight attacked from each beam while a third came in from astern; some dived as low as 800 feet, then screamed across the flight deck below funnel height. The first hit had been on No. 1 pom-pom and the second through a recreation space, exiting through the ship's side and exploding, and causing flooding of some compartments; the next hit had destroyed another pom-pom, killing most of the crew. The after lift had been the next casualty; one bomb had hit the lip and another the platform itself; it had been half-way between decks with a Fulmar and pilot on it and the result was catastrophic, the Fulmar and its pilot being destroyed and the aircraft in the hangar set ablaze. This bomb had also severed many electrical leads, including the ones to the steering motors, causing the ship's rudders to jam hard to port. The situation was then aggravated by a near miss on the starboard quarter. The next bomb penetrated the flight deck and exploded in the hangar, buckling the forward lift and allowing increased draught to fan the fires.

Three more hits had then been received, one of which severed the electric leads to the radar and gyro compass repeaters. To make matters worse, a JU87 that had been shot down crashed into the after lift well, burst into flames and added to the fires already raging. The heat and fumes from the fires had made the engine room almost untenable but the boiler room crews stuck to their posts magnificently.

Within half an hour the steering had been re-connected and the ship was under control again. Fires were still raging but their advance was held up by superhuman efforts on the part of the damage control parties under the Executive Officer, Commander Gerald Tuck RN.

Captain Boyd decided, with the approval of the C-in-C, to head for Malta. His ship then left the fleet, accompanied by two destroyers, and despite conditions below decks the engineers succeeded in providing a speed of 26kts. As she was leaving, a further attack was levelled at her, this time by SM79s as well as some of Fleigerkorps X. The result was two more hits, one of which exploded in the wardroom flat wiping out a number of officers who had been grabbing a cup of tea, and causing further flooding and damage.

The steering gear had failed again and *Illustrious* was now steaming at only 14kts, steering with her engines. When only 5 miles from Grand Harbour a further attempt to stop her was made by torpedo bombers, but an intense AA barrage from her batteries, many of which had been repaired, drove them off. It was 2100 by the time she passed St Elmo's Light and, finally, at 2215, with the aid of tugs, she was secured to Parlatorio wharf.

During the ten days that she spent in Malta, the Maltese dockyard workers made magnificent efforts, day and night, despite many air raids. In the dock she received another hit but with little damage. It was her good fortune that she had not arrived a few months earlier, when the island's only fighter defence had been three Gladiators, lovingly named Faith, Hope and Charity. The air raids were now broken up by Hurricanes, augmented by Fulmars which had reached Malta from *Illustrious*. She reached Alexandria on January 25th.

The casualties had been high: 83 officers and men had been killed, 60 seriously wounded and 40 slightly. It seemed particularly unfair that the officer casualties included many of the aircrew that had survived Taranto. Lieutenants Kemp, Skelton and Clifford, Sub-Lieutenants Perkins, Mandel-Farreira and Wray had all been killed: Lieut. Going had lost a leg and Lieut. Morford had been badly burned.

I was relieved to hear that my friend Sub-Lieut. Angus Hogg had reached Malta safely with his Fulmar and was continuing to shoot down the enemy. He was awarded a Bar to his DSC for this work.

In *Eagle* we steamed into the Mediterranean with some

trepidation. If the Stukas could put *Illustrious*, with her armoured deck, out of action, what chance did we have with our flight deck of thin steel?

We set about the usual routine patrols, helping to cover the convoys heading for the East. The enemy made very little effort to deter us. This good fortune was largely due to weather conditions which were more like those of the North Atlantic than the Mediterranean. The visibility was appalling, with low cloud and haze, which also restricted our own operations.

Two days after leaving Alexandria we received news of an Italian convoy near the Libyan coast: an ideal target for our aircraft. We loaded our torpedoes and headed for its last known position, expecting to be able to do a great deal of damage, as the escort was minimal and unlikely to produce very much AA fire; merchant ships, also, were a different proposition from fast, manoeuvrable warships.

It was a flight of less than an hour to reach the target, which was hugging the coast. Visibility near the land was even worse than that at sea; a khamseen was raging in the desert, and an off-shore wind reduced visibility to virtually nil. We spent nearly two hours searching for the convoy but failed to find any trace of it. Forced to abandon the project before running out of fuel, we returned to *Eagle* highly disgruntled, with our torpedoes intact.

Two days later, all the ships of our convoys having reached harbour in safety, we returned to Alexandria, flying off the aircraft to our old haunt at Dekheila. While disembarked on this occasion we were not called upon to make any forays into the desert nor, in fact, to do anything warlike.

Although able to operate as a carrier, *Eagle* was sadly in need of a major refit and it had been decided in early December that she should return to the UK, sailing south round Africa into the South Atlantic, and looking for raiders on the way. This plan suffered an enforced delay, since the Italians had blocked the Suez Canel with mines, so she could not leave until it had been cleared and re-opened. All was now well and we were no longer essential to the fleet, as HMS *Formidable* had arrived to replace *Illustrious*.

HMS *Formidable* was equipped with Albacores, which none of us had seen before, and most of the pilots found an excuse to go out to Dekheila. The Fairey Albacore was the replacement for the trusty Swordfish and I found that, although still a biplane, it was a larger and cleaner-looking aircraft than its predecessor. The fuselage had a metal skin replacing the fabric cover and it was fitted with a more powerful engine, giving it a slightly greater speed. The cockpits were more spacious, with better instrument layouts, many of the items which had been added piecemeal to the Stringbag being sited permanently. The crew was protected by sliding glass canopies, which vastly improved comfort.

After much 'wangling' I got permission to fly one. It was comfortable and easy to handle but did not appear to have the amazing ability of the Swordfish to let the pilot get away with murder. It lacked the personality of its predecessor and, overall, did not seem a vast improvement. We all thought that it was a remarkable thing that British aircraft designers who had produced aircraft like the Spitfire, appeared unable to give us a really good carrier-borne torpedo-bomber. In fact, the Albacore was shortly to be replaced by the Barracuda, which was another ghastly compromise, and it was not until we were equipped with American aircraft that we had anything really suitable for the job. The British manufacturers, probably with justification, maintained that they were given impossible specifications by the Admiralty which could only be achieved by a botch of bits and pieces. It might have helped if they had consulted the pilots for whom the aircraft were designed.

For the next two weeks, we occupied ourselves with ship's duties, then, as so frequently happens in the Services, without warning we were told that our days in the Mediterranean Fleet were over. We were ordered to a different theatre of war.

Chapter 12

Operation Red Sea

The reason for this sudden flap was the success of the Army. To understand the situation we had to look at what was happening in the rest of the world. The Blitz, as it had been christened, was afflicting England, and London and other cities were being hit by the Luftwaffe almost every night. Convoys were being decimated by U-boats and food was very short. By contrast, in North Africa our army had been doing very great things, and by 7th February had swept right through Libya, captured Tobruk, Derna and Benghasi, and seemed unstoppable.

Hitler, recognising that the Italians were ineffectual as allies, decided to reinforce them with seasoned German troops. On 12th February he sent an appreciable army into the Balkans and, on the 14th, landed an even larger one at Tripoli. This was to be called the Afrika Korps and to be commanded by General Rommel, a most experienced leader.

The Afrika Korps included a formidable detachment of the Luftwaffe. This meant that the RAF could lose the air superiority that it had enjoyed to date.

Commonwealth troops had swept through the Sudan and Eritrea, then into Somaliland where, on 12th February, they had captured Mogadishu. By 16th March they had recaptured Berbera, the capital of British Somaliland. Consequently there were Italian ships in their Red Sea ports which were virtually trapped; in particular, there were four destroyers in the port of Messawa which could menace shipping. This was where we came in.

It was decided that the FAA was ideal for disposing of these ships and that *Eagle* and her squadrons would be available for the job, as she would have to pass through the Red Sea on her way to the Atlantic. Problem: the Suez Canal was blocked by mines! We were required forthwith, so the only solution was to fly there. Another problem! Most of our aircraft were still on board *Eagle* so would need to be disembarked. We had never attempted to fly off in harbour before and had visions of flopping into the middle of Alexandria harbour.

It would be essential to have the wind blowing more or less straight down the deck; strangely enough it was directing itself obligingly, although only 10kts in strength. The experts indulged in numerous calculations and decided that it was possible. It would be necessary to range the aircraft one by one to allow the whole deck to be used; no crew, other than the pilot, could be carried and fuel would require to be drained until there was only sufficient for the short flight to Dekheila.

The first suitably lightened aircraft was ranged at the after end of the flightdeck; the pilot climbed in and started his engine: having run it up and warmed it he opened the throttle wide, holding it on its brakes, until the Flight Deck Officer swept down his green flag. We all watched with our fingers crossed as he gradually gathered speed until, well before the end of the deck was reached, the good old Stringbag lifted smoothly off, as if surprised at all the fuss. When it was my turn I soon found myself rising calmly into the air, then clearing the masts of the shipping, and landing safely at Dekheila after little over five minutes' flying.

As soon as disembarkation was completed, all the aircraft were refuelled. We were then faced with the knotty problem of what we could take with us. Fuel and bombs could be supplied by the RAF, but otherwise we had to be self-supporting. We had to carry pilots, observers, TAGs, ground crews and spare parts as well as our own baggage. This was a case of putting a quart into a pint pot but we achieved an acceptable compromise. The Swordfish looked like overloaded Christmas trees, with spares, including even a propeller, tied to the torpedo and bomb racks.

On the 25th March, we arose at crack of dawn and prepared for take-off. All seventeen aircraft started without problems and we rose into the air, got into formation and set course for the south. Our Commander (Flying), Commander Keighley-Peach, led the whole party.

As we turned on to course I think we all felt some degree of nostalgia at leaving Alexandria. I did not realize at that time that I would be returning in less than two years. We had enjoyed a fair amount of fun, together with many moments of intense fear. We had been involved in a number of successful operations, including a resounding one, Taranto. Some of our friends and colleagues had been lost. This had only to be expected in a theatre of war and, logically, our losses had been remarkably low.

We had decided to split the journey into a series of flights of roughly three hours' duration, and had arranged to make the first stop at Assyut, on the Nile. Our course gave us a straight line which crossed and recrossed the river. Looking down, it was remarkable to see the whole course of the Nile clearly defined by bright green fields of cotton and other plants where the ground had been irrigated from the river. They stopped in a firm line to give way to pure sand and desert. We arrived at Assyut to find that some liberties had been taken in calling it an airfield. It had an appalling surface, and two tail-wheel tyres burst on landing. These were quickly repaired, so we had some lunch while the aircraft were being refuelled.

We managed to take off without accident and arrived, after about three hours flying, at Aswan where the surface was slightly better. Having quickly refuelled, we were again in the air, passing over the great dam controlling the flow of the Nile and heading for Wadi Halfa, where we were to spend the night. The name of this little town was familiar to me from stories of the campaigns of Generals Kitchener and Gordon. It was exactly on the border of Egypt and the Sudan and was almost completely run by the British. The government of the Sudan was a rather unusual arrangement as it was a Condominion ruled jointly by Britain and Egypt.

When we reached the airfield we were surprised to find that virtual runways had been marked on the sand by blackpainted petrol drums. This was because of an almost continual mirage which made it impossible to judge height, and the drums had to be used like the lights of a flare-path at night. Arrangements had been made for us to stay the night in the hotel, which provided us with a reasonable dinner and beds. It also had a bar which we all felt that we needed after eight hours flying. We met some alcoholic and very disgruntled army officers who had been there for some time and thought that they had been forgotten.

Next morning we ran into our first snag. The engine of Commander Keighley-Peach's aircraft had been giving problems and it was found that a cylinder had to be changed. The local RAF volunteered to assist and so, after some swapping of pilots, one was left behind with a TAG and an air mechanic. At last we took off and headed for Atbara where we arrived after another three-hour flight to settle into the Rest House. We had intended to complete the whole journey that day but, after the late departure from Wadi Halfa, decided to have a break.

At Atbara we found that we had made a stupid mistake when leaving Egypt. Since November, in the Mediterranean winter, we had been wearing long-sleeved uniforms but, knowing that we would be flying into considerable heat, had decided to wear tropical shirts. Our arms had lost their resistance to the tropical sun so that our fore-arms, resting on the controls, suffered the full glare. Many pilots found huge blisters rising on their arms. I am one of those fortunate people who tan easily and can normally ignore this problem but, on this occasion, I also suffered burning.

Much of the following day's route took us over pure, sandy desert much more like what I had always imagined: nothing to be seen but long, rolling sand dunes. Twice we passed over caravans of camels travelling in perfectly straight lines across the absolutely featureless terrain. We wondered how they navigated. They had probably used the same route for thousands of years, and it was like looking down upon a page of history.

After flying for two hours we could see ahead of us our familiar element, the sea. We found the aerodrome at Port Sudan and landed safely, unloaded the aircraft, secured them for the night and drove into the town with our personal gear. We found that the officers' accommodation had been arranged in the hotel but that no one had thought of the TAGs and air mechanics. The local naval organisation was totally incompetent and it took us all evening to make provision for our men. Eventually we managed to make temporary arrangement for them in an unoccupied girls' school. The British matelot has an amazing ability to make himself at home almost anywhere so, they settled quite happily, their only complaint being that the girls had left!

The hotel was surprisingly modern and well equipped to suit the hot climate; it even had its own open-air swimming pool. The whole town was virtually new. The port of the Sudan had originally been Suakin, 40 miles further south, but its harbour had become silted to such an extent that larger ships could no longer use it. It had therefore been decided to build a new town, and Port Sudan had been planned, complete with a modern deep-water harbour with full facilities for large merchant ships. The town had been designed to meet the requirements, then a railway extension had been built from Suakin and everything needed for business and domicile was moved, lock, stock and barrel.

The natives caused us much amusement. The Europeans had given them the name 'Fuzzy Wuzzy' in the 19th century and the name had stuck. The reason was abundantly clear, as they wore the most elaborate hair styles, masses of curls piled up like giant mops. They were a cheerful people, always smiling with great flashes of white teeth. They were also extremely brave and, in the Sudanese Wars at the end of the previous century, had elicited admiration from the British troops. They were the only enemy who ever broke a British Square. Kipling had written:

'So 'eres to you Fuzzy Wuzzy, at your 'ome in the Soudan;
You're a pore benighted 'eathen but a first class fightin' man;
And 'ere's to you Fuzzy Wuzzy, with your 'ayrick 'ead of 'air
You big black boundin' beggar – for you broke a British square!'

They appeared to have settled into a more modern existence but still had a few awkward ideas. They found that steel from railway lines was ideal for making knives, so it was common to find parts of the rails missing. The taxi drivers were quite terrifying. Their right feet had only two positions – fully down on either the accelerator or the brake pedal; one thumb was equally firmly down on the horn.

The day after our arrival we heard that we had missed another major victory by our old colleagues of the Med. Fleet. The battleship *Littorio*, previously put out of action at Taranto, had been found at sea with some heavy cruisers and destroyers and been attacked a number of times by aircraft from *Formidable*, which had managed to get one torpedo hit and slow her down, and had also hit and stopped the heavy cruiser *Pola*.

Admiral Cunningham had arrived with part of the battle fleet and, off Cape Matapan, had sunk the cruisers *Fiume* and *Zara* before finishing off the *Pola*. *Barham* had sunk the destroyer *Vittorio Alfieri* and another called *Giosue Carducci* had also been sunk. It was good news but we were sorry that *Littorio*, although damaged, had escaped again.

Quickly we became organised and sent an aircraft down to Messawa each day to keep an eye on the enemy ships. The first one to be sighted at sea was on 1st April, when the daily reconnaissance was being flown by Midshipman Sergeant with Lieut. Lyle as his observer. They found a destroyer and shadowed it, reporting back by radio, but it reversed course and returned to harbour. On their way back to Port Sudan they had to land at Mersa Taklai to refuel. This was a landing ground maintained by the RAF and manned by a handful of unfortunates. It could provide no facilities other than avgas, which had to be pumped by hand from 44-gallon drums.

The following day a high-priority signal was received from Aden, telling us that three destroyers were raising steam in Messawa dockyard. If they were to steam at high speed they could be off Port Sudan by first light the next day. We armed the aircraft with six 250-lb bombs and, at 0530, Commander (Flying) took first turn to look for them.

His crew was Warrant Officer Wallington, an observer who had also to act as TAG and handle the radio. Flying through wispy cloud, they saw one of the destroyers steaming fast along the coastline, followed by two more, so Wallington immediately radioed for the stand-by aircraft, adding that they were about to attack. K-P was a fighter pilot, with no dive-bombing experience, and on his own admission let his bombs go too early so that they hit the sea astern of the target. It was only justice, perhaps, that the next one to attack was Midshipman Sergeant, who had spotted the first destroyer off

Messawa; he sank the *Nazario Sauro* first time. I attacked the *Tigre* and my line of bombs straddled it, one exploding close to the port side and one close to the starboard. It is always infuriating to achieve a straddle without getting a direct hit. The near misses must have been enough to damage her, however, as she was run aground and was later destroyed by gun-fire. Sub-Lieut. Suthers attacked the *Daniele Manin* and managed two hits so that she sank later. In other attacks, a fourth destroyer, *Pantera*, was also damaged and run ashore to be destroyed later, like the *Tigre*, by gun-fire from HMS *Kingston*. Overall, we disposed of the major part of the Italian Navy in the Red Sea and put Port Sudan out of danger from bombardment. We had not suffered any casualties, although the targets had fired their AA armament with enthusiasm.

Kingston presented us with the ensign from *Pantera*, which was a nice gesture. In their report they said that, when they had come up to the ships ashore near Jedda, they had found their decks strewn with dead sailors from our bombing and machine gunning. This left a nasty taste in my mouth. One advantgage of being in a flying service during a war is that the target is normally a solid object and the destruction of humans is not seen.

Between these engagements we had time to see more of the town and to swim in the pool. One day three of us scrounged some transport to have a look at the old town of Suakin. Remarkably, most of the buildings were in very good condition, many still bearing the names of the businesses that had occupied them. It was all very clean and, in some places, there were even brass plates that had been left behind and were highly polished by the blowing sand.

We had been told to visit Kitchener's house, so we searched for it and found an immaculate building flying a Union Flag, which overlooked the harbour. Inside, it was furnished and scrupulously clean. It was staffed by a Sudanese who served us with tea from a silver tea-pot into English cups with matching saucers. The view from the house showed the whole of the harbour and the silting could be seen clearly.

There were a few Arab dhows inside and we were told that these were used partly for trading but often for transporting pilgrims to Mecca on the other side of the Red Sea.

We heard an amusing story about a fairly large dhow that had met an Italian submarine which had mistaken it for a 'Q' ship and had surrendered to it! For this episode the captain had been awarded an OBE of which he was immensely proud. From then onwards he had always worn an enormous Red Ensign on his ship.

We returned safely to Port Sudan, despite efforts to the contrary by our Sudanese driver, with an increased knowledge of history and geography.

We continued the daily flights over Messawa, finding little activity except when Lieut. Slee flew to some islands outside the harbour and found about a dozen ships, many of which had been scuttled and resting on the bottom, but some were still afloat. He found a naval launch which seemed to be the scuttling party and attacked it with front and rear guns, eventually sinking it.

Our final effort was on the day before the port surrendered to the Army, when we found the MTB *Giovanni Acerbi* in the harbour and bombed her. The crew accelerated the effects by scuttling her.

Eagle finally managed to scrape through the canal on 17th April so we arranged to embark the following day. The white population of Port Sudan were very appreciative of our saving them from bombardment, so we felt that we should hold a farewell dance in the hotel, which boasted an attractive outdoor ball-room. This was a great success, particularly for the wives. The sight of all the young Naval officers in tropical mess dress was too much for them and they practically queued to dance with us, while their husbands propped up the bar.

Next day *Eagle* went to sea and we gave a formation fly past and shoot-up of the town to say 'Farewell'. Having collected her brood, *Eagle* steamed south, through the Straits of Bab el Mandeb, round the island of Sokotra and into the Indian Ocean, where we returned to our routine A/S patrols.

Reaching the open ocean, we started long searches in all directions for commerce raiders, about which the Admiralty seemed continually worried, but found no sign of any before we were off Mombasa. We disembarked a few aircraft to Port Reitz aerodrome where the South African Air Force seemed very glad to see us and gave us a good time in the city.

Mombasa, built on an island of the same name, was a thriving place with a very good harbour. All exports and imports for Kenya and Uganda were handled there or at the adjacent port of Kilindini. We only spent three days at Port Reitz but I managed to get a trip in an Anson of the SAAF. The Anson 1 was a fairly elderly Jack-of-all-trades, used mostly for transport. It was a twin-engined monoplane and the fabric-covered wings literally flapped when it was flying. The undercarriage was retractable and was raised by winding a handle over 100 times. In the tropical climate, the operator ended up pouring perspiration.

On 29th April we returned on board to find that a German commerce raider had been reported in the area. For the next few days we searched far and wide but could find no trace of her. On the third day we received a signal to say that she had been found and sunk by the cruiser HMS *Cornwall*. Naturally we were pleased, but thought it strange that *Cornwall* should have found her when we had covered hundreds of square miles of ocean and failed. Had she been given some information that had been withheld from us? Very odd!

With no more reports of raiders in the Indian Ocean, we headed for Durban to refuel. However, we kept searching and, on one flight, I found a rather suspicious-looking ship which proved to be inoffensive. Returning to the ship I found that the routine of landing had become trickier. The sea around the Cape of Good Hope often builds up a nasty swell, the effects stretching quite far into the oceans on either side, and our ship, despite her size, was pitching quite heavily. On my second attempt I managed to thump down safely.

When we reached Durban we had time for only a very short visit, and steamed south around the Cape. We had been joined by HMS *Nelson* which was a battleship of an odd design. All her superstructure was aft, reminiscent of an oil tanker; forward of this were the huge turrets of her 16-inch guns. An international agreement, reached between the wars, had limited the size of warships and had, in fact, resulted in the design of the German 'Pocket' Battleships. HMS *Nelson* and her sister ship HMS *Rodney* had been on the drawing board at that time, and it seemed that the naval architects had simply chopped off a large area of her after deck. The result, in my opinion anyway, was not a very beautiful ship.

As we rounded the Cape we felt that we were dropping the curtain on our last scene in the Eastern Theatre.

Chapter 13

South Atlantic Station

Those of us who had to fly from the ship's deck found a difference in our new ocean. In the Mediterranean, which was enclosed and relatively shallow, quite fierce storms could blow up but there was seldom an appreciable swell. In the South Atlantic the huge area of unprotected water allowed a long swell to develop, despite the sea appearing to be relatively smooth. The motion was hardly perceptible but, on the flight deck, when taking off or landing, the bows rose and fell very noticeably.

We had only been in the new area a few days when everyone was severely affected by snippets of news coming in on the radio – *Bismark*, the mighty German battleship, was at sea. HMS *Hood* and HMS *Prince of Wales* were on their way to engage her. *Hood* was a battlecruiser and probably the most beautiful warship that had ever been built. She had, for many years, been the pride of the Navy and dearly loved by everyone. *Prince of Wales* was brand new and still had some dockyard workers on board when ordered out to chase *Bismark*. The German was being shadowed and it looked as though our ships would meet her somewhere south of Iceland. We waited impatiently for news.

The following morning, May 24th, the news was not what we had been hoping; in fact it was the horror story of the year; our brand new battleship had been hit and damaged and our darling HMS *Hood* had blown up and sunk with the loss of almost the whole of her crew. We could hardly believe it. Apparently, her magazine had blown up after receiving a hit. We had lost ships in this way at the Battle of Jutland and everyone had assumed that the problem had been put right long ago. Obviously, it hadn't. To make matters worse, the shadowers had lost *Bismark*.

Panic was reigning at the Admiralty. They knew that *Bismark* would be making for one of the ports in the west of France and, should she get there, she would become a terrifying menace to our shipping in the Atlantic. She must be stopped. Every available naval vessel which could possibly reach the area in time had been sent to

124

sea; Force H from Gibraltar, with *Ark Royal* was on the way; HMS *King George V*, wearing the flag of the C-in-C Home Fleet and sister ship of *Prince of Wales* was at sea, making over 100 ships in the search.

On 26th a Catalina of Coastal Command found her. We breathed again. News continued to improve: Swordfish from *Ark Royal* had attacked her twice with torpedoes and managed a hit near the stern, damaging her rudders and causing her to leave a trail of oil. Slowed down by this damage, she was caught by the battleships, and HMS *King George V* and HMS *Rodney* had engaged with their main armament and finally sunk her.

On 1st June I flew an uneventful A/S patrol after which I went down to my cabin to write up my Flying Log Book. Epic day! I found that I had reached my first 1,000 hours flying as a pilot of single-engined aircraft, which entitled me to a reasonable claim to being 'Experienced'. Looking at the other columns in the book, I found that I had also made 250 deck landings without a crash. 'Joey' must have been doing his stuff!

Our job as we steamed northwards was, once again, to search for enemy shipping, not raiders this time, but ships supplying fuel and stores to U-boats. Intelligence reports had been specific on this occasion and the targets were the German ships *Elbe* and *Lothengen*, alleged to be in the area into which we were sailing.

To help dispose of them, should we find them, we had been joined by the elderly light cruiser HMS *Dunedin*. I had last seen this ship in the Solent; we used her as a target for our dummy torpedoes while at Gosport.

On 6th June one of our Swordfish found the *Elbe*, so, having armed up with SAP bombs, we went off to deal with her. She was exactly where reported to be so we made a copy-book dive-bombing attack, achieving a number of hits and leaving her on fire and sinking. When we had appeared her crew had abandoned ship in three boats.

We had insufficient fuel remaining to hang around, so flew back to the ship, another Swordfish being sent back to keep the enemy in view and lead *Dunedin* to the lifeboats, so that she could capture the crew.

When our people reached the site they found oil and debris but no sign of the lifeboats, and *Dunedin*, when she arrived, could not find them either.

Some hours later we passed close to a US merchant ship whose course must have taken her very close to *Elbe*, so we spoke to her by light, asking if she had seen the boats. She maintained that she had not, but we did not believe her! At that time, many Americans were pro-Nazi or strongly against becoming involved in the war. We felt sure that the US ship was taking the crew to America to be returned to Germany. There was nothing that we could do about it as we could not threaten a neutral ship.

We had been steaming around for some time since we had last seen an oiler and we had also needed to refuel *Dunedin*. *Eagle* was getting thirsty. Arrangements had been made for an oiler to be at St Helena for us so we wended our way in that direction.

We were not overworked so everyone spent time on deck 'goofing' at the wonderful marine wildlife. The magnificent albatross would glide for days at our stern, using only the air currents to remain airborne and seldom even flicking his wings. Sometimes he would soar up along the side of the ship then, with only a quick twitch of a wing, would hurtle down wind, disappearing under our stern, only to reappear skimming over the surface. Albatrosses never appeared to sleep. No pilot could watch them without envying their superb flying skills. Many years later I saw a fascinating film of their nesting ground near Cape Horn. They spend so much time at sea that they are utterly incompetent on land. This brilliant film, taken, I believe, by Peter Scott, showed them gliding gracefully down and, having failed to take the elementary precaution of turning into wind, rolling head over heels in a volley of squawks and feathers.

Many hours were spent watching dolphins, which some of the crew wrongly thought were porpoises. These highly intelligent creatures would swim alongside the ship, sometimes, we estimated, making more than 30kts.

They seemed to feel that life was designed just for playing and would often leap right out of the water in pure *joie de vivre*. They are remarkably friendly to humans and we had had fun with them when swimming from the beach in Durban. Sometimes, however, they had been led astray by their high intelligence: they obviously appreciated that the human was an animal requiring air so, if you attempted to swim underwater, they would assume that you were drowning and rescue you by coming up underneath and pushing you to the surface. This could be alarming, as they were not particular as to which part of your anatomy they chose to push.

Occasionally, a sperm whale would join us and take station about 100 yards to one side, staying there for a few hours; before leaving to go about his own business. These huge, harmless creatures had a misfortune that, I am sure, they did not themselves appreciate; from the air they looked remarkably like submarines. One of our Swordfish on A/S patrol had encountered one, immediately assumed that it was a U-boat and had dived to attack. Luckily for the poor animal it had lifted its massive tail into the air and brought it smacking down on to the water. As this was a manoeuvre that no

U-boat could have performed, the pilot sheared away before releasing his depth charges. The whale swam onwards without realising how near he had been to a violent death.

Another entertainment was to watch the flying fish, which would rise in shoals out of our bow wave, skimming along the surface for 30 or 40 yards before splashing back into the sea. We all thoroughly enjoyed watching these antics and voted it much better value than a visit to the zoo.

St Helena was reached on a rather grey day and the whole island looked the same colour. We anchored off the capital, Jamestown, a pleasant little town of stone houses. The population, largely white, were very British and many Union Flags were flying, perhaps for our benefit.

I talked to some of the islanders and learned that the place had been found, originally, by a Portugese in 1502. It had changed hands a number of times and for many years had been owned by the East India Company. It had enjoyed great prosperity for some years before the opening of the Suez Canal in 1869, because it had become a main port of call and coaling station for ships voyaging to the East.

For a period it had been a depot for liberated slaves before they were taken to the new country of Liberia, which had been given to them. It had also been a POW camp for Boers captured in the South African war.

The island's greatest claim to fame, of course, had been as a prison for Napoleon from 1815 to 1821. Some of us visited the house at Longwood, some three miles inland, where he had been confined. It had been kept more or less as a museum and had various artifacts relating to his stay. To me it was rather a strange place. I had always found historical places to have an atmosphere almost as though the ghosts of the past still haunted them, but Napoleon's house seemed stone dead. The things that were most alive were the extraordinary, giant tortoises that wandered around: some were alleged to be over 100 years old but this could have been wishful thinking as I could not see much difference between the young ones and the old ones: they all had the same gnarled and prehistoric look.

After only 36 hours at St Helena we sailed northward, still hunting the elusive *Lothengen*. As we had spent thousands of flying hours searching in vain until, a little over a week ago, we had finally found and sunk the *Elbe*, we thought the odds against finding another such were about 1/1,000. How wrong we were. We had only been at sea for two days when we received a report by W/T from one of our searching aircraft. She had found *Lothengen* and was shadowing.

I was a member of the stand-by striking force that day so rushed with the others to take off, armed with four 250-pound bombs. We were bursting with enthusiasm for this break in the monotony, and looking forward to some dive-bombing practice on a real target that would be unlikely to carry very much in the way of offensive AA armament. After less than an hour's flying, looking eagerly ahead, we saw her and slid into bombing formation.

As we approached we were astonished to find a large, modern ship, stopped and wearing no ensign, with our shadowing Swordfish circling round her, at a height of some 500 feet, without so much as a pop-gun being fired in her direction. There was much flashing of the Aldis lamp from the back cockpit of my aircraft, as I was carrying our Squadron Commander, Lieut-Commander Debenham, as observer. It transpired that the captain of *Lothengen*, on sighting our Swordfish, had decided that there was no future in arguing with aircraft, and had surrendered.

We explained the situation to *Eagle* by radio, asking for a relief shadower to home *Dunedin*, who was already on her way. We then made a number of 'show off' passes over the German ship, at a low height, to keep her frightened by a good view of our bombs, then turned back to our ship. We felt a little disappointed at having had no chance to display our skills but were glad, nevertheless, that we would be causing distress to the U-boats which expected to fuel from her.

When we landed on *Eagle* we found an unexpected amount of interest in our rather tame episode. Apparently, it was the first time on record that a ship had surrendered to an aircraft. Once again dear old *Eagle* had made history.

Some two hours later our relief shadower returned to tell us that they had watched *Dunedin* lower boats and her men climb on board the German ship. A signal shortly afterwards confirmed that a prize crew had been put on board to steam *Lothengen* to Bermuda.

There was much hilarity and argument in the wardroom about whether the old rules about prize money were still in force. In the old days a prize was sold and its value divided amongst the crew of the ship that had captured her. The captain's secretary was sent to wade through his manuals of Naval Law to find out. He could find nothing relevant. I never learned the answer, and I certainly never received a penny.

With no other possible targets known, we steamed for Freetown, capital of Sierra Leone, to refuel. As we neared the African coast we sent some aircraft ashore to RAF *Hastings* for compass checks, then re-embarked them before entering harbour.

Freetown was a ghastly place, but possessed a magnificent natural harbour, the finest in West Africa. The same adjective could not be used for any other part of it. Even in the town centre, a high percentage of the buildings were of wood. The only really conspicuous structure was the seat of government, standing on a rise above the town. The shops were poor and a few places masqueraded as hotels and pubs.

It was extremely hot and sticky and every movement caused floods of perspiration. We had arrived in the rainy season and everything seemed to be continually dripping water. We were told that it wasn't always quite so bad! At night the air was fouled by clouds of mosquitoes. There was little in the way of entertainment, although some sites were reasonable for swimming and there was a golf course.

The majority of the inhabitants were black, cheerful and friendly, full of flashing smiles showing beautiful white teeth which would cause ecstasy to any dentist. These people formed the defence force of the colony as the West African Rifles, a smart and efficient regiment. The local naval craft were also manned by them in British Naval uniform. This could have an astonishing effect on a dark night as an approaching boat appeared to be manned by pairs of white shorts and shirts with no visible means of support.

I was surprised by the number of schools, which covered all ages and standards. It was a great centre of education dating back to 1827 when the Fourah College had been founded. The town itself had only come into existence some 40 years before.

We spent a few days at Freetown and then were back at sea to search for more raiders and U-boats, which had been reported in our area. After a week of fruitless searches, we turned again towards Freetown.

It was now early August 1941 and I had been in *Eagle* for two years, the length of a normal peace-time commission. I had assumed that I would remain in her until she returned to the UK, which we understood would be in the near future, as she had been long overdue for a major refit when we were still in the Mediterranean. I was therefore taken completely by surprise when the Admiralty signalled that I was relieved with effect from the 11th August and was to return to the UK forthwith. It looked as though NA2SL* did, actually, examine their records occasionally.

Another officer, Lieut. (E) Sedgewick, who was a qualified pilot as well as an Engineer Officer, was also required to return home.

We wondered by what means we were expected to make the journey to England 'forthwith'. No doubt somebody would make the arrangements. We set about packing our gear, which was a major project as we had joined the ship in peacetime, on the China Station,

* NA2SL – Naval Assistant to 2nd Sea Lord. Responsible for officers' appointments.

so had our European as well as tropical uniforms plus civilian clothes for all occasions. Added to those were the souvenirs we had collected during our wanderings. When we had assembled it all it seemed that we would need a furniture van to leave the ship.

On the way back to Freetown, Captain Bridge sent for us to have drinks and a chat in his sea cabin. He talked about the operations in which we had taken part and finished by shaking us warmly by the hand, wishing us well in the future and saying: 'You have both done very well in this ship and I am only sorry that, as with all the other aircrew, there have not been more decorations to recognise your work.' It was a satisfying farewell to receive from one's captain.

We enjoyed an alcoholic last evening with the other pilots and observers then, on the following morning, toured round the hangars to thank our troops for the way they had looked after our aircraft. Finally, and not without a few pangs of regret, we climbed into our boat, accompanied by most of the duty part of the watch to handle our legion pieces of baggage, and were taken to the *Edinburgh Castle*, an elderly liner used as a depot and accommodation ship, where we were to live while waiting for some convenient vessel to take us home.

Chapter 14

The Road Home

Edinburgh Castle was a tatty old ship that was alleged to be aground on empty gin bottles. A high percentage of her crew had been exiled to her on account of some dreadful misdemeanour. Our cabins had been passengers' staterooms in the days of peace, but had now been selected by an inordinate number of cockroaches.

Our first demand was when and how we were to get passage to the UK. The horrifying answer was that there was a waiting list on which we were at the bottom, some names having been on it for weeks.

We twiddled our thumbs and propped up the bar with little to do but talk. Most of our discussions were about the progress of the war. A look at the general picture did nothing to break our depression.

In the Mediterranean area the arrival of the German reinforcements had, as we feared, changed everything. Rommel had driven our army right back into Egypt. Axis forces had swept down through Greece, then into Crete, and the Navy had been needed, once again, to evacuate our troops.

To our surprise, however, the United States, although neutral, had landed forces on Iceland to avoid a German invasion. We thought this to be excellent, although the Icelanders may have differed. Also, the US Senate had agreed to send arms to any non-Axis country. Probably the best news was that Hitler had thrown away his non-aggression pact with Stalin and had invaded Russia. It seemed to us that he was breaking one of the first rules of strategic warfare by opening a war on two fronts. At least there was even less chance of an invasion of Britain.

After more than a week of humdrum existence, we stood on deck one day to watch the arrival of the escort vessels of a convoy coming in to refuel. They were corvettes and armed trawlers, but the Senior Officer's ship was a rather unusual vessel of about 2,000 tons, called HMS *Philante*.

She did not look like a warship, although armed with guns and depth-charge rails at the stern. As we were standing 'goofing' we were told to report to the Commander in his cabin forthwith. He told us that *Philante* had accommodation for two officers to the UK. He was giving these places to us as he felt that FAA pilots were more needed at home than the others. We had not realised that he had been in the RNAS in the last war! He said that a boat would be alongside in ten minutes, men had been detailed to handle our gear so, 'Good luck and get cracking.'

Overjoyed, we packed our toothbrushes, and within half an hour were boarding *Philante*. Some men took charge of our numerous boxes and led us to our cabins. Opening the door of mine, I stood and goggled. It was a large room, tastefully decorated with expensive wallpaper and wall-to-wall thick carpeting, a double bed with a dial telephone and radio beside it, armchairs and normal bedroom furniture. It had its own private bathroom with lavish fittings and tiled bulkheads decorated with pictures of sea horses and dolphins.

What type of ship was this, I wondered? I soon found out that she was the private yacht of T.O.M. Sopwith, the famous aircraft builder and designer. The Admiralty had requisitioned and armed her; many of the luxury fittings had been removed but such things as cabin furniture had been left.

She was crewed in a most unusual way: the Captain was an RN Commander, there were some RNVR executive officers and the seamen were naval ratings. All the engineers and some others were borne under an agreement between the Admiralty and the Merchant Navy called T124X. I was to know this arrangement well in future years when serving in escort carriers.

The navigator was wearing the uniform of a Lieutenant RNVR but I found that he was the original captain of the ship. I felt that this must place him in an invidious position, but he had accepted the situation most logically, admitting that he could handle the ship better than the present Captain, but knew nothing about naval warfare.

The engineers messed separately, in Merchant Navy style, except for the Chief Engineer, who lived in the wardroom. Although he had been given the rank of Lieutenant (E) RNR, he always wore, on board, the uniform of a Chief Engineer in the Royal Yacht Squadron.

He told us that the ship was driven by two MAN diesels; he had surpervised the building and installation of them in Germany and knew every nut and bolt in them. If there was ever the slightest vibration or sound from them, he would know instantly what was causing it and disappear like a flash to put it right.

We sailed in less than an hour, and spent the rest of the afternoon marshalling the ships of the convoy into formation. Many vessels did not seem to have had much experience of convoy work. Some were incredibly casual about the operation and followed a law unto themselves. Others appeared to think that it was a naval benefit for the pleasure of the escort vessels and that they should make it as difficult as possible for them. They were a motley collection; some looked as though they would have been in a breakers' yard had it not been for the war. There were a few more modern cargo ships, one of the best of which carried the Commodore. They wore the ensigns of many countries or flags of convenience. One was a particular headache; she was an ancient coal-burner and, every few minutes, clouds of smoke would issue from her single funnel causing the escorts to rush up to her screaming abuse and the Commodore to make her furious signals: 'Stop making smoke.'

She just ignored everything and waffled onwards. During the evening, she broke down completely and one of the corvettes had to tow her back to Freetown. Eventually we achieved some semblance of order but we dreaded to think what might happen in the darkness of the night.

All was quiet until the next morning, when one of the corvettes which was sailing under the Free French flag, thought it had a U-boat contact, although nobody else had, and proceeded to hurl depth charges in all directions. She then, for no apparent reason and without orders, started to lay a smoke-screen between us and the convoy. After disappearing into this, she suddenly emerged, pointing towards us; there was a crack and a shell passed over our masts. We assumed that she had gone 'pro-Nazi', sounded off Action Stations and increased to full speed. However, a signal lantern started to flash furiously from her bridge: 'Pardon! I discharge the cannon!' She, undoubtedly had and we trusted that she wouldn't do it again. We ordered her to return to her station on the screen and not to waste depth charges, and were relieved to find that her station was as far away from us as possible.

We spent much of our time sun-bathing, but one day the Captain told me that he had some Ordinary Seamen due for promotion to Able Seamen. As I was a Royal Navy officer with nothing to do on board, would I examine them? I could hardly refuse so, having no idea what they were supposed to know, I appealed to the petty officer who acted as Bo'sun, and studied the Admiralty Manual of Seamanship Part 1. Having primed myself I examined the candidates, who were all young 'Hostilities Only' ratings and very keen and intelligent. I believe I passed them all.

With little to do there is too much time to think. I began to have the nasty feeling that we were sitting ducks, waiting for an unseen predator to creep up in the dark. I wondered if the men of the Merchant Navy crossing the North Atlantic felt like this all the time.

Reaching the latitude of Gibraltar, we were joined by more merchant ships and a few additional escort vessels. One of these was a CAM Ship, a vessel that I had never seen before. In addition to carrying the normal cargo she had, rigged on her fore-deck, a catapult similar to the one we had used at Gosport. On a trolley on this device was a Hurricane. The idea was that, should the convoy be menaced from the air, it would be fired, flown by a young Pilot Officer of the RAF. After completing his mission, in the unlikely event of his being within range of England, he would fly ashore, failing which he would bale out and hope to be picked up by one of the escort. Sedgewick and I felt that some particular brand of guts must be needed for such a manoeuvre.

I tried to keep myself occupied by spending many hours on the bridge chatting with the captain about the Mediterranean and his own experience with convoy protection. Occasionally, I would relieve the officer of the watch if he wanted to go to the heads or had some other essential job to do. I felt frustrated. Everything remained remarkably quiet for some days as we maintained our course, well out into the Atlantic.

I had been asked to mark the chart with the earliest position that we might expect to meet enemy aircraft operating from the west of France and where we could hope for cover from Coastal Command. The captain asked that one of us would now be continually on the bridge for aircraft recognition and to advise him when to order the Hurricane into the air.

We were both on the bridge when we heard the cry of a look-out: 'Aircraft bearing Green 45'. A quick look through the glasses was all we needed to recognise a Fockke-Wolf Kondor which, we told the captain, would sit there and home U-boats on to the convoy. It should be removed rapidly. The pilot of the Hurricane had also identified the aircraft and was already in his cockpit with the engine running. Within seconds of our signal there was a puff of smoke and he shot into the air, climbing steeply into the clouds. The next we saw of him was appearing above the Kondor and diving down towards it. We could clearly hear the chatter of his guns and those of the enemy aircraft, then saw smoke trailing from the target. He attacked again; this time, we saw pieces flying off the Kondor, more smoke, then it started spinning towards the sea which it hit with a great splash. The ships in the convoy sounded their hooters in congratulation as the pilot flew across them doing a pair of fully justified victory rolls.

He spent about an hour circling the fleet lest another shadower should arrive, then flew slowly over from astern, at about 2,000 feet, then, just ahead of the escorts, turned on to his back. We watched with our fingers crossed as his body dropped from his aircraft then, with relief, saw the white canopy of his parachute burst out above him. As he floated towards the sea, the nearest corvette steamed flat out towards him, rigging a scrambling net. It came to a stop; men clambered down and grabbed him: I doubt if he was in the water more than two minutes. It was most efficiently done and they signalled to us: 'Pilot well and guzzling hot soup in the wardroom.' We hoped that they had laced it with something stronger. The Convoy Commodore sent him a signal of thanks and Sedgewick and I asked *Philante* to send him a rude personal signal from us as the only other pilots present.

Unfortunately, that night it became clear that the Kondor had transmitted our position and course. Just after midnight the escorts reported a submarine contact and that they were making an Asdic sweep. They lost contact. Was it another whale? A few minutes later there was a flash and a pillar of flame from the starboard side of the convoy. The captain said: 'There's no merchant ship there: that was an escort'.

He was right: a torpedo, presumably intended for a ship of the convoy, had struck a Flower Class corvette. The lightly armoured ship had simply dissolved with the loss of all hands. It was a horrifying beginning to the night. Another escort searched the area but reported 'no hope'. They had no Asdic contact so one suspected that the U-Boat had crept under the convoy and was hidden by the engine noises from the ships.

The tension increased as we waited for its next attack. I found that I was gripping the bridge rail so hard that the circulation had gone from my fingers. I was shaking my arms to make the blood flow when a ship astern of the Commodore burst into flames, followed by a violent explosion. She was soon surrounded by burning oil and, through binoculars, we could see heads in the fire and waving arms. An escort approached the sinking ship but could do little to save the men in the holocaust.

We shuddered at this horrible way to die and wondered if the people at home really appreciated the cost of feeding them. In future months I met people who told me with pride about how they managed to fiddle extra petrol for joy-riding in their cars. It made me feel sick.

The following day passed quietly, but one waited with trepidation for nightfall. As daylight died the sky became overcast, not a star to be seen, there was no moon and the darkness was Stygean. How could the ships keep station, with no radar? Each had only a tiny blue light on its stern. For two hours the Asdic pinged but not a contact was heard, then there was a thump audible to starboard of us but no flames, only lights appearing on the mast of a ship to indicate 'I have been torpedoed and have stopped'. We heard the sirens of ships altering course to avoid the casualty. An escort closed her and later reported that she had picked up all survivors. As she cleared the sinking ship we heard another thud and, this time some fire but no explosion. Another escort closed this one and managed to save most of the crew. We waited. And waited. And waited. As the horizon lightened in the east, we sighed with relief and went down to find some sleep. Soon after dawn broke a Catalina appeared and circled us for the remainder of the day. Next morning, after an uneventful night, a Sunderland flying boat reached us and these aircraft circled us for the rest of the daylight hours.

We were now well into the Western Approaches and everything remained quiet as we rounded the north coast of Ireland, where the convoy split, part to proceed to the Clyde and the remainder to Liverpool. We had been ordered to Londonderry, which annoyed Sedgewick and me, as we would have a lengthy journey by rail and ferry to reach our homes. The captain turned up trumps: entirely for our benefit he arranged to heave-to off the tiny fishing village of Port Patrick, in Galloway, where we could get transport to the town of Stranraer to catch the boat train. We thanked him warmly and said 'Goodbye' to the ship's officers who had done everything to make life pleasant for us.

On a beautiful evening with a flat calm sea I had my first view of Britain for over two years. The ship came to a stop close inshore and lowered a boat. We climbed on to dry land inside the little harbour, to find that our arrival had caused a furore. Never in history had a warship visited their little village; the Harbour Master was completely overcome; he rushed around organising hand carts for our gear and led us up to his own cottage. Fortunately, in the excitement, he completely forgot that he also wore the hat of the Customs and Excise Officer and made no attempt to see what was in our baggage.

Reaching his house we found that a message had gone ahead of us and his wife had prepared a magnificent repast of home-made scones and jam. While we were tucking in, the Harbour Master was burning the telephone wires, and arranged for transport to come for us from the RAF Sunderland base near Stranraer. He even booked first-class seats for us on the boat trains, one on the London-bound line for Sedgewick and one on the Glasgow train for me, as I was bound for Aberdeen.

When our transport arrived we presented the Harbour Master and his wife with half-pound slabs of chocolate, of which we both had a large supply. They were speechless; they had not seen so much chocolate for nearly two years.

I arrived in Glasgow just after midnight only to find that the Aberdeen train did not leave until 0630. However, by resorting to bribery with more chocolate, I got the train unlocked and snatched a few hours' sleep before reaching my destination at about 1000 the following morning.

I reached home without having been able to give any warning and caused complete chaos. Eventually comparative peace reigned and I was able to have a look at war-time Britain for the first time.

Chapter 15

The Home Front

Aberdeen looked much the same as when I last saw it. It did not appear to have suffered structurally from the war. The most obvious difference was in the women's clothes. They were mostly dowdy, with little sign of anything new. The main shopping centre, Union Street, had always been lined with parked Rolls Royces, but now there were only a few small cars. In the shop windows, particularly those of the bakers, there was nothing on show. In the clothiers the goods were labelled more prominently with the number of coupons required than with the price.

Food rationing was the thing that hit me hardest. It was a shock to find that I was only allowed 1/3 of a pint of milk, a small square of butter per day and one egg per week. I was glad I had brought a box of 'goodies' with me, and so was my family.

Having taken a few days to settle, I telephoned NA2SL to tell them that I had arrived, to scream for some leave and to find out where I was to go next. They told me that I could have three weeks leave, after which I would be required for instructional duties, probably in Scotland.

Knowing the Admiralty, I assumed this would mean an appointment to the other side of the earth for quite a different job.

I spent more than a week in Aberdeen, allowing my relatives to drag me around and to introduce me to their friends then, feeling that I had satisfied their requirements, I travelled down for a restful stay with friends in Bute.

The island had certainly changed! Instead of pleasure steamers and yachts in the bay there was a submarine depot ship with its brood, and other naval vessels were coming and going: the place was full of naval uniforms so I was quite at home. The Powers that Be had made a blunder about rationing, much to the advantage of the local people. They had ordained that it should be self-supporting in dairy produce. No one could have told them that it was a very fertile island that in peacetime had exported eggs, milk and butter to the mainland. As it had now been instructed to keep it for its own use, there was almost a glut of these foods.

After some ten days I received an appointment to HMS *Condor*, which was the RN Air Station at Arbroath, for instructional duties in the Deck Landing Training School. For once the Admiralty were giving me what they had promised, but I was not particularly thrilled. I was pleased that I was to be so near home, but teaching pilots to do ADDL's, and standing on the airfield waving a pair of bats, was not an exciting prospect.

I arrived at Arbroath to find that things were not quite what I had expected. In the first place, RN Airfields had changed somewhat from their state in 1939. The landing area was no longer a grass field but had tarmac runways; the buildings were of wood, but quite well built, and were complete with electricity and bathrooms with hot and cold running water. I was given a fairly large cabin, furnished with two beds although, in the early stages, I was to occupy it on my own. Another innovation was that we had WRNS stewards! They were most efficient and looked after us and our clothes very well; we had to be careful, however, not to wander along for a bath in our 'birthday suits'.

The morning after reaching Arbroath I reported to No. 767 Squadron, to which I had been appointed.

This also differed from my expectations: we were equipped with Swordfish and, to my surprise, some Fulmars, which were now regarded as obsolete. We were certainly required to teach deck landing and, in fact, take each course to HMS *Argus* to qualify. However, I found that I was expected to teach a great deal more than that.

Our pupils had all been taught to fly at Pensacola, in the United States. I could find no fault with the standard of instruction they had received, but they had been trained in a peace-time environment and, at night, in a blaze of light. We had to teach them to handle their aircraft in war and to fly at night over a blacked-out country. The purpose of the Fulmars was for an instructor to sneak around and suddenly jump on the pupils to see if they were keeping alive to the possibility of meeting enemy aircraft. We did not labour the fact that, should they meet an ME109 when flying a Swordfish, they had little chance of survival unless they could rapidly disappear into a convenient cloud. This duty was a popular one, and light relief for the instructors: flying a pleasant and reasonably fast aircraft through the 'streets' between towering cumulus clouds, then diving down to make a fighter attack on an unsuspecting Swordfish, was fine entertainment and valuable to the pupils.

It was amusing to study their faces when they were greeted, on landing, with: 'I'm surprised to see you. I shot you down half an hour ago!'

They also had to be taught to fly in formation low over the sea, which I remembered from my own training at Gosport could be quite hair-raising. I had been warned by my colleagues that instructing at Arbroath was much more dangerous than fighting the Germans. On many occasions I was forced to agree with them.

We also sent our pupils out over the sea to find their way back without the aid of an observer. On one occasion a Canadian pupil became hopelessly lost, eventually found land and came to earth, without breaking his aircraft, in a large field. When the locals rushed up to him he assumed from their voices that he had landed in Germany and set his Swordfish on fire with his Very pistol. He had, in fact, landed near Montrose and had failed to recognise the Aberdeenshire accent!

Quite the most alarming exercise was the one for night flying formation, in total darkness with the only lights visible being the tiny blue ones on the leader's wings. On one occasion I had been waiting ten minutes for my No.3 to find me when I saw him rising up underneath me; to avoid being rammed I had to make a manoeuvre somewhere between a stall turn and a half loop. I had a serious discussion with him when we landed.

Occasionally our pupils lost themselves at night when only circling the airfield. They seemed to have charmed lives. One night an aircraft disappeared without trace until, early the following morning, we received a telephone call from the pilot to report that he had hit a mountain. He appeared to be unhurt apart from a sprained ankle. He had scraped over the top of this mountain so closely that he had removed his undercarriage, then skidded to a halt on a relatively flat plateau. He had damaged his ankle when climbing down the hill!

One pupil force-landed in a field and telephoned to say that he had restarted his engine which seemed to be running alright and should he take off? He was told to remain where he was while another instructor and I came over in our dual Swordfish.

This we did, and found after each making a number of attempts, that there was no way that we could land in that field. Returning to Arbroath, we took our Tiger Moth and tried again, but were equally baffled. Finally we went by road with two mechanics and discovered that it was quite impossible to get a long enough run to take off. The aircraft had to be dismantled. How on earth could this relatively inexperienced pilot have landed in that field without even scratching the fuselage? We felt sure that he must have bounced in the previous field, but he denied it. He was obviously another one blessed with a charmed life!

Arbroath was a happy station and I found instructing very satisfying. It was most encouraging to watch a pupil doing an exercise well after I had taught him. It was easy to slip up to Aberdeen for an occasional week-end, usually by flying a pupil to Dyce, the airport of Aberdeen and leaving him to take it back to Arbroath, then to pick me up again first thing on Monday morning.

I had not been there long before Angus Hogg, the fighter pilot with whom I had become very friendly in Alexandria, joined the fighter unit at the station. As I was still living on my own in a double cabin, it was natural that he should move in with me.

We sometimes visited his home in Edinburgh, staying there for a night or two when we could arrange leave at the same time.

Being stationed in Scotland, I could visit Bute comparatively easily, but one of those intended visits ended in disaster. Angus had gone to Prestwick for a two-week night fighter course, so we had arranged that on the Friday evening we would both fly to Abbotsinch, and from there spend a week-end with my friends in Bute. On the Thursday evening I sat down to dinner opposite the Captain's Secretary, who greeted me with the remark 'Sorry to hear about Angus Hogg; I know he was a friend of yours.' He was most embarrassed to find that I had no idea what he was talking about and had to explain that Angus had been flying in an Anson with others of his course on a radar exercise, when one engine had cut. Although an Anson can be flown easily on one engine, the pilot made a mess of landing and Angus, who had been sitting in the second pilot's seat, had been killed.

One becomes accustomed in time of war to accepting the deaths of friends and relatives, but to learn the news in the manner that I had, when it was the result of a stupid and unnecessary accident, came as a great shock.

The result of shock can be that a careless and thoughtless attitude to work arises and this seemed to happen to me. I was sent for by the Squadron Commander, a man of considerable experience, who explained to me that I was flying in the manner known as 'split arse' and that, although this was no doubt quite safe for a pilot of my experience, it was not a good example to pupils, who would undoubtedly kill themselves if they tried to copy me. He understood why I had started to fly that way and his remarks were fully justified. I took immediate action to get a grip on myself, and succeeded.

Newspapers were now available to me daily, and the radio news was first-hand. Both press and radio were obviously playing down Axis successes and embellishing any of our good fortunes, of which there were all too few.

On November 13th HMS *Ark Royal* had been sunk by a U-Boat only a few miles from Gibraltar. She had enjoyed a most successful career and had done yeoman work. Both the Germans and the Italians had claimed to have sunk her on many occasions but she had never previously received a single hit.

The situation in the United States was very curious. The destroyer USS *Reuben James* had been sunk by a U-Boat, and two others damaged. Their ships were now escorting North Atlantic convoys which were carrying arms and food to us. As they were still a neutral country it seemed most remarkable, although we were not going to complain.

The work of the Squadron progressed well, and every three months we were able to release another course of young pilots to operational squadrons. I broke the routine occasionally by scrounging aircraft that I had not flown before from other units to gain 'experience on type': these included the Skua and the Roc, both of which had very poor reputations. Having flown them, I fully agreed with everything I had been told. The Hurricane was quite a different story; I found it a delightful aircraft to fly and many fighter pilots told me that they preferred it to the Spitfire which, although faster, was less robust and could not accept so much punishment in battle. I experienced a minor alarm in one of those aircraft: on a slack day I was asked to take a Hurricane to the repair yard at Evanton, near Inverness.

This was a pleasant break from flying Swordfish, so I jumped at the chance. I had just taken off, when one of the panels in the port mainplane, that were provided for loading the guns, came loose and started to flap in the slipstream; this did not improve the aerodynamic properties of the wing, so I landed immediately. It was screwed down, thumped, banged and declared secure. I tried again and had only been flying for ten minutes when two of these panels started to flap. Having slowed to a minimum safe speed, I crept into the nearest airfield, Dyce, and they were fixed once again. This time I almost reached Inverness before the same two started their old tricks. I flew slowly into Evanton and was glad to give the aircraft to the repair yard for a much-needed overhaul!

Since arriving in this country I had never heard a single air raid warning and London seemed to be having a rest from the Blitz. We were particularly pleased about this because some of us were given leave to go with our families to an investiture at Buckingham Palace to have our 'gongs' hooked on to us by King George VI. I think that our families were the people who received the greatest thrill from that event.

On 7th December there were headlines in the press and flashes on the radio: the Japanese had bombed Pearl Harbor. The Americans appeared to have been quite unprepared, despite the fact that they had known that the Japanese had been studying our attack at

Taranto and our intelligence sources had warned them of the danger. Many years later, when I attended the Naval Staff Course, I learned the many other peculiarities of the event. To us then it chiefly meant that the United States, with its vast manufacturing and food-producing potential, was now in the war with us.

Within a few days our new enemy was sweeping through the Far East with little opposition. Malaya was invaded and, within two months, Singapore had fallen. When we lost HMS *Prince of Wales* and HMS *Repulse* by attack from torpedo-bombers all the instructors at Arbroath were amazed to hear that these ships had been sailing without any fighter cover. We had decided that capital ships had little chance against a determined attack by torpedo aircraft when overwhelming numbers were used, attacking from different directions. Our point had been proved.

Before the end of January 1942, US forces and equipment were arriving in the UK. Although the war could continue for a long time, we felt we must triumph in the end, with these apparently inexhaustible resources now available to the Allies.

Shortly after these events I moved into very luxurious quarters. More and more units of various types had been arriving at Arbroath and accommodation on the station was becoming very tight. Instructors were therefore allowed to look for suitable facilities outside. I was incredibly lucky in finding a manor house whose owners were charmed to look after a few naval officers. The house had its own vegetable and fruit gardens so the food was much above war-time standard. I had the whole of the comfortable 'nursery suite' to myself.

On the 11th August I heard the distressing news that poor *Eagle* had been sunk by a U-Boat whilst in the 'Pedestal' operation to bring vitally needed supplies to Malta. It was sad to hear of the old girl's demise, but there was, at least, something very suitable about her meeting her end in the Mediterranean, where she had made her name.

The spring and summer of that year passed with long hours of day and night flying broken by occasional week-end leave. One break that I received involved a visit from my uncle, the Rev. Wilfred Currie, now a Padre in the Army. I flew him to Aberdeen in an Albacore and he was thrilled at being piloted by his nephew.

I had been at Arbroath for a year when I was told, one day, that the Captain wished to see me. Immediately I wondered what ghastly crime had been committed, but he offered me a chair and asked if I had heard from the Admiralty. I hadn't, so he passed me a signal which stated that I had been appointed to 815 Squadron, in command. I was very surprised, as I had less than three years' seniority as a Lieutenant, but he said that he considered me quite competent to command a squadron and had recommended me some months before.

815 Squadron had been one of the *Illustrious* squadrons at Taranto and was well kown for its work in other areas; it would be a fine squadron to command. I knew that it was ashore in North Africa and based at Dekheila, so I was on my way back to my old hunting ground in Alexandria.

Chapter 16

Back to the Sand

The Admiralty gave me a few days to collect my tropical uniforms from Aberdeen, then required me to find my way to RAF Lyneham, in Wiltshire. I begged a lift south from the Communications Squadron at Donibristle. This was a most efficient organisation which had been Jersey Airways before the invasion of the Channel Islands, when it had transferred to the Navy complete with aircraft and pilots. They took me in a Dominie to Hendon, where I found transport to Lyneham.

The station was the UK end of the route to Egypt and the East for RAF Transport Command. They used Liberators, huge four-engined bombers which had been converted to carry passengers and priority stores. There were others waiting for the next flight, who consisted largely of senior Army officers and their staffs but included a US Navy Captain and the Chinese Ambassador, Dr Wellington Koo. The latter was an immaculate little Chinese, who was very intelligent and entertaining.

I had a number of conversations with the US Captain, who was complimentary about our efforts to date but gave the impression that the United States would now show us how to win the war.

Two Liberators left Lyneham on 7th October. The senior officers embarked in one that had been fitted with passenger seats, while the less exalted, such as myself, had to pack into one carrying stores. We took off in the early morning, flew well out to sea to keep out of range of enemy fighters, and headed for Gibraltar. We touched down after eight and a half hours flying. There was no time to see the place, as we only stayed long enough to refuel, have a meal and change out of European uniform.

We left as night was falling and climbed towards the south, eventually turning east to cross Africa below the area where we might encounter anything hostile. It took over eleven boring hours before we landed near Cairo.

I spent the night in a hotel, travelling onwards next morning in a dusty train bearing the glorified label of 'Express'. In Alex I found a taxi to take me to Dekheila.

145

The Air Station was much changed since I had been there with the *Eagle* squadrons. There were many more buildings and hangars and a vast improvement in the plumbing arrangements. Having dumped my gear in a cabin, I went in search of the Commander (Flying). Then the problems started.

I was informed that they had no knowledge of my having been appointed to command 815 Squadron, which I found very hard to believe. Only recently, with no reference to the Admiralty, they had made a local appointment of an observer to the command and didn't think it would be a good move to change again so soon.

I was stunned by this blatant disregard of Admiralty instructions. It seemed to me that a private empire was being built in the Middle East and everything that I was to see later tended to confirm this. The Captain had given himself the title of CONAS Egypt (Commanding Officer Naval Air Stations Egypt).

After much discussion the Commander (F) offered me the position of Senior Pilot in 815 Squadron. I objected strongly. He did a rethink and offered me command of the Fleet Requirements Unit while they 'sorted out the situation' with the Admiralty. I had very little faith in anyone doing this, but was not in a strong position to argue, so agreed to take command of 775 Squadron, the FRU, temporarily. Finding an officer about to return to the UK, I briefed him with a message to pass to my old Captain at Arbroath.

775 Squadron was a complete shambles. It was basically used for communications, combined with any odd jobs required by the fleet. The flying discipline was appalling – many of the pilots would have been awaiting court martial had they been serving anywhere else – and it was equipped with a mixed bag of aircraft. I tried to get some semblance of organisation going but it was difficult to put much enthusiasm into the job. After nearly six weeks, it became clear that, as I had expected, nothing had been done by the powers at Dekheila but that my message to my old captain had borne fruit.

We received a peremptory signal from the Admiralty stating that I was to take command of 815 Squadron forthwith. It was clear to the powers at Dekheila that information had gone to England that had not originated from them and it did not make me popular, but I could hardly carry any blame.

I found 815 Squadron to be well organised and running very smoothly, the aircrew all having a fair amount of experience and well indoctrinated into life in the desert. The Senior Pilot, Lieut. Swanton and Senior Observer. Lieut. Hunt were both RN Air Branch and there was one other RN officer, Lieut. Spademan, an observer. All the remainder were RNVR. I had never met a squadron crewed this way but I soon found that they were keen and efficient and compared not unfavourably with 'straight stripe' officers. We were equipped with Swordfish, a number of them with ASV (Air to Surface Vessel) radar. We flew under the direct operational command of 201 Group RAF, which worked unexpectedly smoothly.

Our principal job was to defend the area against U-Boats and cover shipping and harbour approaches. Detached flights had to work from places like Gaza, in Palestine. We also had another duty which was rather unusual.

The Army had stopped the German advance at El Alamein in July and had held it there while building up a force to drive the enemy back. By October this force had become much greater than the German and Italian opposition. Supplies had been pouring into Egypt, in particular American Sherman tanks, vastly superior to the Axis ones, which were mainly Italian and regarded as coffins by their crews. General Montgomery had taken command of the Eighth Army; he appeared to be a tremendous showman but could certainly produce results. It was clear that a major battle was imminent.

During the build-up of our forces the duty fell to 815 Squadron, which was skilled in night operations, to keep the enemy disturbed and short of sleep, by cruising around over their lines, dropping one bomb every five minutes. At dawn the RAF took over, to spend the day bombing while fighters straffed the enemy positions. This was not a particularly dangerous frolic, as the AA fire was desultory and seldom came near us. One night, however, I was surprised to meet more fire than usual and some of it passed remarkably close to me.

On returning to Dekheila I found that I had inadvertantly switched on my navigation lights so had been flying around in full view of everybody! I had to hang my head in shame and apologise to my crew.

On 29/30th October there was a tremendous barrage which we could hear in Alexandria, some 60 miles away. Then came the news that the Eighth Army was sweeping forward. For the next few weeks we covered shipping and naval vessels around the coast, at night, until it became clear that the Axis forces were being driven right out of Egypt and were already falling back through Libya. We were instructed to go forward and set up a Squadron Headquarters at Mersa Matruh. This was to be a more or less permanent camp and it took a masterpiece of organisation to move everything required, including living and messing equipment, some 200 miles. I was astonished at how smoothly this happened. Everyone pulled his weight, appeared to know what was required and got on with the job.

By air, road and rail we set off, and laid our camp out on the side of the airfield. Tents blossomed all around the site and marquees were rigged for dining rooms, rest rooms and wardroom. A tall flag-pole, complete with yard arm, was raised and the White Ensign hoisted.

We had some RAF personnel, including a most efficient Flight Sergeant named Burlington-Green, who took charge of the diesel generator and soon had electric lights in all the tents.

Our transport section included lorries, vans and, I was pleased to find, a comfortable Humber shooting brake as CO's car. After a short time we 'won' some ex-Italian and ex-German vehicles; one was a massive machine with a body resembling a 1908 touring car, a powerful engine and four huge wheels like those of a farm tractor. It was designed for travelling over the desert, and became invaluable. We also acquired two BMW motor cycles.

With the remarkable ability of the British matelot to make himself at home, in no time there were white-painted boulders marking paths to the messes and even some palm trees in pots at the entrances. There were some dug-outs, built by the Italians, one of which we cleaned, disinfected and fitted out as our operations room. We were a most self-contained unit, even having our own Doctor and sick-bay. I put Lieut. Hunt, the Senior Observer, in charge of camp organisation generally, in the capacity of First Lieutenant. He was brilliant at this, and one of the best 'scroungers' I have ever met.

We had just started to get the operations room working, when we received signals from 201 Group requiring our services. Convoys of ships were passing east and west almost continuously, supplying our advancing army, and we were to provide anti-submarine and anti-E Boat cover during the hours of darkness. We rapidly arranged a programme covering patrols of three hours each, and laid out a flare path and night-flying equipment so that all flights ran smoothly.

From then onwards we were required almost every night to cover either convoys or warships. One frequent duty was to escort mine-layers such as HMS *Manxman* en route for Malta. These ships were sometimes used to carry essential stores to the island as they were fast enough to make the dangerous part of the voyage mostly in darkness. We felt rather redundant, as their speed was such that no U-Boat was likely to achieve a hit.

One night I had a radar contact which seemed very definite from my observer's interpretation of his screen and I prepared to attack; as I dived it became rather exciting: the convoy was flying balloons and my direction of attack took me through them. I managed to avoid them, but before dropping depth charges we lost contact. I ordered, by radio, more aircraft to search the area but nothing could be found.

On one unfortunate occasion we attacked one of our own submarines. When any friendly boats were approaching harbour a 'submarine sanctuary' was declared and we were given exact times that it would be in force. On the night in question the submarine decided to 'warm the bell' and arrive early. One of our aircraft saw it and, obeying the rules, attacked at once, damaging it but failing to sink it. We met the captain and officers later and they admitted that it had been their own fault and presented us with a model of a bent submarine, which was a nice gesture. I often wonder if that model is still in existence.

Gradually we had to cover greater and greater distances, so I had to form detached flights to operate from airfields as far apart as Gaza and Benghasi. I had to ask for more and more Swordfish and many of those were practically worn out, so that maintenance became a major problem. Another difficulty that arose from the far-flung detachments concerned was the lack of suitable transport to enable me to keep in touch. I screamed about this and was given two Fulmars, which proved a godsend.

Between flying operations we steadily improved our camp. I found another two-roomed dug-out which, after cleaning out and furnishing with fittings from a sunken Italian liner, was most comfortable. Our greatest addition, however, was to build the only hot-and-cold shower in the Western Desert. This wonderful construction of corrugated iron with a brick furnace was the brain-child of Lieut. Hunt. Some three miles away we had found a water hole which was too brackish for drinking but adequate for washing so was ideally suited to our shower. It became famous far and wide.

More and more personnel had joined us: we had Maltese cooks and stewards and a party of Italian POW's, one of which was an experienced bartender: almost all of them had some kind of useful trade.

Suddenly I received a signal one day informing me that I had been granted the rank of Acting Lieut-Commander, which was pleasing as, apart from the increased salary, it gave me more clout with the other services.

At 11.00 o'clock one night we had our flare path lit and had just landed two aircraft when we saw what was obviously a Liberator circling the airfield and appearing to wish to land.

We flashed green lights at it but it would not come down and eventually disappeared over the escarpment and seemed to crash land. I could not allow anyone to look for it on the ground, at night, as there was a huge minefield between ourselves and the site where it seemed to be, so I ordered an air search at dawn. A few hours later I was awakened by cries of 'Who goes there?' from my sentries. Two US officers had walked right through the minefield! I opened the bar for them. One of the officers had been the captain of the aircraft and the other the navigator. They told me that they had been bombing near Algiers but when I asked what had been the target the captain replied 'Gee. I guess the bombardier is the only man who knows that!' I wanted to know why they hadn't landed when we gave them a green light and they replied that they thought it was an enemy trap. We were only 150 miles behind the lines!

At first light we rescued the other seven members of their crew and sent details of the situation to HQ Middle East. They replied that the Americans would be collected the following day and would we look after them meantime? The following night no fixed operational flights had been demanded so, apart from two stand-by crews, no one else was needed on duty other than the operations room staff.

We decided to entertain our guests with a wardroom party. It developed in the usual way and there was soon a deal of horse-play. At one stage, when I had become involved in a melée with some Sub-Lieuts., the duty observer had come in, disentangled me and reported that there had been a U-Boat sighting in the area. I had, of course, risen to my feet and shouted 'Shut up everyone,' which they did. I then ordered the stand-by crews to the Ops. room and went there myself, telling the others to carry on with the party.

The following morning the US captain greeted me with 'Gee, Commander, that was amazing last night.' I assumed that he meant that he had enjoyed the party but what had, in fact, astonished him was that I had been involved in a wrestling match with some very junior officers but had only to say 'Shut up' for everyone to do so, had then arranged an operational flight and allowed the party to continue. He told me that a US commanding officer had to place himself on a pedestal and never let his hair down in view of his juniors or there would be no respect for him. He couldn't understand how we Limeys could maintain what he admitted seemed a smooth and efficient discipline when we behaved like that. I suppose it must be based on our history and tradition.

They were collected that day and we received a signal from a US senior officer, giving effusive thanks for the way we had looked after his men. He sent us a case of Bourbon, which was very welcome, although we would have preferred Scotch.

By this time we were required to form and train a flight for spotting fall of shot when battleships and cruisers were shelling shore targets. We were given four Albacores for this purpose and I put Lieut. Spademan in charge. After exercises with ships of the fleet they had to move forward and were finally based at Benghasi. This meant another distant detachment for me to visit.

For the more complicated maintenance inspections it was necessary to send aircraft to Dekheila and I used those occasions to give the aircrew a break in the fleshpots of Alexandria. I sometimes managed to have a 'jolly' myself. My uncle, Wilfred Currie, the Padre in the Army, arrived in Egypt. I spent a night with him in the Cecil Hotel in Alex. Another arrival from Bute was a school friend, Arthur Christie, whose sister I later married. He had obtained a commission in the RAF, had been trained to fly in Rhodesia and had now arrived at Heliopolis, near Cairo. I flew down in a Fulmar, spent a night with him in the city then flew him to Mersa Matruh to spend a few days seeing how the Navy operated.

Since we carried out most of our flying at night, we tried to work a routine which left the afternoons free for relaxation: usually swimming and lying around on the beach. There was a fine stretch of sand and a rocky area with deep water for diving. Amidst the rocks was a deep pool which did not appear to be entirely natural. It was alleged to have been Cleopatra's swimming pool.

We were frequently called upon for other duties. A not very popular one was ferrying replacement aircraft for Malta. It had been decided that this was not a job for the normal ferry pilots and should be done at night to avoid enemy fighters. The aircraft had to be flown as far west as possible then, during the dark hours, flown to Malta, where the crew remained until taken back to Egypt the following night. The day spent in Malta, mainly in an air raid shelter, gave an insight into the sufferings of the islanders and the marvellous way they endured their lot. They had been awarded the George Cross, and we all felt that it had been richly deserved.

The FAA Swordfish Squadron based there had done magnificent work destroying convoys attempting to supply Rommel's Afrika Korps.

Another duty that sometimes fell to us was to take personnel or urgently needed items to the Long Range Desert Group at Siwa Oasis. This unit did outstanding work infiltrating behind the enemy lines.

As most of our operational work was searching for remarkably rare U-Boats and E-Boats, I felt that we were in danger of getting into a rut, so arranged dummy dive bombing attacks, at night, on Mersa harbour and torpedo attacks on the RAF Air Sea Rescue launch, using radar. The crew of the launch loved these exercises as they had become very bored waiting in vain for someone to fall in the sea.

Although we found our work routine, it was recognised as the reason why so much shipping was travelling safely up and down the North African coast. However our aircraft were becoming worn out and requiring continual repairs; engines were on their last legs and we were making frequent emergency landings.

I reported the situation officially and this resulted in an

unexpected order to report to the AOC 201 Group. I was greeted most cordially and the work of 815 Squadron greatly praised. I was then told, after warnings of the greatest secrecy, that we were about to invade Sicily and that it was essential that we keep going until then. I was asked what I would need to do this and said 'Every Swordfish and spare part in the Middle East.' To my amazement I was told 'You can have them!'

Without being able to give the reason, I told our Air Engineer Officer that he could now demand and get anything he wanted. He could hardly believe me but soon found that extra aircraft were arriving and any spares that he wanted were delivered with high priority.

We managed to keep going for a further two months, until our poor old Swordfish were literally falling to pieces and, more often than not, having to cut their patrols short due to failing engines. I had to report that we had reached the end of our tether. We collected everything together, packed up all items worth keeping and returned to Dekheila.

On Sunday 18th July 1943 I disbanded 815 Squadron, apart from the Albacore Flight, which had now reached Sicily and was still in a reasonable state to operate with the fleet. It was sad to see the end of a famous squadron but I had no doubt that it would soon be re-formed with modern aircraft.

The AOC 201 Group sent a very appreciative signal to Commander-in-Chief Levant, repeated to HQ RAF ME, CONAS and 815 in which he said:

The Camel's back is broken. I understand that 815 Squadron have now been flown to the limit of their resources and will have to be withdrawn. I would be most grateful if you could convey to the aircrews and all other officers and ratings of this squadron our appreciation for the very gallant effort which they have made in maintaining their aircraft to this time. Their co-operation with this Group has been magnificent and may we wish them every success on being re-equipped and taking up their new role.

Instructions were received to return squadron personnel to the UK. I was to be given priority air passage. It looked as though they had another job already arranged for me.

A few days were needed to clear up all the paper work, including listing stores to be written off, some of which dated from before I had joined the squadron and had been abandoned when everyone had been obliged to flee before the advancing Germans. I had marked these as 'Lost during the retreat from the desert'. Later I was to receive a cold message to inform me that our army had not 'retreated' but had made a 'strategic withdrawal'.

As my flight to the UK was not due for a week, it gave me time to do something that, with my penchant for history, I had wished to do ever since I had arrived in Egypt. I took one of our reasonably serviceable Fulmars to tour the so-called Biblical Lands of Palestine.

Leaving Dekheila after breakfast I flew east, passing over the Suez Canal some 80 miles north of the point where Moses, having consulted his tide tables, was alleged to have led the Children of Israel across the Gulf at low water with the Egyptians, according to some historians, chasing them furiously in an effort to retrieve the loot that the Israelis had stolen, only to be stymied by the rising waters.

I landed at Gaza to refuel, then turned south-east to fly around Beersheba. It looked like any other small Middle East township so I turned north to pass Tel Aviv on my left and hit the coast again north of Haifa. I wanted to see Tyre, which is on an island reached by a causeway originally built by Alexander the Great in 382 BC. The next site of historical interest was Sidon which had been an important sea port, not only in Old Testament days, but later to both Romans and Phoenicians. Some 30 miles further north I landed at Beirut, and next morning I flew south over much of the area where Moses, Joshua and various 'prophets' had set a pattern for Napoleon and Hitler by invading and massacring the inhabitants. Passing over Lake Tiberius, I circled Nazareth then, following the River Jordan, I found Jericho where there were some obvious ruins and archaelogical sites north of the modern town. I imagined that these sites were probably of the old city where Joshua, with a surprising knowledge of civil engineering, seems to have known that, by marching an army in step around the mud walls then giving a blast on trumpets, they would fall down. It would have been a miracle if they hadn't.

On reaching the Dead Sea I turned eastward to find Jerusalem which I flew over a few times, at a height much below the legal limit, in search of famous places. Having decided that some were recognisable, I circled Bethlehem then headed for Ismailia, where I would need to refuel.

With a few days still in hand I spent some time at the Sporting Club in Alexandria. Returning to the city centre from the club was, in itself, a history lesson. The tramway route from Gamel Abdul Nasser goes through 'The Region of the Dead' by the old, walled boundary of the city. It is a cemetary which has existed for some thousands of years and is still used. Alexander the Great is supposed to be buried there. The tramway terminates at Ramleh, where Cleopatra's Needle and its twin stood before we stole one and set it up on the Thames Embankment and the Americans stole the other and put it in Central Park, New York. Actually they had nothing to do with Cleopatra as they had, originally, been at Heliopolis long before her time and had been moved to Alexandria just over 200 years ago. Also at Ramleh are the ruins of the Caesareum, a huge temple built in honour of Mark Anthony. It had been knocked about a good deal over the centuries but not, oddly enough, by us, although we did bombard the town in 1880-82 for no apparent reason.

On 28th July I left for England in a Liberator. We landed at Gibraltar in the afternoon, refuelled, had a meal and changed into European uniform then left in the evening to fly overnight to Lyneham. We passed over the south coast just after dawn to feast our eyes on our 'green and pleasant land' after the colourless sand of North Africa.

I soon had an inclination to delete the word 'pleasant'. Including the diversions to keep clear of fighters, it had taken some 20 hours to come all the way from Egypt – it took 36 hours to reach Aberdeen in trains covered with smuts from inferior, wartime coal and crammed with service personnel of every nationality. There was, I suppose, 'a war on'.

Chapter 17

Escort Carrier

I spent a week with the family, during which I telephoned NA2SL to report my return. They told me that I could have a few week's leave and then would probably be sent back to sea: they would not be more specific. I assumed that I would be given command of another operational squadron but this time in a fleet carrier.

I had been a little concerned about my next appointment, because of the unfortunate row in Egypt about commanding 815 Squadron. However, I was surprised to discover that I had been given quite a glowing reference as a 'most efficient squadron commander'. I must have been forgiven.

I had spent some ten days in my old haunts in Bute, before my new appointment arrived. I was to join HMS *Biter*, in Belfast as 'Wings' (Commander [Flying]). I had a fit. I suspected that *Biter* was a thing called an Escort Carrier – some sort of converted merchant ship. I had heard about British liners being converted, such as HMS *Nairana* but knew little about them otherwise.

Moreover I had not served in a carrier since *Eagle* and then I had only been a squadron pilot, so had little idea of a carrier's air department organisation. Now I was to be responsible for the whole operation of aircraft! I thought they might have given me a short course or a period as understudy before dropping me into it. Panic reigned.

I 'phoned everyone I could think of who might be able to give me any useful facts and figures, and learned that *Biter* was an American conversion from a merchant ship, had a composite squadron of Swordfish and Wildcat fighters and would probably be used for convoy protection. I was also told that her sister ship, HMS *Dasher*, had blown up and sunk due to an electrical fault. I was far from reassured.

On the due date I crossed to Belfast in the ferry from Glasgow and found a taxi to take me to Harland and Wolff's shipyard, where *Biter* was completing a refit. I found her lying alongside a wharf, looking much bigger than I had expected. She was like a large merchant ship

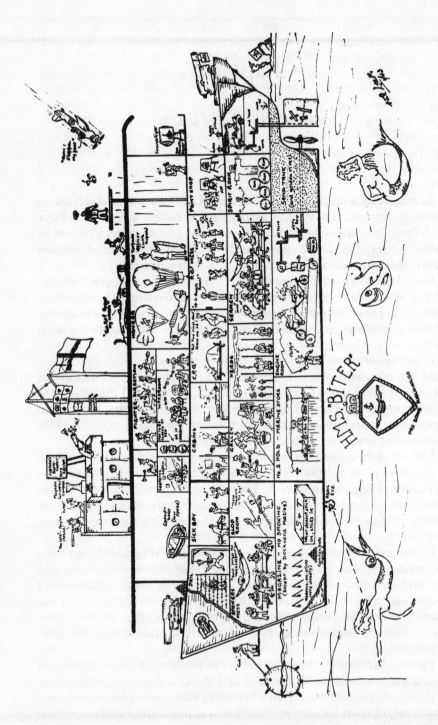

HMS *Biter* – How she really worked

with the upperworks sliced off and a flat platform stuck on top. On the starboard side was a structure resembling a child's effort with matchboxes; radar aerials rose on the top of it.

I was vastly relieved to find that my predecessor, a very experienced Lieut-Cdr. RN, was still on board and able to give me a few days' briefing.

My cabin was a cheering surprise. It was much larger than the usual style in naval ships, was well furnished and, through a door in one bulkhead, was a shower and heads compartment. Outside the entrance door was a plate reading, in the American style, 'Senior Air Officer'.

As a merchant ship she had been named '*Rio Parana*' and designed for fast refrigerated cargo, and many of her original fittings remained, including the forward hold, now empty apart from some stores. The flight deck was of timber with hydraulically-operated arrestor wires and crash barriers and a catapult which could only operated US-built aircraft. She had, to my surprise, an open bridge which, in the Navy, we called the Compass Platform. It would be horribly exposed in winter weather. My flying control position was on the port side of the island and was fitted with quite modern instruments. It was not enclosed either so I decided that I had better look to my winter woollies in the near future.

At the after end of the flight deck was an aircraft lift descending into a hangar, which I estimated could take about 20 aircraft, with workshops etc. at the forward end. Below the flight deck were Operations, Aircraft Direction, Briefing and Ready Rooms. She was astonishingly well equipped.

The AA armament was impressive. At intervals down each side of the flight deck were sponsons with Bofors guns, as there were on the forecastle and on the after deck, known, as termed by the Americans, as the 'Fan Tail'. There were also Oerlikens on the island. *Eagle* would have been glad of such armament.

Biter was driven by two diesel engines working a single large propeller and capable of giving her a speed of 18kts. Orders to the engine room were made by a telegraph using expressions that I had not met before. In addition to the usual British words, stop, slow, half and full speeds, ahead and astern, was an additional one, 'flank', meaning 'go like hell'. In this ship there was a further instruction: 'manoeuvring procedure'. On receiving this the engineers would run one engine ahead and one astern', then, depending upon the orders from the bridge, would throw the clutch to one engine or the other.

Failure to remember this could have most alarming results, as I found to my cost on one occasion when the Captain let me 'play' with the ship. Not having asked for 'manoeuvring procedure' the engine room could not react to a demand for power astern, and the ship charged around Lamlash harbour in an unnecessarily exciting manner.

Biter was manned under a system which I had first heard of in *Philante* in 1941 but in which I had never previously been involved. Our Commanding Officer was Captain Boswell, who was RN, but the Commander (Executive Officer) was RNVR, as were the watch keeping officers, other than the navigator, who was a Lieutenant RNR. The Operations officer, when I joined, was Royal Navy but was soon relieved by Geoff Coy, a Lieut-Cdr. (A) RN. The only other 'straight-stripe' officer was Lt. (A) Campbell who combined DLCO and Flight Deck Officer. The Chief Engineer held the rank of Lieut-Cdr. (E) RNR but was under the T124X agreement as were all the other engineers who held the rank of Sub-Lieut. (E) RNVR, apart from the 'Senior' who was a Lieut. (E) RNR. The Paymaster Commander and all his staff were also T124X. Stewards and galley staff came under the same agreement but the seamen were mainly 'hostilities only' ratings with a leavening of RN Chiefs and PO's.

I found that Captain Boswell had been in command of HMS *Dasher* when she had sunk. It seemed to me rather heartless to have given him a sister ship in those circumstances.

After a few days' briefing by my predecessor, meeting the others in the Air Department, and touring the ship, my panic began to abate. Everyone seemed to know his job; the Flight Deck Officer, the Flight Deck Engineer and the aircraft handlers were fully competent to keep that vital area running smoothly. Only experience would show if my time as an instructor and as a Squadron Commander, plus an element of common sense, would qualify me to handle the job. One of the greatest responsibilities of 'Wings' in a carrier is to calculate the windspeed required over the deck, and its angle for safe take-off and landing. An error on my part could cause the death of an aircrew; this was a heavy responsibility.

We crossed to the Firth of Clyde to work up the ship and act as a Deck Landing Training Carrier. Aircraft would be landing and taking off continuously, so I would start right in the thick of it.

During the days spent working up, I exercised and tested everything testable and could find little fault with the hangar and flight deck organisation. Anything I changed was my own personal idea, and not a criticism of the current arrangement.

We were told that the first aircraft for deck landing training would be Seafires. Once again I was alarmed. The Seafire was simply a Spitfire with an arrestor hook. It had not been designed for carrier operation, and the undercarriage was too narrow and delicate. The long, in-line engine caused the pilot's cockpit to be well aft so that, in the landing attitude, he had a very restricted view forward.

Ten minutes before their arrival I broadcast 'flying stations', and all the right things happened. The DLCO was on his platform, the aircraft handlers were ready, the fire party in asbestos suits were beside the island and the barriers and arrestor wires were raised. Three Seafires appeared, so I asked for the ship to be turned into wind, gave the 'ready to receive aircraft' signal to the DLCO and stood in my flying control looking calm and collected with my crossed fingers hidden in the pockets of my reefer jacket. All three landed smoothly.

For the next two weeks we continued to be training carrier for 768 Squadron from Arbroath, accepting various different types of aircraft. We had only two barrier crashes, resulting in nothing worse than bent propellors and undercarriages. I was becoming much more confident and felt that I could handle the job, although we had yet to start operations.

All these exercises took place in the Firth of Clyde, an area where I felt that I could recognise every wave from the sailing days of my youth. Depending on the wind direction, we steamed from the Sound of Bute in the north to Ailsa Craig in the South, passing along the coast of Arran and getting superb views of her mountains, which resembled a knight in armour lying on his back, known as the Sleeping Warrior.

The next requirement was to embark our own squadron and work up with it before starting convoy duty in the North Atlantic. It was 811 Squadron, a long established FAA Unit with an honourable history. It was equipped with 'pregnant' Swordfish, thus named because of the ASV (radar) dome fixed where the torpedo rack would normally be. The fighters were Wildcat IV's, robust little US-built aircraft. The Squadron Commander was Lieut-Cdr. E.B. Morgan RANVR. He was an Australian, and from earlier connections with members of their forces. I felt a little apprehensive about discipline.

They all landed on without problems and we started a very concentrated period of exercises with them by day and night, including trying out some new ideas.

The first one was brilliant and worked most efficiently. It was designed to assist Swordfish to take off from escort carriers, at low wind speeds, when heavily loaded. It was called RATOG (Rocket Assisted Take Off Gear) and, with a little imagination, could be considered as making the good old Stringbag the first and only 'jet' biplane.

A rocket was attached to each side of the fuselage and, at a calculated point, the pilot fired these electrically; there was a roar followed by a flash of flame and sparks, and the aircraft visibly accelerated. On many occasions it saved me much worry.

We also had to practise, on a towed target astern of the ship, a new type of anti-submarine attack. Now that many convoys contained escort carriers, the U-Boats could expect to find themselves attacked by a Swordfish almost anywhere in the ocean. They had decided to augment their close-range AA armament and fight on the surface rather than to submerge and be depth-charged. Our reply to these tactics was to accompany an attacking Stringbag with two fighters. One Wildcat would attack from one side, raking their decks with his guns, followed by the second aircraft repeating the process from the other side, causing the U-Boat gunners to swing their weapons in opposite directions thus, hopefully, causing panic and confusion. At this point the Swordfish would attack with rocket projectiles designed to puncture the pressure hull, then explode inside. In practice attacks the system worked extremely well.

We were on our way to Tail o' the Bank to refuel and store, prior to covering a convoy to the US, when we received from the Admiralty a surprising signal for action by me, personally. It simply said: 'Where is 815 Squadron?' Considering the number of documents that I had signed in Egypt to report the disbanding of the unit, I could not believe it. The Captain suggested that it would be best to wait until we reached port, then go to the office of FOCT (Flag Officer Carrier Training) at Largs and 'phone the Admiralty. This I did and, after being pushed from one department to another, managed to trap the originator of the signal. I explained that 815 Squadron had not existed since July. He said, rather coldly, that he was aware of that so why was he receiving copies from various naval offices in Italy of demands for spare parts, stores, pay and allowances emanating from 815 Squadron? The bell rang! I had last heard of the Bombardment Flight being in Sicily; they had obviously followed the fleet up the Italian coast and Lieut. Spademan had continued to call his unit 815 Squadron, as it had no other name.

I explained this and he told me, as though it was my fault, that it was causing much confusion. I felt like suggesting that it would give him something to do between his Civil Service cups of tea, but simply wished him luck in his efforts and rang off.

As we prepared for our convoy duty, a change in everyone's feelings was clear to see. Merchant ship losses had dropped noticeably, due to increased numbers of escort vessels and air cover from escort carriers; the Russians were advancing on the Eastern Front; US forces were taking the offensive in the Pacific; the Allies held the whole of North Africa; we were driving the Germans, slowly, out of Italy. Now, in October, Italy had surrendered and had immediately declared war on Germany. We no longer felt like losers.

It was strange to know that the epoch of Calabria, Bomba, Taranto and Matapan was fading into a memory. Admiral Sir Andrew Cunningham had provided a superbly worded epitaph to that era with his signal to the Admiralty: 'Be pleased to inform their Lordships that the Italian Battle Fleet now lies under the guns of the fortress of Malta'.

After a few days at Tail o' the Bank we left to join a convoy which we were to cover as far as Newfoundland, where a US escort would take over.

There were about 40 merchant ships, but a much larger number of escorts than in the early days. There were corvettes and frigates as well as some of the over-age US destroyers. The latter looked like relics of the First World War, which in fact they were. They had four funnels, were very narrow and rolled like barrels in a flat sea.

We were allowed a wide lane in the centre of the convoy to give room to manoeuvre when operating aircraft. All day and night we flew A/S patrols of two Swordfish, while two Wildcats remained at immediate readiness. I found that my main difficulty was lack of sleep. I had to be available for roughly one hour in every two-and-a-half hours, only getting, if I was lucky, about one hour's sleep at a time. Despite doses of Benzedrine I felt that I could be in danger of making some howling blunder if required to make a quick decision when half asleep. Some arrangement for a relief system in Flying Control seemed necessary but there was no one competent to spare. I had to struggle on and hope for the best.

For the North Atlantic the weather was remarkably good. There was always some motion on the ship, but flying went very smoothly, and we were not attacked. After some twelve days we left the convoy and called into Argentia in Newfoundland to refuel and await the Merchant ships which we were to escort homewards.

Argentia was an excellent harbour and one of the ports that we had leased to the Americans in return for the destroyers. It was highly organised, with wonderful facilities for officers and men.

We decided to hold a ship's company dance and so invited the nurses from the hospital which the US had built. We immediately found another astonishing thing about the US Forces. The Matron visited us, looking rather embarrassed, and regretted that her nurses would not be able to attend as there would be 'enlisted men' there. What an extraordinary piece of snobbery, we felt, from a republic with no aristocracy!

We stayed in Newfoundland for nearly a week, then joined our homeward bound convoy, which was roughly the same size as the outward bound one.

The weather remained good and we crawled along, averaging

about 7kts. Everything went smoothly until we reached the midway point when, just after midnight, a U-Boat managed to sneak in. The first that we knew of its presence was a blinding flash: of all possible targets she had torpedoed an ammunition ship. The explosion could have been heard for many miles; a mass of flame and smoke shot 100 feet into the air and parts of the ship rained down into the sea, some landing on other ships in the convoy. The wreckage sank almost immediately. When an ammunition ship explodes like this there are no survivors.

No Asdic or radar contact could be obtained either by our aircraft or the escort vessels, although the latter dropped depth-charge patterns to deter any further attacks. However, the U-Boat must have been both lucky and determined, because she also managed to hit a tanker; fortunately the torpedo only damaged her slightly, so that she was able to continue, albeit with a noticeable list.

We suffered no more attacks and arrived safely in the Western Approaches.

During the following months we covered more convoys, using the same route, and lost few ships. With more escorts and continuous air cover from carriers we seemed to be turning the tide in the Battle of the Atlantic.

It was on our third trip across from Newfoundland that the North Atlantic showed what it could do. The Met. Officer reported that a violent storm was raging over the eastern side of the United States and its low pressure system was moving to pass to the south of us, putting us into storm-force winds between east to north-east.

Everything was reasonably quiet when I flew off two Swordfish for A/S patrol and landed-on their predecessors. Less than two hours later I began to be concerned; the swell was increasing and coming from almost dead ahead, so that the flight deck was pitching more than I liked. It was starting to rain, reducing visibility. I decided to cancel further flying and recall the A/S patrol. At that point one aircraft appeared with his navigation lights burning and signalling with a shaded Aldis lamp; his message read that the cloud base was down to less than 600 feet and the sea returns on the radar was making it impossible to differentiate between them and anything else. I replied that they were to circle the ship while we recalled the other aircraft, then switched on the flight deck lighting to help them.

We could not contact the other aircraft so, as no U-Boat or shadowing aircraft could be operating in that weather, I ordered a search-light to be aimed at the base of the clouds. This worked, and soon both of them were circling. My wind indicator was showing gusts over 45kts, so I asked for the ship's speed to be reduced to the lowest possible to retain steerage way. Each made two attempts before the DLCO was happy enough to give a 'Cut' signal. They both landed safely but it took the whole aircraft handling party to hold them down while the wings were folded and they were struck down.

I went through the hangar myself to be satisfied that all aircraft were firmly secured with double lashings and that no other equipment was loose. After a quick visit to my cabin to collect oilskins and more sweaters I dragged myself up ladders to the inside of the island, intending to check that the flight deck gear was properly tied down, because heavy transport like 'Jumbo' the mobile crane, fork lift trucks and tractors could do a great deal of damage; we could even lose them over the side. In the passageway I met the Flight Deck Officer and his Petty Officer who assured me that they had moved everything to the relatively sheltered area abaft the island and secured it with wire strops and bottle screws. They strongly advised me not to attempt to go on to the flight deck as it was no longer possible to keep one's feet, so I hauled myself up to the compass platform.

It was now well into the middle watch and as I reached the open bridge the full force of the storm struck us; the ship shuddered and seemed to gasp; it was a world of noise and blackness. The Captain was jammed in his chair on the port side of the platform, the Navigator on the other and the Officer of the Watch had his arms round the gyro repeater; I heard him calling urgently for more engine revolutions.

The wind was howling out of the east as though in personal hate. It screamed through the rigging and slammed against the island structure. Although protected by armoured glass screens and shields, a man's breath was pushed back down his throat if he attempted to speak. Hail and sleet were blasting down like icy needles. As the bows dipped, stinging salt spray hurled over us. The screw rose clear of the water to scream in protest as it over-revved. As our prow plunged into the troughs, tons of black water crashed on to the foredeck.

It seemed to me that the flight deck would be torn off the steel pillars supporting it. This had happened to an escort carrier in a North Russian convoy; she had been left with the forward end bent upwards like the gaping mouth of the world's biggest shark.

Having a wide lane to ourselves and reasonably powerful engines, we could maintain our position by care and hard work, and the skill of the helmsmen. Our powerful radar sets kept us in comparative safety from collisions but needed a very experienced operator to differentiate between ships and sea returns. It showed the convoy in chaos. The lighter ships and the many elderly ones could not hold station and some had even turned right around and given way to the screaming brute that had them in its clutches. Collisions seemed inevitable.

I could do nothing constructive and was simply getting in the way, so told the OOW that I would be in my sea cabin if required and clambered below in a series of wild lunges.

When the bulkhead clock read 0600 I thought that there should be some signs of dawn so struggled into my oilskins. The door opened to reveal my steward clad in foul-weather gear and dripping water in floods on to the deck. He was clutching a Thermos flask and a tin mug. 'Thought you might fancy a cuppa before you went on deck, Sir.' I looked at him and said: 'Good God, man, have you been on the upper deck?' Said he: 'Thought the officers on watch could do with a cuppa in this weather so took some up to the bridge.' Some of these Merchant Navy stewards were first-class lads. With great skill he poured me half a mug of dark fluid without spilling a drop. 'Nice bit of strongers, Sir,' he said. It was, indeed; he must have poured half a bottle of rum into the Thermos.

Feeling fortified, I made a gymnastic progress to the compass platform. The ship was still reeling, bucking and juddering; the wind speed indicator was swinging between 75kts and 90kts. The forbidding black overcast had delayed the dawn but now a sullen grey light was beginning to reveal a scene of chaos. The rain and sleet had eased to give visibility of, perhaps, a mile. I could only see eight ships of the convoy. The Commodore, in a 10,000 ton cargo liner with twin screws, was still in position: the heavily loaded tankers, lying low in the water, were suffering least: although water was continuously sweeping right over them, their gyrations were much less impressive and their powerful engines were holding them on course. A few of the more modern cargo ships were still in station; the remainder of our 40 ships could be anywhere.

Occasionally we caught a glimpse of the escorts. They would disappear almost completely under the waves then become virtually airborne as they climbed a huge, surging mass of sea until two-thirds of their hull reared into the air before crashing down to repeat it all again. Life on board must have been pure hell. I knew that, in much less violent weather than this, the crews of these frigates and corvettes spent days soaking wet with no dry clothes, no hot food, and water a foot deep sloshing through the mess decks. We enjoyed comparative luxury; apart from the discomfort of the ship's wild motion we were, below decks, warm and dry with hot food and drinks.

The storm raged all day until, in the early evening, the wind began to fall away and change direction through north to north-west bringing it on to our port quarter and driving much of the viciousness out of the sea and sting out of the air.

The Commodore signalled that he was increasing speed to 6kts and that 15 ships were missing. Two frigates were sent off to find them and I arranged to fly off a search of three Swordfish when conditions improved. Meantime I ordered two wildcats to be at readiness lest a shadower should appear.

Our Captain, who had been on the bridge for nearly 36 hours, was frozen and wet with red-rimmed eyes. The Commander, Navigator and I assured him that we were fully capable of handling the situation and practically dragged him down to his sea cabin.

During the night the sea lost much of its violence so, as a glimmer of dawn struggled through the breaking overcast, I ranged two Swordfish for A/S patrol, then three to search for stragglers, flying them off from a flight deck which, to my relief, was still flat. Finally, we rounded up eleven of the wayward ships but four had disappeared. These, in fact, did finally reach port safely, two of them towing the other two until met by tugs.

A few days later we broke away, to come to rest at Tail o' The Bank feeling somewhat tired and jaded. I wondered if the people at home appreciated what it cost in human endeavour to feed them.

We managed to have a few days leave over Christmas, but returned to the unpleasant news that we were to cover a convoy to Russia. We had learned from others about the ghastly weather, intense cold, continual attacks by U-Boats and aircraft, and hostile treatment at Murmansk. We were not enthusiastic, but the project was cancelled for a most embarrassing reason: one of our T124X engineers had decided that there was no way he was going on a North Russian convoy, and had sabotaged the engines! It took over a week for them to be returned to a fully serviceable condition, after which we were sent off with another Atlantic convoy which was only a rather dull repetition of the preceding ones. On our return we disembarked the squadron to Limavady in Ulster, as we had not been detailed for any immediate operation.

While we were in harbour we found that their Lordships had decided that Captain Boswell, with his experience in *Dasher* followed by an appointment to *Biter*, had suffered escort carriers long enough. He was replaced by Captain Bingley, known for some reason, as Baron Bingley, a wonderful captain with whom to work. He knew nothing of aircraft carriers, so just told us to get on with it while he learned. He had a tremendous sense of humour and preached the doctrine that, in any alarming event, one's first act must be to put the incident into perspective: to do this he considered it necessary to look for the funny side and laugh at it. He practised what he preached and the result was a very happy ship.

We were sent on another convoy to Argentia where we were

supplied with a most cunning device designed as a 'homing depth charge'. When dropped from an aircraft it sniffed around to find the nearest engine noise and 'homed' on to it at a speed of 15kts. We christened it Oscar. It was terribly hush-hush and no-one in the convoy was allowed to know anything about it. We gave strict instructions that it must not be dropped near a ship and the escorts were warned that, if a Swordfish used one, it would broadcast 'Oscar, Oscar' on hearing which they must steam away from the aircraft's position at a speed over 15kts.

On the second day of the homeward voyage we found that the boffins who had designed Oscar had failed to fit him with a device to make him 'safe'. Returning to the ship one of our Swordfish came to grief with complete engine failure, ditching near the convoy. As might have been expected, the weapon was torn off, sniffed around for a target and exploded on the hull of a tanker. Fortunately the damage was not disastrous, but the tanker had to return with an escort to Newfoundland. She had assumed that she had been torpedoed, and was surprised and upset that the naval vessels had not reacted more.

The following day Oscar struck again. There was a noticeable swell, and a Swordfish attempting to land-on managed to scrape over the round-down, tearing off the missile, which landed in the sea astern of us. The windspeed was such that I had asked for 8kts ship's speed, only half that of Oscar, who decided that our propellor noise was exactly what he wanted. The ship shook and a huge volume of water rose high over the stern. There were immediate cries for damage reports. The engine room assured us that everything seemed to be working as it should, the shaft was rotating smoothly and that we were not taking any water. We increased speed, steamed ahead of the convoy and carried out high speed trials, and the ship appeared to be handling satisfactorily.

In due course, we sailed up the Firth of Clyde and approached our allotted anchorage at Tail o' the Bank. At a suitable slow speed we crawled up through the anchored ships and were pointing towards the liner *Queen Elizabeth*, which appeared to cover most of the horizon. The captain said: 'Starboard 20'. Absolutely nothing happened! We continued straight towards the huge ship. He had no time to look for the funny side.

By going 'Full astern' and with the aid of our attendant tug which pushed our bows around, we found clear water and dropped anchor. A diver despatched over the stern reported that our rudder was only one third of its proper size! Oscar's disposal of the rest of it had not been noticeable at higher speeds.

It was decided that it would be safe for us to proceed round to

Rosyth for a new rudder, so the following day we returned down the Firth, rounded the Mull of Kintyre and turned north. The weather became absolutely appalling: the ship pitched and rolled and did everything short of capsizing. I ordered double lashings on all the aircraft in the hangar but the picketing points were being bent on the wings. We were forced to reduce speed and the Captain decided that we might not be able to round Cape Wrath, across the huge seas, without danger of losing control. He therefore signalled for an ocean-going tug to stand by us. This arrived and escorted us round the top of Scotland, then through the vicious Pentland Firth until we could turn south in the North Sea, protected by the land from the westerly storms. We arrived in the Firth of Forth and were met by four tugs that nudged us into a dry dock. I would not care to repeat such a voyage.

While we lay at Rosyth, Geoff Coy and I were bidden to report to HQ Western Approaches in Liverpool. There we met Admiral Max Horton, who had been doing a magnificent job handling the problems of North Atlantic shipping. He briefed us on his latest idea for putting an end to the U-Boat 'wolf packs'. Hunter-Killer Groups, consisting of an escort carrier and three frigates, were being formed to tour the mid ocean area, independent of convoys, to search for and destroy these groups of submarines. As soon as ships became available we were destined to be the carrier of one such group. We were keen about this idea and returned to Rosyth, only to find that we were to cover another convoy before starting our new rôle.

We were three days out when the fighter boys had the opportunity to show their mettle. A Heinkel 177 with a glider bomb appeared astern of the convoy. I despatched two Wildcats which we could see clearly as they climbed away, clawing for height to dive down on the German aircraft. We watched them hurtling down to attack, heard the rattle of their guns, then saw smoke issuing from the Heinkel.

White parachutes blossomed out below it, then it spun down to crash into the sea. The ships of the convoy sounded their sirens and the Wildcats returned to land-on amidst general acclaim. It was good to see some action at last.

On our return we found our frigates ready, and spent a week working-up, establishing a communication system and a method of combined A/S attack.

When we felt that we were ready we rushed off into the Atlantic, hoping to find a U-Boat prepared to fight on the surface, as we had all wanted a chance to try the attack that we had practised so assiduously. We did not find any such, but had four definite contacts, two of which we attacked and one of which we were sure was a kill, by the combined efforts of a Swordfish and the frigates.

After only two of these sorties we were sent on convoy duty once again, but this time with a more interesting object.

We were to provide A/S cover for a fast convoy of troop ships, ammunition ships and others carrying army hardware to the Mediterranean. A large escort had been provided, and another carrier with fighters. It was a much enjoyed change to sail southward into beautiful, warm, sunny weather. Before we turned east to Gibraltar we had changed into tropical rig and this gave Captain Bingley a chance to show another original idea. He wore, on the bridge, a wondrous pair of white braces covered with gaily coloured foxes' heads.

At the Straits of Gibraltar our part of the proceedings was over and we turned into harbour to lie alongside and refuel: I now had the opportunity to see Gibraltar, so made the most of it. So did the catering department. In particular, the wardroom bar did very well. Sherry cost only coppers per bottle and could be bought in bulk. The sight of city lights at night startled everyone after years of black-out. There was no point in turning off lights, since the Rock could be seen by anyone and the fully illuminated towns of Spain gave its position away.

The proximity of Spain had caused a silly situation right through the war. Enemy agents sat openly in their deck chairs with binoculars, noting the ships passing through the Straits. One simple attempt to confuse them was for ships arriving from the east with the crew wearing white cap covers to pass through at night, change hats, and arrive from the opposite direction in daylight, the idea being employed in reverse by ships arriving from the west. I have no idea whether this worked or not. Refreshed, we joined another convoy for an uneventful cruise back to the Tail o' the Bank.

The whole country seemed to have only one thing in mind – the Second Front. Up north we were well out of the way but we knew that the South of England was a massive armed camp. Any convoys that we covered seemed to carry mainly army equipment, with deck cargoes of tanks.

On June 6th the Allies invaded Europe. All spare time was spent listening to the radio.

Convoys were now including MAC Ships – Merchant Aircraft Carriers – usually tankers or grain ships with a flight deck built over their holds. These ships carried their normal cargoes but also a flight of A/S Swordfish. This wonderful old aircraft was still earning its keep.

Back at Tail o' the Bank, we received information that, whatever our next job was to be, we would not need 811 Squadron, so decided to fly it off to Ireland while at anchor. I calculated that this would be no problem using RATOG and decided that I would go myself.

I did my proper job of controlling the aircraft until only the one I had borrowed was left on deck with a squadron observer sitting in the rear cockpit. Running down the deck, I jumped in and prepared to take-off. Never having taken off from a deck with RATOG before, I was looking forward to the experience. We trundled down the flight deck until, abreast of the island, I fired the rockets and was most impressed by the instant acceleration.

The weather was typical of summer in the West of Scotland. Cloud base was less than 1,000 feet with some drizzle and poor visibility but the route could be covered entirely over the sea, provided we avoided Ailsa Craig and the Mull of Kintyre. It was not pleasant flying weather but we had no difficulty in finding Sydenham airfield near Belfast, which was our destination. When we landed I found that we were the only ones there. The Squadron Commander had decided that the weather was too bad and had diverted to Prestwick. For an operational squadron this performance did not impress me.

The following day I flew another Stringbag to Abbotsinch, carrying a spare pilot to take it back to Sydenham.

After scrounging transport to Greenock I rejoined the ship to find that the Captain was screaming for me. He had received a 'Most Immediate' signal from Admiralty that I was to join HMS *Empress* forthwith at Rosyth, in the same job, to arrive not later than 1400 the following day. This was totally unexpected.

I spent the night packing madly and saying 'goodbye' to the ship's officers and men of the Air Department.

She was a good ship and I was sorry to leave her.

Chapter 18

Last Lap

I knew that HMS *Empress* was one of the newer escort carriers which, although built on the same 'Liberty Ship' hull as *Biter*, was not a converted merchant ship but had been designed as an aircraft carrier. There my knowledge ended.

In the early morning of 29th August, 1944 I disembarked with my gear and climbed into the ship's jeep, which we kept ashore at Greenock. Accompanied by a driver to bring it back, I set out for Rosyth. In those days it was a long and involved journey but we reached our destination before the appointed time, to find a boat waiting for me.

Approaching the ship, I thought that she was larger and more solid looking than *Biter* but this must be an optical illusion, as she was built on the same hull. I climbed on board to be greeted by the First Lieutenant who, rather to my surprise, was Royal Navy. He told me that Special Sea Dutymen had already fallen in and that we were proceeeding to sea to steam around to Tail o' the Bank.

What genius at the Admiralty could have arranged for me to dash across Scotland to join the ship, which had no aircraft on board, only to lie within 100 yards of *Biter* some 48 hours later?

While everyone was getting the ship to sea, I thought it best to keep out of the way, so found my cabin, which was on the port side under the flight deck, in an alleyway opposite the SDO (Signal Distribution Office) and adjacent to the Captain's quarters. It was not so luxurious as the one on *Biter* but was well furnished and had its own shower and heads. My only complaint was that the sole source of natural light was from scuttles (port-holes) into the forward lift well, which was excellent when the lift was down but not when it was at flight deck level.

When we had cleared Rosyth I reported my arrival to all the right people and gained the feeling that the ship's atmosphere was much more 'genuine Navy' than its predecessor. She was commanded by Captain Henry Traill, RN known for some reason as 'Jane'. The Executive Officer was Commander Sam Davenport, also RN, as was the Navigator.

The Operations officer was Lieut-Cdr. (A) D. Brian Shaw RNVR. My first impression of him was that he had about a week to live, being thin and cadaverous, but I learned later that he always looked like this. He was a fellow countryman and a qualified Scottish solicitor. I was to find him one of the best 'Ops' with whom I ever served and we became great friends. The Flight Deck Officer caused me some surprise. He was an RNR Lieutenant named Gordon Wray-Sudlow whom I considered to be a strange choice. However, he proved to be a man of boundless energy who drove his flight deck party unmercifully while himself doing three times as much work as anyone. The engineers and supply branch were, again, T124X.

Comparing the ship with *Biter* I found the hangar to be much bigger, with better facilities and well equipped workshops. The flight deck layout was similar but with a lift forward of the barriers, which much improved aircraft handling. The island was larger, with much better protection from the weather and the Operations and Briefing rooms had some improvements. Radar and radio were more modern. There were even more AA guns. I felt that we could do great things with this ship. In September 1944 no squadron had yet been allocated to *Empress* but she had previously operated Avengers of 850 Squadron.

This was a considerable change from the Stringbag and I was determined to fly one as soon as possible, as I did not feel that I could appreciate a pilot's problems in an aircraft that I had not flown myself. The Captain fully supported me and I made arrangements with Abbotsinch to borrow one of their aircraft.

Accompanied by a pilot experienced on the type, I examined a Grumman TBF Avenger. It was very large for a single-engined aircraft and had a solid appearance. The fuselage was all metal and the wings folded hydraulically. It could carry bombs and torpedoes in a bomb bay closed by doors; there were none of the external brackets and wires that festooned the old Stringbag. Both cockpits were covered by perspex canopies and the air gunner had a proper turret with twin machine-guns. The undercarriage was fully retractable with sturdy and well spaced wheels. The engine was a Wright R-2600-8 with variable pitch propellor, which I was told gave her a top speed of about 250kts, but she was comfortable when dived at well over 300kts.

I climbed into the pilot's cockpit and found it very roomy but, as in all American aircraft, there were far more dials, switches, levers and wheels. My guide gave me a thorough briefing on everything and a copy of the Pilot's Notes. Having sat in the cockpit for some time, I could find everything necessary and could translate the US terminology on all the warning notices. The engine started without problems, giving a very satisfying impression of power. After a remarkably short run she rose into the air and climbed away, gaining height quickly.

I flew around the Clyde for an hour, trying various manoeuvres, then returned to the airfield. She touched down easily with a feeling of solidity and no tendency to bounce. This really was an aircraft for the FAA. I hated to have to admit that it was in a different league from misfits like the Barracuda.

We found that the first task for *Empress* was DLT for 768 Squadron pupils from Ayr. The squadron provided a mixed gaggle of aircraft for these courses; sometimes they sent Hellcats, on other days Avengers, then Fireflies. We even had odd days working Seafires and Sea Huricanes and, once, some Swordfish and a Fulmar.

We suffered the usual number of hair-raising landings and the occasional barrier crash. On one of these a young man in a Firefly made three hopeless attempts to land and was waved off each time by the DLCO. I told the squadron commander that, if he failed to make a better approach on his next attempt, I would send him ashore before he killed himself. His next attempt was equally hopeless and, once again, he was given furious signals to abort. He totally ignored them and also my red Very light which was the final signal not to land and, without even touching the deck, hurtled along until his undercarriage caught the barrier and his aircraft or what was left of it, slid along towards the bows, fortunately stopping before it reached them. I suggested that his future would be more assured in a second-line unit. On the whole, however, the pupils did very well and reflected credit on their instructors.

Our next duty was DLT for 772 Squadron, who were equipped with Fireflies. They gave a very satisfactory performance and seemed ready for their operational role on HMS *Ruler* in the British Pacific Fleet. While they were with us I asked the Squadron Commander, Lieut-Cdr. (A) A.H.D. Gough RN, if he would do some interception exercises for the benefit of our Fighter Direction Team, which was screaming for a chance to practise. The FIDO (Fighter Direction Officer) was Lieut. Donald Eccles RNVR who was most efficient and a very amusing character. He was the brother of Sir David Eccles, the Minister of Health; he had been an actor in peace-time.

His method of complaining to me that his team needed practice was to arrive in Flying Control and fall on his knees before me, with a beseeching look and hands held up in prayer. The ship's company thought him completely mad.

After a few more sessions of DLT we were sent down to Devonport where we arrived just before Christmas and gave leave to both watches. I was on board over the holiday period, as it was the practice to give the Scottish members of the crew their leave at New Year. Actually, we had some good fun with dinners and parties in the ship and visits fron ENSA, who gave shows on a stage we built in the hangar. Captain Traill and Commander Davenport both had their families nearby so I was left in command of the ship. This caused a silly situation which I feel sure that the Captain had not appreciated. As an Air Branch officer I had not had the opportunity to obtain the necessary qualifications such as a Watchkeeping Certificate, although I had kept watches at sea and, in *Biter*, Captain Bingley had often let me 'play' with his ship. However, nothing ghastly happened that I was unable to handle.

On return from leave I found that we were packing the hangar and flight deck with F6F Hellcat fighters to be transported to India after which we were to join the East Indies Fleet based in Trincomali in Ceylon.

This was no surprise, as the war in Europe was grinding onwards towards an Allied victory. Our troops were over the German border, the Russians were sweeping all before them on the Eastern Front, the Balkans were in our hands and Paris had surrendered. General de Gaulle who had been something of a thorn in Churchill's side, had returned to France and been greeted as a hero. There had been some hiccups, like the disastrous action at Arnhem and the V-2 bombs which had rained on London but lights were now being switched on all over the country.

We were on our way to another war, although the US Forces had achieved a number of victories there, had bombed Tokyo and regained the Philippines. Some time soon there must be overall victory and the mopping-up would start.

We sailed south with an escort: we were virtually a cargo ship with no way of protecting ourselves. Refuelling at Gibraltar we were left on our own to make our way to the Suez Canel. It was extraordinary to be steaming, like a cruise liner, through the Mediterranean where previously I had either been dodging bombs and torpedoes or dropping them myself.

It being winter time, we were still wearing blue uniform but as we ran into the Red Sea, I had to unearth my tropical gear. The heat caused a problem with the lack of scuttles in my cabin so I arranged for our workshops crew to cut a large 'window' for me into the lift well.

Clearing the Red Sea we turned east and, after a few days, entered Cochin in Western India. This little town is believed to have been the first European settlement in India. It had been occupied by the Dutch for a time and some of the buildings showed this influence.

We passed through the excellent harbour to lie alongside a wharf near the airfield which was the collecting and delivery base for aircraft of the East Indies Fleet. We disembarked our cargo of Hellcats, working overnight in a blaze of floodlights. Gordon Sudlow was in charge of the operation, which he carried out with his usual drive and energy. We left the following morning to sail round to Ceylon and join the fleet at Trincomali.

I had known this place well in the days of *Eagle* and the vast harbour had changed little, apart from being packed with ships. I could see two huge battleships, one of which was the French *Richelieu* which was a magnificent-looking ship but marred by strings of washing in her rigging. A cruiser squadron occupied part of the harbour and there were many destroyers, frigate and smaller ships. Depot ships and oilers with other supply vessels were scattered here and there.

To most of us, however, the most staggering sight was the number of escort carriers. I could recognise HMS *Khedive*, HMS *Ameer*, HMS *Shah*, HMS *Emperor* and HMS *Smiter*: there were others, we were told, presently at sea.

We learned that there had been fleet carriers, capital ships and other cruisers which had left to join the Pacific Fleet now consisting of nearly 300 British ships. The maritime situation in European and Atlantic waters had changed to such a degree that ships were being released almost daily for service in the Eastern Theatre. Shortly we would also grow to 300 ships so that the British Pacific Fleet and the East Indies Fleet would, together, amount to 600 units and be the largest accumulation of British Naval vessels ever to have assembled in one part of the world.

In the carriers were many people I knew. I was soon visiting them to find what was happening and what operations we would be doing. When we had left the UK all talk and news had been about the invasion of the continent and the progress of our armies and of the Russians. There had seldom appeared in the press more than a few short paragraphs about the advance of US forces in the Pacific. Seldom was the considerable British fleet mentioned.

We were told some disquieting stories of life in the Pacific. Some US admirals had turned out to be anti-British and to regard our fleet as muscling in to their private war. They were being as uncooperative as possible and giving us the most unpleasant jobs. Some had been extremely critical of our fleet carriers, which they considered unable to carry sufficient aircraft because of their armoured flight decks which the US carriers, of course, did not have. They had, therefore, been upset to find that their ships, when hit by Kamikaze bombers, had been put out of action and, in one case, sunk. Our armoured ships when hit had been able to operate aircraft in less than an hour after the event.

Keeping the ships supplied had proved a major headache. In the past, virtually anywhere in the world, the British Navy had a port within easy reach where they could oil and store ship, but this was not so in the Pacific at that time. The US Navy, on the other hand, had enjoyed many years' experience of operating in the vast area of the Pacific Ocean and had built up a magnificently organised Fleet Train which could replenish their ships with everything down to luxuries. The US Admiral had catagorically refused to allow its use to our fleet. We had produced our customary compromise: a polyglot collection of oilers, depot ships, escort carriers and merchant ships, which hardly achieved the same standards as the US Fleet Train, particularly regarding luxuries, but nevertheless did a marvellous job.

We found the Japanese in a state of some confusion as Lord Louis Mountbatten, Allied C-in-C, was sweeping down through Burma and the Japs were evacuating troops from that area and from the islands, to put them in Malaya and Singapore. They had sent most of their heavier surface craft to the Pacific and their convoys of troops and supplies were hugging the coast with relatively light escorts. Our destroyers were attacking these convoys and bombarding harbours.

Our job in the carriers was fighter and A/S cover for the Fleet, searches, straffing airfields, railways and lines of communication, as well as a great deal of photographic reconnaissance. We worked principally in the Nicobar and Andaman Islands, the Burma and Malay coast and Sumatra.

To date, our aircraft had not been bothered by enemy fighters, but had met intense AA fire. When at sea the fleet had been attacked from the air quite often and these attacks had included suicide bombers which, so far, had not done any damage. It was difficult for a Westerner to understand the mentality of a people who could feel honoured to be a Kamikaze (Divine Wind) pilot. We understood that they received the minimum of flying training necessary to aim their aircraft then, complete with Samurai sword, would take off to fly straight into the side of a ship, destroying themselves in the process. They were always led by a twin-engined aircraft which had to return safely to be able to tell the Emperor that they had done their duty. I could not imagine anything more inconvenient than trying to fly a small aircraft while armed with a whacking great sword.

We only remained in harbour for a few days but in that time I arranged to fly a Hellcat. I thought that it was ideal for carrier operation. It gave the same feeling of solidity that I had found in most US naval aircraft and was pleasantly manoeuvrable, though less so than the Spitfire or Hurricane. The engine was a 2000HP Pratt

& Whitney R-2800-8 Wasp, which gave it a speed of 330kts, greater than that of any current Japanese fighter. Armed with 6 × ·5 calibre guns and able to carry rockets or bombs, it was a formidable straffing machine, but I did not think that it would be agile enough for me in a dog-fight. One great thing in its favour was that, like the Avenger, it could be thumped down on its main wheels with very little tendency to bounce back into the air.

For this first jaunt we embarked 845 Squadron of Avengers and Hellcats, the former to carry out A/S Patrols and searches and the Hellcats, CAP's. Each carrier had a particular duty – fighter cover, photo recce, straffing etc.

This was my first time at sea with an operational fleet since the days of *Eagle*, and I found things greatly changed. There were now at least three times as many ships in the screen as we had had in 1940. We were surrounded by a curtain of destroyers and frigates: inside them were cruisers and, in the centre, eight escort carriers, one or two of which were always operating aircraft. With relatively light winds and heavier aircraft, most take-offs were made by catapult and I was relieved to find that we were doing this at least as fast as the other ships, so weren't looking like the new boy. We only spent about a week at sea before returning to Trinco. For our first foray in this theatre it had been very quiet.

While we dashed around in large fleets, flotillas of destroyers often had very exciting cruises amongst the islands and close in to the coast, where they attacked convoys and bombarded harbours. This type of mission could be highly dangerous, as the Japanese had confused both themselves and us and we seldom knew which islands or harbours they had already evacuated. Sometimes, while clearing everything of importance, they would leave manned batteries of quite heavy calibre guns, which would suddenly open up when the destroyers came within range. At other times our ships bombarded bases enthusiastically, only to find that there was nothing of importance there. One such action occurred on 21st February, when the destroyers *Rotherham, Roebuck, Rapid* and *Rocket* bombarded Great Coko Island. Having expended 991 rounds of HE and 18 Star-shell only to find that everything of use had been removed, they had made a further sweep and bombarded Port Blair dockyard, sinking 3 coasters and destroying or damaging 5 sailing vessels and blowing up an ammunition store.

We were soon off to sea again, this time in a very exalted position, because Admiral 'Hooky' Walker had decided that this operation was to be based on carrier work and that he should therefore fly his flag in one. For some reason he had chosen *Empress* to be his flagship, which raised the problem of accommodation for all his staff, but we managed somehow. The Admiral was a remarkable character. Having lost a hand in the attack on Zebrugge in the earlier war, he had replaced it with a hook with which he was incredibly agile. If he required a messenger he would simply hook any passing seaman. We were told that he had two hooks, a stainless steel one for daytime and a silver-plated one for the evening, designed to be a perfect fit for a gin glass.

The object of this operation, which had been named 'Stacey', was mainly very detailed reconnaissance. The Allied armies, under Mountbatten, were sweeping down through Burma. He was shouting for detailed photographs of the Japanese positions and bases and also wanted damage and confusion in their troop ships and supply lines. B29s of the US Air Force had tried to be helpful but, as they normally flew at 30,000ft their photographs didn't give him enough detail. Our Hellcats of 896 Squadron were very experienced in this work and could take photos at low heights while other Hellcats straffed the area to negate the AA fire.

Just before leaving on these operations two very studious-looking gentlemen, dressed as Lieuts. (Special Branch) RNVR, would sneak over the side and disappear into the bowels of the ship. They were known as 'The Cloak and Dagger Boys'. They spoke fluent Japanese and could decipher their codes as well as analysing photographs.

We embarked 888 Hellcat Squadron, a very experienced and well organised unit. I detested the system of taking bits and pieces of different squadrons every time we went to sea. These could be 804, 888 or 896 Hellcat Squadrons, or 845 Avenger Squadron. These were never with us long enough for me to know the individual aircrew, their reliability or their standard of flying skill. Most flying units have pilots who do exactly what they have been briefed to do, return to the ship at the specified time and land in a calm and copybook manner. Others arrive at any time, from any direction then hurl themselves at the deck as though determined to make their arrival the end of everything rather than just the end of a flight.

When we first met 896 Squadron it was commanded by Lieut-Cdr. R.M. Norris but, by July, Lieut- Cdr. Zegers de Bejl of the Royal Netherlands Navy took over. He ran it well and was popular with everyone. His English was excellent but could be quite amusing. One day I asked him if he intended to remain in the Dutch Navy after the War. His reply was: 'Ach, No. In ze Nederland Navy, before you are promote, you haf been dead for twenty years and nobody told you.'

On this occasion we took six escort carriers, five cruisers and the usual screen of destroyers and frigates and steamed straight across to the Andaman Islands, then through them to a position which I felt to be so close to the enemy-occupied mainland that we were inviting attention from their Air Force. We spent 24th and 25th February cruising around there and two or three times small groups of Japanese aircraft were picked up on the radar screens; however their attacks were not pressed home and a number were shot down by our Hellcats; the few that reached the fleet were met by such an intense barrage that they broke away without doing any damage.

We spent two days of extremely intensive flying, in which we made photo recce of the Kra Isthmus, all the adjacent islands and Penang. By 4th March we had moved to a position off Simalur Island where we made similar missions over Sumatra and Sabang. When we had achieved all that was required of us we returned, still unscathed, to Trinco.

Having so many carriers it was no problem to give them, one at a time, a highly welcome holiday. When we reached harbour we were delighted to hear that we were to go to Colombo for a week to give the crew a break from the ghastly discomfort that we suffered on board.

The cause of this was that these ships had not been 'tropicalised'. There was no air conditioning, and far too few compartments with any access to the open air. The ADR (Aircraft Direction Room), which was frequently packed with men, was completely enclosed with an atmosphere of hot air circulated by the ship's fans. The engine room was an inferno. The cabins of the Captain, Commander (Ops) and myself were immediately under the flight deck so that, with the sun scorching down upon it, they became ovens. Conditions were particularly bad in harbour when there was no movement of the ship. At sea, operations permitting, I always kept the lifts slightly down to allow some air, even though it was hot and sticky, to flow through. At night I kept the lifts fully down and most of the crew slept on them or on the hangar deck. During the day uniform regulations went by the board and everyone worked in the lightest and smallest pair of shorts that they could find, despite which we all suffered from the dreaded 'prickly heat'.

When we returned to Trincomali we found that some of the destroyers had been engaged in a nasty brush with the enemy. *Saumarez, Volage* and *Rapid* had been in the Stewart Sound, between the North and Middle Andamans, some distance apart, searching for targets. On 19th March there was a cry for help on the radio from *Rapid. Saumarez* dashed to her aid to find her stopped and badly damaged by gunfire from shore batteries. Her guns were out of action and the bodies of the gun-crews were lying round the deck with dismembered parts horrifyingly entangled in the rails. The shore batteries were still firing but *Saumarez* laid alongside *Rapid* and took her in tow. *Volage* came rushing in to help but was immediately hit by a shell which penetrated the engine room so that she, also, stopped. They were well within range of the enemy guns. Fortunately, *Volage* soon got her main engines going again and, shortly after, *Rapid* managed to steam on one shaft, so all three escaped.

On 25th March four destroyers, including the repaired *Volage*, met a convoy of two merchant ships escorted by two minesweepers. They set upon these with more enthusiasm than necessary because, although they sank them all, with the help of two RAF Liberators, they expended 18 torpedoes, and 3,160 rounds of 4.7 HE plus Bofors. The Admiral regarded this as a gross waste of ammunition.

A few days after our return from Colombo we were off to sea again, this time with a very powerful force including the battleship *Queen Elizabeth* (Flag of Vice Admiral Walker), *Richelieu* and the usual assembly of escort carriers and destroyers. We split into separate groups and our aircraft continued their reconnaissance missions as well as making strikes on Japanese airfields, bases and railways, while the battleships and destroyers bombarded harbours and shipping. Our sister carrier *Khedive* had a very unpleasant time. When 808 Squadron was embarking, one of the Hellcats flew into the ship's stern, killing the pilot. Two days later another of her Hellcats missed all the arrester wires, bounced over the barriers and crashed into the aircraft park forward, carrying an aircraft over the side and killing the pilot and several others.

On 11th April a large formation of Oscars and Dinahs was reported by radar and the Hellcats went in to attack, shooting down a number of them. While doing so, 808 Squadron lost another aircraft; they seemed to be dogged by misfortune. Despite losing some of their force from fighters and being greeted with our formidable AA barrage, the enemy pressed home their attack. It was very uncoordinated and we gained the impression that the Japanese were scraping the bottom of the barrel for aircrew.

The attack included some Kamikaze which I always found to be the most unnerving experience, but the attitude of the men on deck quite astonished me. Many of them seemed to treat it as a game, jumping up and down in excitement and screaming encouragement to the guns crews like fans at a football match: they had to be ordered to take cover – not that there was much cover to be found in an unarmoured escort carrier. I had no gun to fire and nothing to do but stand like an idiot in the open Flying Control position behind the bridge watching a guided bomb being steered straight at me. Two Kamikaze seemed to have chosen to target our ship. One approached the stern, but we had the wheel hard over to starboard and, like all Kamikazes, it was very badly handled and flew into the sea well clear of us. The other was much more dangerous; it seemed to bear a charmed life; the air around it was filled by the tremendous barrage put up by our port Bofors turrets. It came straight at us, closer and closer and closer; there seemed no chance of it missing us; it was less than 100 yards away when the two port forward turrets were at last successful and it blew up in the air with a tremendous blaze of flame and collapsed into the sea in a cloud of debris. We all gasped with relief and there was a roar of cheering but the incident almost caused civil war between the crews of the two turrets, who both claimed to have shot it down.

On the following day, the 14th April, one of our aircraft failed to return. Our Hellcats had been detailed to straff railways and stations but one of ours had ditched. The pilot, Sub-Lieut. Tomlinson, had been an unusual officer to find in an FAA squadron: he was a US Citizen who had joined the RNVR before the US had entered the war then trained as a pilot. His last radio message had been: 'Ditching; goddam these Yankee engines'. We could only assume that he had suffered complete engine failure. He had been a cheerful and popular lad and he was sadly missed. He might have been picked up by the Japanese but, regrettably, this would not have helped him. They beheaded all aircrew that they captured.

We were returning to harbour when the Flight Deck Engineer Officer came to me to tell me that the main cable that operated the hydraulic catapult was on its last legs because of the continuous use that I had made of it in the almost invariably light winds. He said that I could disembark the aircraft when near Trinco but it could not be used again until we could fit a new cable. I had complete faith in his opinion as he was a first-class Flight Deck Engineer who maintained the arrester wires, barriers and catapult with painstaking efficiency. He was a Sub-Lieut. (E) and, like all the engineers, was under the T124X Agreement. People we carried under that agreement varied tremendously from the brilliant to the utterly useless.

On our way in we received a signal from the Admiralty to say that Captain 'Jane' Traill, who had been in command of *Empress* since she commissioned in America, was to return to the UK and his relief was on his way. We dined him in the wardroom and then, the next day, rowed him ashore in the best naval tradition. A soon as we had reached harbour the FDEO rushed ashore to the dockyard stores for a new catapult cable, only to find that there wasn't any. I was horrified, and a signal was made immediately to Admiralty who promised to have some flown out at once. It was incredible to find that, with sixteen carriers, all with the same equipment, in the fleet, no one had ordered enough spares.

Empress had been lying in harbour, a useless hulk, for some two weeks. I took the ship's jeep to the airfield to meet our new captain, who was arriving by the Communications Squadron from Colombo. He was Captain JRS Brown and had not had any previous experience in carriers but was keen and enthusiastic and very disappointed to find that we were out of action. I assured him that, as soon as the cable arrived, we would be fully operational again in a few hours. I briefed him on the type of operation that we had been doing and the general situation in the Fleet. He was determined to get to sea as he felt, as did we all, that we were approaching the final stages of the war.

When we reached the harbour, one of the ship's motor boats was waiting for us. The best that we had was a small, open boat which the Americans, to our great amusement, called a 'gasoline gig'. Captain Brown's next shock was when he saw the ship. Most captains have some eccentricity and Captain Traill's had been the belief that paint caused a fire hazard. As a result the ship looked distinctly scruffy. This had caused us all some embarassment and had prompted fights ashore between our crew and those of other ships. Our new captain had no such inhibitions and, at once, the crew were hanging all over the outside of the ship slapping on paint.

At last our cable arrived and we were fully serviceable again and it was not long before we were off on another mission of reconnaissance and straffing.

While we had been in Trinco we had received continuous reports of the progess of the war in Europe. Our army had swept through Belgium and Holland into Germany; futher south the US Forces had been equally successful; the Russians were through Poland and at the gates of Berlin. Obviously the end was near. It had also been announced that Mussolini, who had been keeping well out of sight since the collapse of Fascist Italy, had been caught and executed by partisans.

On 2nd May we received news that Hitler had committed suicide and Germany had surrendered. We reached Trincomali on 8th May, which we had been told was to be VE Day. The expected signal arrived from the King: 'Splice the main brace.' There was, of course, much celebration and the bar stocks were given a hammering. Like many others on board I had been fighting the Germans and, for a time, the Italians, for nearly six years, and today we should have been overjoyed. Of course, we were all happy that we need no longer worry about our families being bombed and the fate of brothers, sisters and relatives in the services in Europe but it all seemed to belong to another world and another war. Our own war was not over and there might be many thousands killed or mutilated before we could really celebrate.

A great difference between our war and that nearer home was that we were unable to understand the mentality of our enemy. Here we had a people who had sufficient technology to design and build high-performance aircraft, aircraft-carriers and battleships but who had a total disregard for human life, including their own. They perpetrated acts of the most barbaric horror. Only recently, when short of food in the Andamans, they had transported 300 Civilian 'useless mouths' to an uninhabited island, without food, and just left them to die. Only eleven survived. We often felt that the dyed-in-the-wool Nazi showed a loyalty to Hitler that was excessive to the point of imbecility, but the Japanese took it far further. One example was the Kamikaze but there were many others. When our ships attempted to pick up Japanese survivors in the water, they would swim away to avoid being rescued. On one occasion a destroyer with a scrambling net over the side had steamed to the debris of a sunken ship, to find a Japanese clinging to the net with one hand while, with the other, banging a shell against the ship's side in an attempt to make it explode.

The never-ending list of atrocities engendered strong anti-Japanese feeling amongst everyone in our ships. This resulted, particularly in the destroyers, in their shelling and sinking small sailing craft and fishing boats which were, no doubt, being used by the Japanese but were owned and crewed by the natives. Admiral Walker condemned these actions, which he described as pure butchery.

In the afternoon of 9th May, the day after VE Day, many of the ships' companies of the fleet were ashore and trying hard to start a war of their own. Huts were set on fire, and a battle was raging between destroyer crews and ratings from the *Richelieu*. Suddenly, all serviceable vessels in the East Indies Fleet were ordered to prepare for sea, and naval patrols rushed around shepherding everyone back to the ships' boats which were running a non-stop ferry service. *Empress* and most of the other carriers, all of whom had a large proportion of T124X in their crews, hoisted Blue Peter in the hope that men of the Merchant Navy would more easily appreciate the urgency of returning on board.

The cause of the panic was an Intelligence report that the Japanese cruisers *Ashigara* and *Haguro*, with the destroyer *Kamikaze*, were evacuating troops from the Nicobar and Andaman Islands to take them to Singapore. A signal from the submarine *Subtle* (Lieut. B.J.B. Andrews) had reported a cruiser and destroyer to the north of the Malacca Strait. She had attempted to attack but had been forced to break off, as the target was out of range. It was fortunate that she had not fired torpedoes as, on attempting to dive more deeply, she had struck the bottom at 33 feet, contrary to the depth shown on the chart. She had been depth-charged for three hours but had finally escaped with only internal damage. Another submarine, *Statesman*, had also tried to attack but been foiled by the high speed and zig-zagging of the target. RAF Liberators also reported that they had found Japanese ships in the Andaman Sea which they had attacked, claiming to have sunk the escorts.

The fleet steamed rapidly towards Sumatra, the intention being to split into groups, each with sufficient power to dispose of the cruiser, and make air and surface sweeps to find her. Unfortunately, we were not destined to take part in this operation.

On the morning of 14th May I had the Avengers of 845 Squadron on deck ready to launch and was about to give the order to start up when there occurred that sudden deathly silence which, in a ship at sea is louder than the banging of a drum. Normally one absorbs without conscious thought the rumble of machinery, the faint vibration, the hum of circulating fans, the clicking of gyro repeaters on the bridge: when all those stop without warning the effect is stunning. We became a dead object, wallowing uselessly. The Chief Engineer came tearing up to the bridge, breathless and pouring perspiration. We were suffering 'condenseritis'. We would need dockyard assistance before the main engines could be used again. He said that he could provide auxiliary power to give electricity and essentials but nothing more. We were left with the embarrassment of an ignominious tow back to Trincomali. The cruiser *Black Prince* was detailed to be our tug and she picked up the lines in a most seamanlike manner, treating the matter as an evolution. She had her seamen doubling round her decks taking in the slack in the style of an old sailing ship and all carried out in time to music supplied by their ship's band, which played rousing marches. To the fury of our crew they chose to render 'Wings over the Navy'.

Empress having ceased to be any use as an aircraft carrier, I had little to do except catch up with my paper work. I made a point however, of being on the bridge for a time in the evening. Each day, before sunset, when the flight deck was not in use, pallid troglodytes whose duties normally kept them out of the light of day, would appear from the bowels of the ship to see one of the few sights which compensated in some way for the meteorological horrors of the East Indies. On an evening clear of lowering monsoon clouds, when the sky was the brooding tropical blue with a few tiny clouds on the western horizon, the great orange orb of the sun would slowly subside towards the sea. As it lowered it would seem to accelerate and fall quickly into a blaze of golden light then, as its upper rim slid below the ocean horizon, a flash of green would streak across the gold to leave a prismatic glimpse of the spectrum's final colour.

The following day we arrived quietly and, we hoped, reasonably unobtrusively, in Trinco and secured to a buoy. It would be some days before the main engines could be returned to their normal inferno of sliding valves and clattering connecting rods so I catapulted the Avengers whilst tied to the buoy to let them operate from the airfield.

We were all disappointed at missing what looked like the most exciting operation since we had joined the fleet. It should end in a surface action against heavy enemy units. We were, therefore, avid for news of developments. Gradually information filtered through and, in the end we were able to build up a fairly clear picture.

On 14th May our cruisers and destroyers and aircraft from the carriers had been making sweeps to the north of the Malacca Straits, when one of the Avengers found the enemy ships. The aircrew had been briefed that the first one to find them was to make an enemy report, then keep out of range and shadow. However, the young Sub Lieut. flying the aircraft thought that he knew better than the Admiral so, having made an enemy report, then given a wrong position, he ignored his instructions and attacked. He missed his target and was shot down by AA fire. Later it was found that he had drifted ashore on the Burma coast and been captured.

The 26th Destroyer Flotilla, led by Captain Power in *Saumarez*, had heard the position given by the *Avenger* and was steaming towards it at 27kts. At 1041, he was horrified to receive a signal from the C-in-C to break off. This, he felt, must have been made without the knowledge that the enemy had been found. He therefore decided to emulate Nelson's blind eye act and to steam at high speed to the east-north-east while making a somewhat delayed signal asking for confirmation. He considered that the Naval Fighting Intructions which cautioned against breaking off contact with the enemy prematurely, could be interpreted as giving him freedom to disregard an order believed to have been given in ignorance.

At 1150 an Avenger of 851 Squadron, flown by the CO Lieut-Cdr. M.T. Fuller RNVR, signalled that he had found a cruiser and a destroyer steaming 140° at 10kts and gave the correct position. *Haguro* and *Kamikaze* had been found just in time; they were only one day's distance from Singapore.

The destroyers were keen to get in to the attack but Captain Power was apprehensive about meeting the Japanese ships in daylight, as *Haguro* was over 13,000 tons, with a speed of 33kts and armed with 10 × 8″ guns, 8 × 5″ and 8 torpedo tubes. She could easily keep out of range while picking off his ships one by one. The situation would be very different in darkness.

The Avengers had attacked but only achieved near misses;

however, these had been sufficient to cause *Haguro* to alter course, which was to the advantage of the destroyers. The Captain's main concern now was that he might miss her, as there was far more water than he could cover.

At 0100 on the following morning *Venus* reported a radar contact at 68,000 yards. This was greeted with the utmost scepticism, as that was far beyond the range of a destroyer's radar. The operator was insistent and he was proved to be correct, as the other ships soon picked up the same contact. This unusual performance of the equipment was later attributed to a phenomenon called 'anomalous propagation'. They soon closed with the Japanese, and utter confusion reigned. *Haguro* was zig-zagging at high speed; there were ships in all directions. *Venus* was first to fire torpedoes but missed. *Saumarez* was hit by a shell in her boiler room and almost the whole engine-room watch was killed. *Venus* fired again and achieved one hit. *Virago* managed to hit with two torpedoes. This brought the cruiser to a halt, in a sinking condition. *Venus* was detailed to finish her off. It was fortuitous that none of the destroyers had been hit by torpedoes from each other as these had been running in all directions. The Engineer Officer of *Venus* had heard two passing close to the side of the ship. *Kamikaze* had sustained only minor damage and, after our ships withdrew, returned to pick up survivors.

This was to be the last major gun and torpedo action in the war.

The following morning the flotilla was attacked by Oscars, one of which gained a near miss on *Virago*, killing four and badly injuring eight.

While we had been languishing in harbour and missing the operation we had been visited by Lord Louis Mountbatten. He impressed everyone, speaking to all the officers and many of the men. He told us how valuable had been our photo reconnaissance and said that he could never get enough of it but now he wanted us to concentrate on causing the maximum possible confusion to the Japanese by destroying their railways and communications and sinking their convoys of troops, which they were trying to evacuate from Burma, the Andamans and Nicobars to reinforce Singapore and Malaya. He had that most valuable gift of any leader; he could climb on to a box, gather the troops around him, tell them nothing that they did not already know but leave them waving flags and ready to take on the enemy single-handed. A visit from him could be guaranteed to raise morale to a peak.

Meanwhile, on *Empress*, I received some staggering information from the Flight Deck Engineer: he had been visiting the dockyard stores for some items that he needed and had noticed a huge drum of cable which seemed familiar. On asking what it was he had been told that they had no idea; it had arrived many months before with no markings that they could find in their lists. It was hydraulic catapult cable! I wondered how we were managing to win this war.

With no longer any enemies to deter aircraft and ships between the UK and ourselves, we were now receiving mail and newspapers with regularity, full of stories of lights coming on again all over the country, church bells ringing, arrangements for demobilisation and the gift of free suits to everyone leaving the Services. There was some news about US successes in the Pacific but virtually no mention of the tremendous work being done and casualties being suffered by our British Pacific Fleet, and seldom a murmur about our not having been entirely idle in the East Indies. It seemed that the press was determined that we should earn our title of 'The Forgotten Fleet.'

We only had one operational sortie during the month of June as only sections of the fleet now needed to be at sea at any one time. Those sections sometimes included a battleship but always cruisers and destroyers and three to four carriers to provide A/S and fighter cover and for straffing convoys, ports and railways. The destroyers and submarines were at work continuously, sinking large numbers of troop and supply ships, landing-craft and oilers. Seldom were our ships attacked by any appreciable number of aircraft. It looked as though the Japanese were hard pressed for pilots and equipment. On this occasion we embarked 896 Squadron commanded by Lieut-Cdr. R.M. Norris.

A new duty had fallen upon my shoulders. Captain Brown was determined that the ship's company should always know what we were doing, and the reason for our aircraft disappearing into the blue, then returning with no bombs or ammunition remaining. When time allowed, he would clear lower deck and, with the aid of a blackboard, put everyone in the picture. This was a great morale-booster, because hundreds of men worked very hard in the engine room and other regions below deck with no clear idea of the reason for their efforts. Between bouts of operating aircraft I often enjoyed a little spare time: I also had, in the Flying Control, my own Tannoy (broadcasting system) by which I could make announcements to all parts of the ship. In addition I could plug into the radio from our aircraft, so was always up to date with where they were and what they were doing. As a result the Captain lumbered me with giving running commentaries of what was happening. I found that the crew had nick-named me 'Alvar Liddell'. He was one of the BBC news readers and, I suppose, I could take the choice of his name as something of a compliment, as he had distinguished himself one night when Broadcasting House had been hit by a bomb. The ceiling of the studio had collapsed onto his head but he had continued to read the news, without pause, in his usual unruffled manner.

We were off again during July with *Ameer* and *Emperor* and, from the 5th to 9th, the Hellcats from the carriers joined the surface ships in bombarding the Nicobars and covering our minesweepers, who were clearing the channels between the islands. Due to intense flak, four Hellcats were lost including the CO of Ameer's squadron, Lieut-Cdr. R.M. North. On 7th July we lost one of our pilots in a way that particularly upset us. Although he had been wounded he had managed to fly back to the fleet but, before he could attempt a landing, we saw him slowly lose height until he crashed into the sea. A frigate that immediately dashed to the spot could find no trace. He had been one of a formation of 24 Hellcats whose mission had been to attack the airfields in Northern Sumatra.

On returning to Trincomali we had a week in harbour, then embarked 896 Squadron again for a mission entitled 'operation Livesy'. We were accompanied by HMS *Queen Elizabeth*, six other carriers, cruisers, destroyers and minesweepers. We were to help the Army which was fighting its way into Malaya, and to cause confusion to the Japanese efforts to evacuate the northern part of the peninsula and the Andaman and Nicobar Islands. They had made repeated attempts to do this during the last few months, but had suffered a series of disasters due to the efforts of our aircraft and the destruction of their convoys, largely by our destroyers. They were also bombed by Liberators of the RAF and Fortresses of the US Air Force. Our Hellcats struck at airfields in the Kra Isthmus and at railroad and marshalling yards. Once again we lost an aircraft. It had been bombing Dhung Song Railway station, then attacking locomotives with gun-fire. The pilot had left it too late to pull out of his dive. This was a danger that I had frequently warned our pilots about, as the exploding boiler of a steam loco could hurl debris to an astonishing height. I knew from my own experience how, when diving down on to a target, one tended to get a fixation and continue to dive much lower than wisdom dictated in an attempt to ensure a hit. 896 Squadron was also used for its specialisation of photo recce.

During our operations in the last few weeks we had suffered very few air attacks of any magnitude, but this trip was to be the exception. On 26th July radar twice gave warning of aircraft approaching, and Hellcats were launched to intercept. They shot down a number of the enemy without loss to themselves but, as usual, some Kamikazes managed to get through. In the first raid our Bofors disposed of one and the cruiser *Sussex* destroyed another. In the second wave *Sussex* shot down one more but the minesweeper *Vestal* was hit, leaving her on fire with many casualties. Destroyers picked up survivors, then sank her by gunfire. She was the only ship in the fleet to be damaged.

We steamed back to Ceylon, not knowing that we had been involved in the last offensive action by the East Indies Fleet in World War II.

On the return journey Lieut-Cdr. de Bejl, who was a perfectionist, told me that he wanted to take the squadron to the Naval Air Station at Puttalam, where there were practice bombing ranges, as he felt that his pilots were not accurate enough. I thought this would be a good opportunity to show that I was not just a pretty face and could still handle operational aircraft so, with the Captain's approval, I flew across with them in a borrowed squadron Hellcat.

Putalam was built on a lagoon where the water was affected by some form of volcanic activity, and the atmosphere was permeated by the stench of sulphur which was obvious even when flying above 1,000ft. It was not very pleasant but there was no option but to accept it and try to become accustomed to it. I spent a few days there flying with the squadron and was relieved to find that I did not disgrace myself. On my return to *Empress* I was told that we were to sail again on 6th August, so signalled the squadron to be ready to embark on that day.

We were just leaving harbour when we received a news flash. A Superfortress of the US Air Force had dropped an atomic bomb on the Japanese industrial city of Hiroshima, almost totally destroying it and causing hundreds of thousands of casualties.

We had never heard of an atomic bomb. The only information that we could glean was that it was comparatively small, being only about one tenth of the size of the 'blockbusters' that the RAF had dropped on Germany but its destructive power was cataclysmic and, in addition, it caused radioactive fall-out which made the area uninhabitable far outside the boundaries of the city. The radio news told us that the Japanese had been given the ultimatum of immediate surrender or their industrial cities would be systematically destroyed. We all felt that no country could withstand such destruction and that this must be the end of their war.

We steamed rather slowly towards the East only maintaining essential A/S and fighter cover until, on 9th August, the radio told us that the shipbuilding city of Nagasaki had been destroyed by another atomic bomb.

We flew no offensive missions. I am sure that the Admiral felt, as did most of us, that lives should not be risked within a few days of what must surely be the end of hostilities. However, the anti-Japanese feeling ran so high that some of our pilots and, I heard later, the crews of the destroyers, complained that they were being swindled out of a last chance to kill some more of them. For four days we steamed lethargically back and forth, gradually edging towards Ceylon.

On 14th August the long-awaited signal arrived from the Admiralty. It was a message to all ships of the Royal Navy and Allied Navies under our control and simply read: 'Cease hostilities against Japan.' With those four words our war was over. Japan had surrendered unconditionally. We aimed for Trincomali and increased speed, but felt it wise to keep some fighters at readiness and maintain A/S patrols, lest some of the ex-enemy had not received the message or would rather die than surrender.

The Captain spoke to the ship's company as soon as we received the signal. Lively music was blasted forth from the Tannoy and everyone not on essential duties came on to the upper deck. There was much cheering and flashing of cameras, official and unofficial. In honour of our closest allies in the area and, in particular, our own Squadron commander Zeggers de Bejl, we hoisted a Netherlands flag on one of our radio masts. The ship's photographic section was called up to take for posterity a picture of Captain Brown with all our most senior officers.

The expected signal arrived from His Majesty the King: 'Splice the main brace.'

In the late afternoon we secured to a buoy and found that the ships already in harbour had dressed over all with ensigns and code flags and those with their own bands were banging out cheerful music. As the sun set and the tropical darkness dropped over the anchorage, the flags changed to strings of twinkling lights stretched between masts; searchlights played across the sky; a firework display of Very lights and any other pyrotechnics that could be found shot up all around the harbour; decks were crowded with crews behaving like idiots and at one stage I found myself dancing eightsome reels on the flight deck with fellow Scotsmen.

As the hands of the clocks moved round towards midnight a reaction seemed to be setting in. Searchlights and fireworks died and the loud music faded to an occasional solo from some distant ship.

I found that I had climbed up to Flying Control and was standing leaning over the flight deck as I had done so often in the preceding months. Below me the games had ceased and men were walking singly, in pairs or small groups while others were sitting on the edge of the deck with their legs dangling over the gun sponsons. There was only quiet conversation and occasional bursts of laughter to be heard. I wondered how often I would see aircraft taking off or landing on that deck again. Probably *Empress* would be returned to the United States, there to be converted to a merchant ship and join the thousands of vessels that would be needed for a long time to ferry the food and equipment necessary to rebuild the war-torn world.

My thoughts dwelt over the last six years. Finally we had overcome the horrors of Nazi Germany and the barbarism of the Japanese. Always, illogically, I had been sure that we would eventually triumph. Most of the time, during those years, I had been in the front line but I was standing here physically unscathed while, for others, their lives had finished on their first brush with the enemy. Mentally, I felt little different from the days of 1939 but I must certainly be more mature. I wondered about my own contribution to events. Many had given much more than I but many had given much less. I felt that my conscience could be reasonably clear.

What of the future? Was World War II to be really 'The war to end all wars'? I thought it doubtful. I was Royal Navy, and another job would be found for me. I would not be joining the many friends that I had made as they stripped off their uniforms and started to rebuild their different lives.

The book of war had closed, and would reopen at another leaf. How would my story fit into those future pages?

I climbed slowly down, crossed the flight deck to my cabin and flopped on to the bunk to await the dawning of the first full day of Peace.

Appendix I

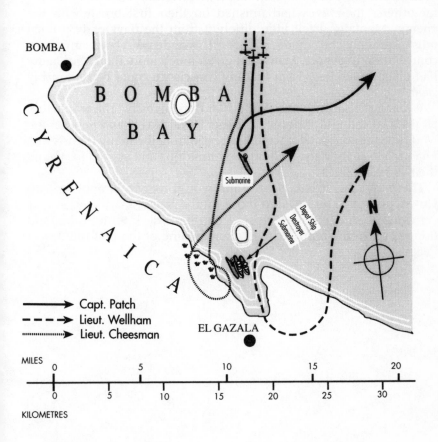

The Swordfish Strike in Bomba Bay – August 1940

191

Appendix II

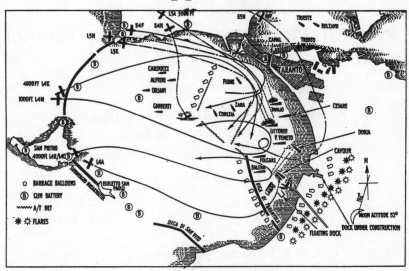

The Attack on Taranto

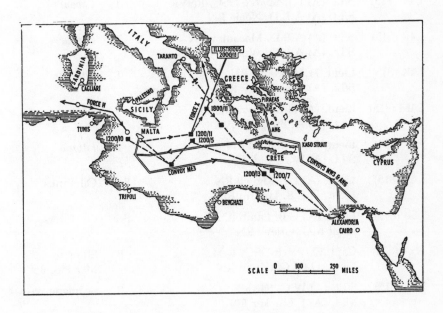

Operation MB8

Appendix III

Aircraft and Crews in Attack on Taranto

Aircraft bearing initial L belonged to Illustrious,
those with initial E to Eagle.

T = Torpedo. B = Bombs. F = Flares.

1st Strike

Aircraft (Squadron)	Pilot/Observer	Load	Target
L4A (815)	Lt. Cdr. K. Williamson RN Lt. N.J. Scarlett RN	T	Cavour
L4C (815)	S/Lt. (A) P.J. Sparke DSC, RNVR S/Lt. (A) A.L.D. Neale RN	T	Cavour
L4R (815)	S/Lt. (A) A.S.D. Macauley RN S/Lt. (A) A.L.O. Wray RNVR	T	Cavour
L4K (815)	Lieut. H.M. Kemp RN S/Lt. (A) R.A. Bailey RN	T	Littorio
L4M (815)	Lieut. (A) H.I.A. Swayne RN S/Lt. (A) A. Buxall RNVR	T	Littorio
E4F (813)	Lieut. M.R. Maund RN S/Lt. (A) W.A. Bull RN	T	Littorio
L4P (815)	Lieut. (A) L.J. Kiggell RN Lieut. H.R.B. Janvrin RN	B.F.	Oil Tanks
L5B (815)	Lieut. (A) C.B. Lamb RN Lieut K.G. Grieve RN	B.F.	Oil Tanks
E5A (824)	Capt. O. Patch DSO, R.M. Lieut. D.G. Goodwin RN	B	Ships in Mar Piccolo
L4L (815)	S/Lt. (A) W.C. Sarra RN Mid. (A) J. Bowker RN	B	Seaplane Base
L4H (815)	S/Lt. (A) A.J. Forde RN S/Lt. (A) A. Mardell-Ferreira RNVR	B	Ships in Mar Piccolo

Aircraft (Squadron)	Pilot/Observer	Load	Target
E5Q (824)	Lieut. (A) J.B. Murray RN S/Lt. (A) S.M. Paine RN	B	Ships in Mar Piccolo

2nd Strike

Aircraft (Squadron)	Pilot/Observer	Load	Target
L5A (819)	Lt. Cdr. J.W. Hale RN Lieut. G.A. Carline RN	T	*Littorio*
E4H (813)	Lieut. G.W. Bailey RN Lieut. H.J. Slaughter RN	T	*Gorizia*
L5H (819)	Lieut. (A) C.S.C. Lea RN S/Lt. (A) P.D. Jones RN	T	*Duilio*
L5K (819)	Lieut. F.M.A. Torrens-Spence RN Lieut. A.F.W. Sutton	T	*Littorio*
E5H (824)	Lieut. (A) J.W.G. Wellham DSC, RN Lieut. P. Humphreys EGM, RN	T	*Veneto*
L5B (819)	Lieut. R.W.V. Hamilton RN S/Lt. (A) J.R. Weeks RN	B.F.	Oil Tank Area
L4F (815)	Lieut. (A) R.G. Skelton RN S/Lt. (A) E.A. Perkins RNV.R.	B.F.	Oil Tank Area
L5F (819)	Lieut. E.W. Clifford RN Lieut. G.R.M. Going RN	B	Ships in Mar Piccolo
L5Q (819)	Lieut. (A) W.D. Morford RN S/Lt. (A) R.A.F. Green RN	B	Aborted after loss of external tank

Appendix IV

Fleet Air Arm and German, Italian and Japanese Aircraft used in Maritime Operations

N.B. Maximum speeds vary with height.
Many Fighters could also carry bombs or other missiles.
Armament was often variable.
F = Fighter TB = Torpedo Bomber
TBR = Torpedo/Bomber Reconnaissance.
R = Reconnaissance FB = Fighter/DiveBomber DB = Dive Bomber

Aircraft	Role	Speed (mph)	Load	Armament
Swordfish	TBR	137	1T 4 Bombs etc	2 × ·303
Albacore	TBR	161	1T Various	2 × ·303
Sea Gladiator	F	245	-	4 × ·303
Skua	FB	225	Various	5 × ·303
Roc	F	219	-	4 × ·303
Fulmar	F	255	-	8 × ·303
Barracuda	TBR	228	1T Various	2 × ·303
Sea Hurricane	F	315	-	8 × ·303
Seafire	F	352	-	2 × 20 mm. 4 × ·303
Avenger	TBR	271	2T Various	2 × ·303
Martlet	F	300	-	6 × ·5
Wildcat	F	310	-	4 × ·5
Firefly	F	315	-	4 × 20 mm
Hellcat	F	380	-	6 × ·5
Corsair	F	400	-	6 × ·5

Aircraft	Role	Speed (mph)	Load	Armament
German				
F.W. Kondor	RB	225	4,500lb Bombs or 2 × Hs 293 Missiles	2× 7·92 mm 3 × 13 mm 1 × 20 mm
Heinkel 111	TB	200	4,400lb Bombs or 2 × Torpedoes	6 × 7·92 mm
Junkers 87 (Stuka)	DB	230	1100lb Bomb	3 × 7·92 mm
Junkers 88	TDB	290	4400lb Bomb	2 × 13 mm
Me 109	F	350	-	1 × 20 mm
Me 110	F	350	-	4 × 7·9 mm 1 × 7·92 mm 2 × 20 mm
Italian				
Cant Z501	R	155	-	2 × 7·7 mm
Cant Z506	R	195	-	2 × 7·7 mm
Cant Z1007	TBR	280	4400lb Bomb or 2T	2 × 7·7 mm 2 × 12·7 mm
Fiat CR42	FB	265	2 × 220lb Bombs	2 × 12·7 mm
Macchi Mc 200	F	310	-	2 × 12·7 mm
SM 79	TBR	260	2200 lb Bomb or 2T	1 × 7·7 mm 3 × 12·7 mm
Japanese				
Aichi D3A2 (Val)	DB	280	1 × 550lb Bomb 2 × 130lb Bombs	3 × 7·7 mm
Kawanishi H6K4 (Mavis)	R	230	-	4 × 7·7 mm 1 × 20 mm
Hawasaki N1K1J (George)	F	410	-	2 × 7·7 mm 4 × 20 mm
Mitsubishi G4M2 (Betty)	TBR	280	2200lb Bombs or 1T	4 × 7·7 mm 2 × 20 mm
Nakajima B5N2 (Kate)	TBR	235	1650lb Bombs or 1T	1 × 7·7 mm
Nakajima B6N2 (Jill)	TR	320	1T	2 × 7·7 mm

Appendix V

The East Indies Fleet – August 1945

RIN – Royal Indian Navy; D – Royal Netherlands Navy;
F – French; IT – Italian

Battleships	3 (1 F)
A/C Carriers	16
Cruisers	13 (2 D)
Destroyers	43 (2 D; 1 F; 1 IT)
Frigates	42
Corvettes	16 (2 RIN)
Minesweepers	21 (15 RIN)
Sloops	9
Submarines	14
Monitors	2
Gunboats	3
Fighter Direction Ships	2
Destroyer Depot Ships	2
Sub. Depot Ships	2
Ante-Sub Patrol Vessels	2 (2 RIN)
Danlayers	4
Depot & Repair Ships	10
Survey Vessels	7
Boom Carriers	2
Net Layer	1
Minelayers	2
Salvage Vessel	1
Landing Ships	21 (1 RIN)
Base Ships	23 (9 RIN)
RN Air Stations	8
	269

Appendix VI

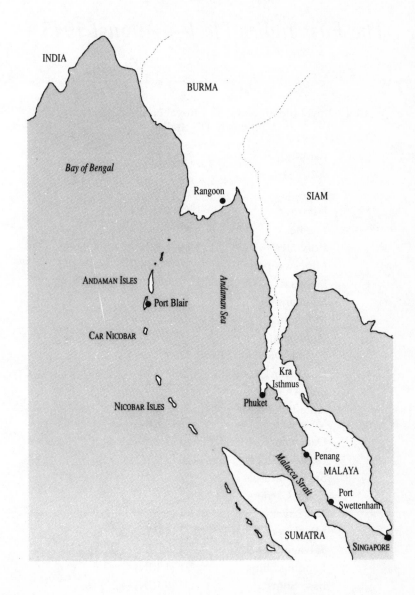

INDIA

BURMA

Bay of Bengal

Rangoon

SIAM

Andaman Sea

ANDAMAN ISLES

Port Blair

CAR NICOBAR

Kra
Isthmus

NICOBAR ISLES

Phuket

Malacca Strait

Penang

MALAYA

Port
Swettenham

SUMATRA

SINGAPORE

East Indies Fleet – Area of Operations